PRESENTED TO:

....

FROM:

....

DATE:

....

EVERYDAY
Joy and *Peace*

MyDaily DEVOTIONAL

An Imprint of Thomas Nelson Publishers

THOMAS NELSON
Since 1798

Cover design by Meg Schmidt.
Interior design by Kristy L. Edwards

ISBN 978-1-4041-1889-8

Printed in China

23 24 25 26 27 DSC 10 9 8 7 6 5 4 3 2 1

Introduction

The devotions in *Everyday Joy and Peace* were created to encourage the reader and reveal the timeless truths of God's joy and peace through a whole year. Each entry begins with one or more verses to meditate on, followed by a devotional thought, and finally a short prayer. As you start your journey with these devotions, I invite you to remember the instruction in Joshua 1:8: "This Book of the Law shall not depart from your mouth, but you shall meditate in it day and night, that you may observe to do according to all that is written in it. For then you will make your way prosperous, and then you will have good success." So let these Scriptures and words of encouragement live with you and in you throughout your day, that God may fill your heart with the joy and peace that only He can give. Keep each closing prayer close to your heart, and pray it repeatedly as you go about your day, always returning to God in your focus. As Psalm 19:14 says, "Let the words of my mouth and the meditation of my heart be acceptable in Your sight, O Lord, my strength and my Redeemer." May God bless your year with His everlasting joy and peace.

O.S. Hawkins

O.S. HAWKINS, PhD
Bestselling Code Series Author
Dallas, Texas

CONTENTS

Everyday Joy and Peace

It's Your Choice

Choose life . . . that you may love the LORD your God, that you may obey His voice, and that you may cling to Him.

DEUTERONOMY 30:19–20

An amazing aspect of God's love for us is the fact that He gives us choices. We are not His puppets. The Almighty is not some master puppeteer pulling our strings so we play out our lives onstage exactly as He wants.

Instead, you are God's cherished creation. He loves you so much that He allows you to make choices in life. While most of these choices are small, some have the potential to be life altering.

One of those life-altering choices is your decision about whether to love God. He wants you to know of His great love for you. He loves you so much that He demonstrated that love by sending His Son. You are deeply loved by the Lord, who both knit you together and died for your sins. How will you respond?

The love you voluntarily return to Him is indescribably valuable to Him.

You are free to choose what you want to do. But, like all of us, you want to sin. It is in our nature. But God's love reaches you right now, wherever you are and whatever you have done. Choose life. Choose Christ.

....

Lord, I love You, but before I ever gave thought of You, You first loved me. In Jesus' name, amen.

O.S. Hawkins, PhD, Bestselling Code Series Author, Dallas, TX

The Word of God Is Ageless

All Scripture is given by inspiration of God, and is profitable for doctrine, for reproof, for correction, for instruction in righteousness.

2 TIMOTHY 3:16

We do not have to defend the Bible. As preacher Charles Spurgeon said, "There is no need to defend a lion when he is being attacked. All we have to do is open the gate and let him out. He will defend himself."

The Bible will still be the Book of all books when all the other writings throughout the centuries have passed into obscurity. Let's open the gates. The Bible can defend itself.

Consider that the Bible is a library of sixty-six books written over a period of more than fourteen hundred years by at least forty different authors from all walks of life. Some were fishermen, and others were prophets, kings, shepherds, doctors, and rabbis. Yet this Book has come together with one theology, one plan of redemption, and one theme running throughout its pages, leaving no explanation for its unique nature outside of God Himself. It is "given" by God Himself.

The Bible never grows old or out-of-date; it is ageless. Relevant to every passing generation, it has withstood the test of time and will still be the Book of all books when all the writings of humanity have passed into obscurity.

....

Lord, open my eyes to behold wonderful truth from Your Word today. In Jesus' name, amen.

Free Gift

God, who is rich in mercy, because of His great love with which He loved us, even when we were dead in trespasses, made us alive together with Christ (by grace you have been saved).

EPHESIANS 2:4–5

Today's young people often want something for nothing. People on both ends of the economic spectrum have an entitlement mentality. On one end, government programs have reinforced this compulsion. On the other end, wealthy parents have given their children every material need or want imaginable, and they have never had to work for anything.

What Christ has to offer is free, so He is the very thing for which these young adults are searching. Jesus is able to offer relationship for free because He paid the ultimate price: He died on the cross. By His blood Jesus purchased a way for us to be in relationship with the Father. That privilege is neither earned nor deserved, and it cannot be bought. It is provided freely to us through the sacrifice of Jesus' blood.

We like the word *free*! You can't earn your salvation. You don't deserve it. You can't purchase it. It is the *free* gift of God, which He already purchased for you with His own blood.

....

Lord, the most expensive gift I have ever received is eternal life through You. And You gave it to me as a free gift. May my life be my thank-You note. In Jesus' name, amen.

O.S. Hawkins, PhD, Bestselling Code Series Author, Dallas, TX

Justified by God

Whom He foreknew, He also predestined to be conformed to the image of His Son. . . . Whom He predestined, these He also called; whom He called, these He also justified; and whom He justified, these He also glorified.

ROMANS 8:29-30

A God-choreographed series of events happens in the lives of individuals who choose to follow Jesus. Those people—whom God foreknew—He predestined to be His followers. Those whom He predestined to follow Him, He called. Those He called—and who, by His Spirit, responded with faith—He justified: God accepted the shed blood of Jesus as the sacrifice that paid for our sins. And those individuals the Father justified, He also glorified. This blessed calling of God upon our hearts is a significant part of His total redemptive plan, wrapped as it is in the mystery of predestination and free will.

One day "every knee should bow . . . and . . . every tongue should confess that Jesus Christ is Lord" (Philippians 2:10–11). We are blessed to have been called to recognize that truth now and to walk through this life with Jesus.

A court of law may acquit, it may pardon, but it cannot justify, make as if something never happened. But God can, and did, for you. It is one thing to be forgiven, but quite another to be justified.

Lord, such knowledge is too wonderful—You took my sin and made it as if it never happened. In Jesus' name, amen.

Everyday Joy and Peace

Guard Your Heart

No temptation has overtaken you except such as is common to man; but God is faithful, who will not allow you to be tempted beyond what you are able, but with the temptation will also make the way of escape, that you may be able to bear it.

1 CORINTHIANS 10:13

I t is not a sin to be tempted—and we will be tempted. One should not confuse temptations with trials. Most often, trials are allowed—or even sent—by God to strengthen the Christian. Temptations, however, are sent from the devil to cause the Christian to stumble.

Arriving in a variety of shapes and sizes, temptation is a reality that is not going to go away. But our minds are like a hotel. The manager cannot keep someone from entering the lobby, but he can certainly keep that person from getting a room. Likewise, when a temptation passes through our minds, we haven't sinned. We sin when we give that thought a room in our mind and let it dwell there.

Guard your heart and mind today as temptation comes knocking on your door. Don't give it a room.

....

Lord, put a guard over my mind and keep watch over the door of my thoughts. In Jesus' name, amen.

O.S. Hawkins, PhD, Bestselling Code Series Author, Dallas, TX

Walk in the Light

"I am the light of the world. He who follows Me shall not walk in darkness, but have the light of life."

JOHN 8:12

Note carefully what David said in Psalm 23:4: followers of Christ never walk through the valley of death, only through the valley of the shadow of death.

The Lord Jesus Himself, however, walked through the valley of death. For three days and nights He walked that valley—and then emerged from the empty tomb and said, "Behold . . . I have the keys of death and of Hades" (Revelation 1:18 NASB).

So the believer walks through the valley of the shadow of death. A shadow may horrify, but it cannot harm. And David walked "through the valley of the shadow of death" because that is what we do with a shadow: we simply walk through it.

Also, the only way you can have a shadow is to have a great light shining. Jesus said, "I am the light of the world" (John 8:12). We believers therefore deal with only the shadow of death.

The light of the whole world is Jesus. If you are walking through a shadow experience right now, it simply means He is near—very near.

....

Lord, surprise me today with Your presence as I seek to walk in Your light. In Jesus' name, amen.

On Secondary Issues, Chill

I know and am convinced by the Lord Jesus that there is nothing unclean of itself; but to him who considers anything to be unclean, to him it is unclean. Yet if your brother is grieved because of your food, you are no longer walking in love. Do not destroy with your food the one for whom Christ died.

ROMANS 14:14-15

My oldest son is always using the word *chill*. To him it means "pause, breathe—it's not worth getting all worked up and worried." In the church, we have made so many secondary issues first-order issues—things that have nothing to do with the gospel.

I like to be right. I believe most people do. It is easy to try and justify ourselves as to why we are right on issues of no importance, even sometimes at the detriment of hurting others. As a follower of Jesus, I have to remember that love lays down the desire to be right. What matters is pleasing Jesus and building each other up.

When I put so much weight on secondary issues that it leads to division with another brother, I remember how many times I have been wrong in my spiritual life. And yet God still has never stopped accepting me! Who am I, then, to reject someone else? In other words, chill. I love how the gospel constantly teaches me this truth. Over and over in my life I am reminded that God accepts me despite my daily sins and mistakes. That amazing grace should influence how we accept one another. Remember—Christ also died for the one you disagree with.

....

Lord, may we as Your church be known for a stronger love of the gospel than of our preferences. Amen.

Dr. Chad Grayson, Life Community Church, Jamestown, NC

Desperate for God

Because Your lovingkindness is better than life, my lips shall praise You. Thus I will bless You while I live; I will lift up my hands in Your name. My soul shall be satisfied as with marrow and fatness, and my mouth shall praise You with joyful lips.

PSALM 63:3-5

This world and especially our modern culture is constantly challenging us to get more and learn more—to continually expand our capacity for knowledge, for earning, and for excellence. But rather than placing so much importance on those things, God is saying through David in today's passage, why not learn how to worship Me with all your heart and every fiber of your being?

When David wrote psalm 63, he was away from the temple in Jerusalem and missed worshipping there surrounded by the presence of God. Through the rest of the psalm, David reflected on the good and the bad. He shared his utter dependence on God and desire to "praise [Him] with joyful lips." Remembering who God is, David meditated on Him and acknowledged, "Your right hand upholds me" (v. 8).

Nothing compares to the love of God. It is better than life itself. No gift will ever satisfy you the way God can. God can't hold Himself back from those who are desperate for Him, who are madly in love with Him, who delight in worshiping Him, and who earnestly seek Him. May Christ truly be our life, and may our capacity for worshiping Him ever expand.

....

Oh God, may I never stop loving You with every fiber of my being, living to bring You glory, and sharing Your amazing grace with my lips. I love You, Jesus. Amen.

If Yes, Then Do

> *If there is any consolation in Christ, if any comfort of love, if any fellowship of the Spirit, if any affection and mercy, fulfill my joy by being like-minded, having the same love, being of one accord, of one mind. Let nothing be done through selfish ambition or conceit, but in lowliness of mind let each esteem others better than himself. Let each of you look out not only for his own interests, but also for the interests of others.*
>
> PHILIPPIANS 2:1–4

I can hear the passion in Paul's words in this scripture. Verses 1–4 are a response to Paul's circumstances in Philippians 1. He was in prison, and he was telling the church in Philippi that he rejoiced in jail because the gospel was being advanced. He reminded them that to live is Christ and to die is gain (1:21) and that their citizenship was in heaven. He instructed them that they had been given the *privilege* of suffering with Christ, and that all this had been given to them together.

Therefore, Paul asks, are you encouraged from belonging to Jesus? Does His love comfort you? Do you have that sweet fellowship of walking with Him and talking with Him and hearing that you are His? If yes, then love one another and have unity. Don't be selfish, but be humble and patient. Think of others the way Christ has thought of you. Today, determine to *do* based on the truth that is found in His promises to us. In Christ Jesus, we live and move and exist. Christ is our life, and we act in love because of it.

....

Thank You, Lord Jesus, for loving us with an everlasting love! May we love one another the same way. Amen.

Dr. Chad Grayson, Life Community Church, Jamestown, NC

Cause and Effect

Justice will dwell in the wilderness, and righteousness remain in the fruitful field. The work of righteousness will be peace, and the effect of righteousness, quietness and assurance forever.

ISAIAH 32:16-17

Justice, righteousness, peace, quietness, and assurance forever? Sign me up! How can I obtain that kind of righteousness? Work really hard and do a lot of good deeds? Make sure I say my prayers every morning and read from my *Everyday Joy and Peace* devotional? The answer to those questions is an obvious no. Many believe that if you live a holy or moral life that means you are a righteous person. When I read scripture, it appears to be the other way around. In other words, righteousness leads to holiness, justice, and peace. As Matthew 5:6 says, "Blessed are those who hunger and thirst for righteousness, for they shall be filled."

Righteousness does have an effect. I believe if we are going to receive this effect we need to become less sin conscious and more righteousness conscious. You don't get this way by constantly thinking about what a worthless sinner you are. You get this way by learning who you are in Christ Jesus. Knowing the truth about who you are in Him will give you peace, quietness, and assurance forever!

.....

Lord, today I will remember that I have been bought with a price, sealed with Your Spirit, and accepted in the Beloved. I rejoice that I am clothed in Your righteousness and will abide in You. Amen.

Carpe Diem

Nothing is better for a man than that he should eat and drink, and that his soul should enjoy good in his labor. This also, I saw, was from the hand of God. For who can eat, or who can have enjoyment, more than I? For God gives wisdom and knowledge and joy to a man who is good in His sight; but to the sinner He gives the work of gathering and collecting, that he may give to him who is good before God. This also is vanity and grasping for the wind.

ECCLESIASTES 2:24-26

S ome people might read these verses as saying, "There is no point, so you might as well just have fun when you can." But I don't think this is what Solomon is saying at all.

Many scholars call these verses "carpe diem" passages. *Carpe diem* is probably one of the most well-known Latin phrases, meaning "seize the day." Often throughout Ecclesiastes, Solomon came to the conclusion that all one can do in life is simply seize the day.

Don't misunderstand Solomon. He is not saying that since there is no point in life, you might as well live how you want. He is saying that there will be days when you have no clue what is happening, why it is happening, and how it is happening! Even though those days may come frequently for many of us, there is still a point to each day. This is the day that the Lord has made; rejoice and be glad in it (Psalm 118:24). Jesus is still Lord. His grace is still amazing. His salvation is still available to a lost world. And His mercies are new every morning (Lamentations 3:22–23).

Father God, may we seize this day for Your glory! Amen.

Dr. Chad Grayson, Life Community Church, Jamestown, NC

Saved and Secure

Blessed be the God and Father of our Lord Jesus Christ, who according to His abundant mercy has begotten us again to a living hope through the resurrection of Jesus Christ from the dead to an inheritance incorruptible and undefiled and that does not fade away, reserved in heaven for you, who are kept by the power of God through faith for salvation ready to be revealed in the last time.

1 PETER 1:3-5

In my opinion, there no passage of scripture that brings more joy, assurance, and anticipation in all the Bible than these verses. Peter was writing to give hope to believers who were facing certain persecution. The city of Rome was burning. The evil emperor Nero was the one guilty of setting these fires. Seeking a scapegoat, he found one in the infant church. He already hated the Christians because they made it clear that they worshiped only Christ and Him alone!

Peter was reminding them of their Living Hope, the eternal salvation that comes through Christ's resurrection. Even in the worst suffering, a believer can never lose his or her salvation. The question is often asked, Can a person truly have eternal security in salvation from Jesus? The answer is yes! But what if that person lives for Jesus for twenty years and then falls into sin? There will be consequences for sin, but a believer's salvation is never in jeopardy. How can someone that bad still have salvation? Because Someone that good secured it!

....

My hope is built on nothing less
Than Jesus' blood and righteousness;

On Christ, the solid Rock, I stand;
All other ground is sinking sand.[1]
Amen!

Building with Joy

On the twenty-third day of the seventh month he sent the people away to their tents, joyful and glad of heart for the good that the LORD had done for David, for Solomon, and for His people Israel. Thus Solomon finished the house of the LORD and the king's house; and Solomon successfully accomplished all that came into his heart to make in the house of the LORD and in his own house.

2 CHRONICLES 7:10-11

Tasks to be completed are a normal part of the day. An unending to-do list usually accompanies a cup of coffee every morning. At work, there are deadlines for multiple projects that require attention. Some tasks are more daunting than others, but even the most minor task completed can bring a level of joy. For Israel, there was a lingering task that needed much attention.

Completing the temple of the Lord was no small task. Simply completing this project should have brought Israel much joy, but this was different. Their labor brought great joy because of what they were accomplishing. They were sent away joyfully, knowing the temple would provide a dwelling place for the Lord. Joy is often absent because the projects we are laboring to accomplish have nothing to do with God's purpose. Our labor and God's purpose must be tethered for joy to exist. Paul said that your body is a temple for the Holy Spirit to dwell within (1 Corinthians 6:19–20). Joy will invade your life when you build it according to God's design and purpose.

....

Lord, will You give Your wisdom, counsel, and guidance to keep me aligned with Your purpose and design for my life? Help me build my life so You may dwell richly with Your joy within me.

Dr. Michael W. Gossett, Green Acres Baptist Church, Tyler, TX

Ingredients for Peace

The word which God sent to the children of Israel, preaching peace through Jesus Christ—He is Lord of all—that word you know, which was proclaimed throughout all Judea, and began from Galilee after the baptism which John preached: how God anointed Jesus of Nazareth with the Holy Spirit and with power, who went about doing good and healing all who were oppressed by the devil, for God was with Him.

ACTS 10:36-38

I n the baking of any dish, ingredients make all the difference in the outcome. The chef has determined which ingredients are necessary to make the dish taste the way it should. Often in life, we attempt to substitute the ingredients for true peace. If the exact recipe for peace in life is known, it would be unreasonable to attempt any substitutes, knowing that the outcome will be different.

One of the primary ingredients of peace is knowing that Jesus is the Lord of all. Living under the lordship of Christ provides a pathway for peace at every step. Another ingredient for peace is the dwelling of the Spirit in the believer's life. Every believer is promised this Helper within them at the moment of conversion. Because Jesus is Lord of all, nothing can remove the Spirit from the believer. To have peace in life, these ingredients cannot be substituted. With Jesus as Lord and with the fullness of the Spirit, you have the ingredients of peace in your life.

Lord, will You reign supreme in my life and fill me with Your Spirit so I may experience the peace only You offer? Help me live a life of peace, knowing my life is in Your hands.

Serving with Perseverance

*Pharaoh sent and called Joseph, and they brought him quickly out of the
dungeon; and he shaved, changed his clothing, and came to Pharaoh. And
Pharaoh said to Joseph, "I have had a dream, and there is no one who can
interpret it. But I have heard it said of you that you can understand a dream, to
interpret it." So Joseph answered Pharaoh, saying, "It is not in me; God will give
Pharaoh an answer of peace."*

GENESIS 41:14-16

One of the most significant tests of perseverance for any team is continuing to play hard while they're behind. Perseverance requires a unique mental toughness and a sense of resolve to continue the game with little hope of coming back or winning. Perseverance requires seeing beyond the circumstance and not letting an unfavorable situation control your actions. The life of Joseph provides a glimpse of perseverance amid difficulty.

Joseph's life is a story of perseverance. Joseph continued walking faithfully with the Lord, serving the Lord, even when circumstances were against him. The key to understanding Joseph's perseverance is to understand that it was not the power of Joseph but rather the power of God within him that allowed him to serve so well. Serving with perseverance is only possible with God's power and presence in the believer's life. Although Joseph was in difficult situations, the Lord was always with him. Without God's presence or His power, perseverance is not possible. Joseph served with perseverance because he understood that it was more than him doing it. It was the Lord in him.

....

Lord, I pray that You will help me serve You with perseverance. Help me continue to walk faithfully with You. Thank You for Your power and presence in my life.

Dr. Michael W. Gossett, Green Acres Baptist Church, Tyler, TX

Carrying Peace

"Whatever house you enter, first say, 'Peace to this house.' And if a son of peace is there, your peace will rest on it; if not, it will return to you. And remain in the same house, eating and drinking such things as they give, for the laborer is worthy of his wages. Do not go from house to house."

LUKE 10:5-7

Hiking multiple miles and camping multiple nights is not a vacation for everyone, but it is the desired trip for some. Campers will need a tent, food supplies, a change of clothes, a water filter, and many other essential items. Packing only essential items is vital because everything packed must be carried throughout the trip. In the same way, in life, everyone carries something with them daily. Disciples of Jesus have been called to carry His character wherever they go. Everyplace His disciples go, they pack the peace of Jesus with them and go from house to house.

Have you ever thought about what you carry with you? Whatever you carry is entering every house you visit. In the gospel of John, Jesus extended His peace to the disciples. "Peace I leave with you, My peace I give to you; not as the world gives do I give to you. Let not your heart be troubled, neither let it be afraid" (John 14:27). The peace of Christ in the believer is carried from the believer and given to others. Let the peace of Christ rest on others today.

....

Lord, thank You for the peace You have left with me to carry. Help me to be a good steward of what You have given and take this peace with me as I go from house to house.

Satisfying Joy

Thus says the Lord God: "Behold, My servants shall eat, but you shall be hungry; behold, My servants shall drink, but you shall be thirsty; behold, My servants shall rejoice, but you shall be ashamed; behold, My servants shall sing for joy of heart, but you shall cry for sorrow of heart, and wail for grief of spirit."

ISAIAH 65:13-14

We experience a level of satisfaction after finishing a good meal. A person gets hungry, eats, and is satisfied, but only momentarily. Jesus fed the five thousand in Matthew 14, and each ate until full. But the next day, those who were previously satisfied would be hungry once again. Satisfaction from the things of this world will always be temporary. Jesus told the crowds that He alone is the bread of life. The life that Jesus offers has the power and the ability to give eternal satisfaction.

The Lord is the only One who offers true satisfaction. Often, satisfaction is thought of in temporal ways, but the satisfaction from Jesus is eternal and complete. A level of completion is available even on this side of eternity. For this type of satisfaction, true joy is possible by serving the Lord, surrendering to Him, and praising Him.

....

Lord, help me trust You entirely for my joy and satisfaction. Please give me the wisdom to know when I am filling my life with things that are not eternally satisfying. Lead me toward Your satisfaction with the fullness of Your joy.

Dr. Michael W. Gossett, Green Acres Baptist Church, Tyler, TX

Pursuing Peace

Who is the man who desires life, and loves many days, that he may see good?
Keep your tongue from evil, and your lips from speaking deceit. Depart from evil
and do good; seek peace and pursue it.

PSALM 34:12–14

I t is a common practice for many to pursue the latest and greatest technology. Many believe that the latest product will provide something different or better than the former product could. Whether we realize it or not, every person pursues something. We need to be intentional to stay up-to-date with the latest technology. To have the latest, consumers intentionally save up, drive to the store, wait for sales, and take many steps toward making their purchases. Consider your pursuits in life and whether those pursuits draw you into the Lord or away from the Lord. Not every pursuit is beneficial, but the psalmist tells us what to pursue.

Pursue peace with intentionality. It seems like a simple task, but the foundations of peace are difficult to maintain. Pursuing the latest product will never provide peace or a good life. But if we want to see good days, the psalmist says we must be intentional in the pursuit. Pursuing peace means that you are running in the opposite direction of evil. Do not allow the tongue to be used for evil or deceit. Instead, run from evil, and cultivate a desire for good. This is what true peace can look like in the believer's life.

....

Lord, give me a desire for You and for Your peace. Give me the strength to pursue peace ultimately. Help me to be intentional in pursuing the things that breed life within me that only You can provide. Thank You for Your peace in my life.

God's Spirit

He who establishes us with you in Christ and has anointed us is God, who also has sealed us and given us the Spirit in our hearts as a guarantee. Moreover I call God as witness against my soul, that to spare you I came no more to Corinth. Not that we have dominion over your faith, but are fellow workers for your joy; for by faith you stand.

2 CORINTHIANS 1:21-24

Today, focus specifically on these words from the apostle Paul: "God, who also has sealed us and given us the Spirit in our hearts as a guarantee." The moment you trust Christ for your forgiveness and salvation, you receive the Holy Spirit. You now have almighty God dwelling within you, and His Spirit begins to work in and through you, not just for your good alone but for the benefit of the world around you. As you go to work today, as you spend time with your family, as you interact with others, you are the light of the world. You are God's representative.

I take from this wonderful passage that Christ-followers should be fellow workers for the joy of others. The same Spirit who worked in Paul to change the world forever is still working today in the life of every Christ-follower.

How are the power and presence of the Holy Spirit working in and through your life today? God has given you everything you need to influence the people in your life. If you will learn to listen to His promptings from His Word and follow His voice, you will have an amazing impact for the cause of Christ.

Lord, lead me and empower me through Your Spirit. I want to be a fellow worker with You for the joy of others.

Chris Dixon, First Baptist Church Bentonville, Bentonville, AR

Grace to You

To the saints and faithful brethren in Christ who are in Colosse: Grace to you and peace from God our Father and the Lord Jesus Christ.

COLOSSIANS 1:2

P aul begins the letter he writes to Colosse with the words, "Grace to you." In three simple but powerful words, Paul pens our story. My story and hopefully your story is a story of grace. We do not deserve forgiveness from God because all of us have gone our own way and done our own thing (Isaiah 53:6; Romans 3:23). We did not and cannot earn forgiveness for our sin because the price was impossible for us to pay (Romans 6:23; 8:3; Ephesians 2:8–9). The curse of sin is the story of humanity. However, "Grace to you."

There is grace from God in the person of Jesus Christ who paid the penalty and took the wrath for sins. There is grace from God, who gave His Spirit and His Word as an encouragement and guide to truth for daily living (2 Thessalonians 2:16). These wonderful truths of grace are personal. Paul writes, "Grace *to you.*"

Now, grace really is amazing, but then Paul adds, "Grace to you and peace from God our Father and the Lord Jesus Christ." Not only does our generous God give grace, but because of His grace, we can also experience peace. How? Paul writes in Romans 8:32, "He [God] who did not spare His own Son, but gave Him up for us all—how will He not also, along with Him, graciously give us all things?" (NIV). Today, if you have grace you can have peace. The same God who generously provided for the work of salvation is still graciously at work in and around your life today (Romans 8:32). If you have trials today, then let me encourage you: *Grace to you.*

Lord, please show me how to drink from the endless wells of Your grace anew every morning.

God in Us

The children of Israel, the priests and the Levites and the rest of the descendants of the captivity, celebrated the dedication of this house of God with joy. And they offered sacrifices at the dedication of this house of God, one hundred bulls, two hundred rams, four hundred lambs, and as a sin offering for all Israel twelve male goats, according to the number of the tribes of Israel.

EZRA 6:16-17

I want you to take an Old Testament celebration and make it a celebration in your house today. The celebration in Ezra was for a building, but Christ-followers today celebrate not just God with us, but God in us—for we are living temples of God (1 Corinthians 6:19–20).

Why celebrate? God loves you with an overwhelming, extravagant love that can never be taken away. It is beyond comprehension. He loves you on your good days and your bad days. But God does not just want you to recognize this love intellectually. He wants you to recognize it spiritually and emotionally—to know Him intimately. He wants to speak to you, comfort you, direct you, and guide you daily through the Word of God and prayer as you spend time with Him. Love is God's nature, and He wants you to experience that love.

Many people say they love you. God *showed* you how much He loves you. He sacrificed His Son to connect with you (John 3:16). That's the kind of love only God has for you. Never think that we are left to ourselves to face the challenges of life. God is not just for us; He is with us because of His love for us. That is indeed worth celebrating with great joy.

....

Lord, I celebrate Your incomprehensible love for me—a love that never changes.

Chris Dixon, First Baptist Church Bentonville, Bentonville, AR

Choose Grace, Not Bitterness

Pursue peace with all people, and holiness, without which no one will see the Lord: looking carefully lest anyone fall short of the grace of God; lest any root of bitterness springing up cause trouble, and by this many become defiled.

HEBREWS 12:14-15

These verses are about choosing grace, not bitterness. Bitterness is a wound, a frustration, or a disappointment in someone that is allowed to stay in a heart and mind until it builds to the point of anger, ultimately altering a person's behavior. Bitterness ruins lives and relationships, and it allows the past to imprison us. It takes away joy and peace and brings brokenness and resentment.

The danger of bitterness is that hurting people hurt people. When this happens, the very people who are hurt now become a tool that is used to hurt others. But today's verse challenges Christ-followers to pursue peace and holiness (God's way of living) to protect their lives from trouble.

When today's verses refer to a person who can "fall short of the grace of God," they are not referring to a person who loses their salvation. They are referring to a person who receives grace but does not apply grace to others. Therefore, the challenge here is to live a grace-filled life. Scripture would teach us: Mercy should produce mercy; grace should produce grace; compassion should produce compassion.

It is important for us to see the challenge God's Word gives us in the context of pursuing peace. This doesn't mean we give up our convictions, allow people to repeatedly hurt us, or ignore injustice. It means we pursue the attitude of Christ and show the world who He is and the change He has made in us.

Jesus, show me how and whom to forgive, so bitterness will not take hold in me. I want to live in Your peace and grace.

God Has a Plan for You

Jesus knew that they desired to ask Him, and He said to them, "Are you inquiring among yourselves about what I said, 'A little while, and you will not see Me; and again a little while, and you will see Me'? Most assuredly, I say to you that you will weep and lament, but the world will rejoice; and you will be sorrowful, but your sorrow will be turned into joy."

JOHN 16:19-20

In John 16:19–20, Jesus was referring to His imminent death and His coming resurrection. But this confused and concerned His disciples because they did not understand the plan or the timing Jesus had in mind. One of the greatest frustrations of life is that God's plan and timetable are rarely the same as ours.

But great people—God's people—are grown through struggles, storms, and seasons of suffering. Be patient with the process.

In Ephesians 2:10 we are told, "we are His workmanship, created in Christ Jesus for good works, which God prepared beforehand that we should walk in them." He has promised to work in your life toward specific plans that He has for you! That is why we have to stay in constant communication with and surrender to Him—because it is *His* work. If we begin to pursue our work and our plans, we can become frustrated because His ways are not our ways (Isaiah 55:8–9).

Take time every day to seek God in His Word, speak to Him, and listen for His voice. God has a great plan for your life, but it is His plan. It is impossible to know without Him. So listen and watch as God works His good works in and through you!

Lord, I surrender to Your timetable and welcome Your works in me.

Chris Dixon, First Baptist Church Bentonville, Bentonville, AR

Praise His Name

Let Israel rejoice in their Maker; let the children of Zion be joyful in their King. Let them praise His name with the dance; let them sing praises to Him with the timbrel and harp. For the LORD takes pleasure in His people; He will beautify the humble with salvation.

PSALM 149:2–4

All of us take time to praise people, places, and things. I know I give a lot of praise when it comes to Krispy Kreme Doughnuts, my favorite sports team, my wife, and my children (and not in that order!). Of course we use words and actions of praise for the things we care about. That is why the psalmist takes time to sing this challenge to God's people.

The greatest commandment Jesus taught in Matthew 22 was to "love the LORD your God" (v. 37). We are to love Him with all that we are, and that includes our words and our actions. Take time today to pay attention to your words and actions. How much time do you spend expressing admiration for who God is and for all that He has done for you? Praise is an outward expression (words and actions) of our inward love! Be sure that your social media, your conversations, your relationships, and your home are filled with words of praise to His name.

Worship is more than just music. I worship God when I turn my attention to Him and when I tell Him I love Him. I worship Him when I praise His name. How wonderful that He takes pleasure in it.

....

Lord, I cannot find enough words to fully praise You, but I want to try! Show me how to make praise and worship of You a way of life.

Everyday Joy and Peace

Chasing Peace

Let us pursue the things which make for peace and the things by which one may edify another. Do not destroy the work of God for the sake of food. All things indeed are pure, but it is evil for the man who eats with offense. It is good neither to eat meat nor drink wine nor do anything by which your brother stumbles or is offended or is made weak.

ROMANS 14:19–21

One of the greatest daily goals we'll ever set for ourselves can be found right here in this scripture—to pursue peace. Strange, isn't it, that we don't have to pursue conflict? It'll find us. Especially in the world we live in today. Read just about any comment thread on social media and you'll see the anger and dissension spill out. As God-followers, though, we've been called to live a different way.

In the first line of today's scripture, we're reminded that today will set before us opportunities for conflict and "things which make for peace." Unlike conflict, peace has to be pursued or chased. That implies that the things that produce peace can be elusive. In practical terms, we may have to go against our own instincts to choose the actions and words that calm situations and build others up. But the outcome is worth it!

Why not make this your goal today? Pursue peace with and encourage everyone you meet. It might just change the trajectory of their lives—and you'll sleep better tonight!

....

Lord, help me today to be an agent of peace and encouragement to everyone I meet. Amen.

Mark Hoover, NewSpring Church, Wichita, KS

You Have a Singing Engagement!

Make a joyful shout to God, all the earth! Sing out the honor of His name; make His praise glorious. Say to God, "How awesome are Your works! Through the greatness of Your power Your enemies shall submit themselves to You. All the earth shall worship You and sing praises to You; they shall sing praises to Your name."

PSALM 66:1-4

When I read today's scripture, one word jumps off the page to me. Maybe it's because it's there three times: the word *sing*. You and I are being invited to sing *to God*! That's way bigger than being asked to sing at Carnegie Hall or the Super Bowl! Many of us are thankful that singing to God doesn't require a beautiful *voice*, but instead a *heart* full of worship and praise.

If you'll pardon a personal reference, I'd like to share something I experienced sometime back. I was recovering from a tough case of COVID, and even after it passed, my diminished lung capacity affected my voice. It was so thin that I sounded like a different person. One day when I was driving alone in my car, I had an idea. I turned on worship music and started singing at the top of the voice I had left. In a few days, my full voice returned. But that's not what I remember most. It was those awesome worship services I had in my car, with just God and me.

Whatever you're going through today, why not change the whole atmosphere? Sing to God. He wants to hear you!

Lord, lead me to songs of praise today. Amen.

Look Forward, Not Backward

Not that I have already attained, or am already perfected; but I press on, that I may lay hold of that for which Christ Jesus has also laid hold of me. Brethren, I do not count myself to have apprehended; but one thing I do, forgetting those things which are behind and reaching forward to those things which are ahead, I press toward the goal for the prize of the upward call of God in Christ Jesus.

PHILIPPIANS 3:12-14

P aul must have really loved sports. On several occasions he compared aspects of the Christian life to athletic contests. He was doing that in today's verses. He was talking about running a race. No longer a young man, he'd been a believer for many years. His Philippian audience knew that Paul had been used by the Holy Spirit to accomplish perhaps unparalleled tasks for the kingdom. So he was writing to let them know how he saw the time he had left.

Most of all, he wanted them to understand his past failures hadn't sidetracked him, nor had earlier achievements made him feel he'd arrived. Sports fans know all too well what can happen when a team that's far ahead in the third quarter begins to act as though the game is already won. It's not over yet.

Paul's advice works for us today. Forget, or don't focus on what's behind—either failures or successes. Put past sins under the blood of Jesus, and lay yesterday's successes at His feet. Focus on the goal of living out God's perfect will for your life. Paul believed his best days of serving God were ahead. So are ours!

....

Lord, help me keep focused on Your plan for my life, and let me glorify You today by giving You my very best.

Mark Hoover, NewSpring Church, Wichita, KS

The Greatest Choice

"Do not think that I came to bring peace on earth. I did not come to bring peace but a sword. For I have come to 'set a man against his father, a daughter against her mother, and a daughter-in-law against her mother-in-law'; and 'a man's enemies will be those of his own household.' He who loves father or mother more than Me is not worthy of Me. And he who loves son or daughter more than Me is not worthy of Me. And he who does not take his cross and follow after Me is not worthy of Me. He who finds his life will lose it, and he who loses his life for My sake will find it."

MATTHEW 10:34-39

Today's scripture feels like one of the most challenging things Jesus ever said, and yet it's more relevant now than ever. Certainly, Jesus wasn't saying He wanted families and friends to be enemies. He is, after all, the Prince of Peace. But Jesus' very person necessitates life's greatest choice. There's no middle ground.

We must choose between two ways of living, two kingdoms, and two eternal destinies. That's what Jesus meant when He referenced a narrow road that leads to eternal life and a broad road leading to destruction (Matthew 7:13).

When Jesus spoke about division here, He was stating the inescapable truth. Just as we can't be ambivalent when it comes to making the most important choice of our lives, others may have a hard time accepting our decision. Jesus knew it, and He wanted us to understand something clearly: Whatever losses we sustain for choosing Jesus, even if it means those closest to us walk away, He's still worth it.

Jesus, thank You for coming into my life. I treasure You above all else. Amen.

Day Brightener

He led them out as far as Bethany, and He lifted up His hands and blessed them. Now it came to pass, while He blessed them, that He was parted from them and carried up into heaven. And they worshiped Him, and returned to Jerusalem with great joy, and were continually in the temple praising and blessing God. Amen.

LUKE 24:50–53

Today's scripture is, of course, the account of the ascension of Jesus into heaven. But here is an interesting nugget I don't want you to miss: Notice that the disciples are said to have returned to Jerusalem with *great joy*. Jesus, their Savior, had just left them. Back in the sixteenth chapter of John, when He had simply *told* them he was going to leave, sorrow filled their hearts. What turned their sorrow at the prospect of Jesus leaving into joy when He actually left?

To be sure, the resurrection of Jesus and the promise of the Holy Spirit had a lot to do with it. But the best answer may come from Dr. Luke's other account of the ascension, in Acts 1. The angels assured them that the same Jesus they saw rise into heaven would return in the same way He left (v. 11).

Here we are, nearly two thousand years later, and the same truth that brought great joy to the disciples is there to fill our hearts. Jesus is coming again. This broken world we live in has sorrows, disappointments, and losses that can bring us down; but when we remember that at any moment Jesus could return, our sorrow is turned into joy.

....

Lord, help me remember that You are returning, and that it could be today. Amen.

Mark Hoover, NewSpring Church, Wichita, KS

Nothing Is Stronger than Our God

The LORD has redeemed Jacob, and ransomed him from the hand of one stronger than he. Therefore they shall come and sing in the height of Zion, streaming to the goodness of the LORD—for wheat and new wine and oil, for the young of the flock and the herd; their souls shall be like a well-watered garden, and they shall sorrow no more at all. "Then shall the virgin rejoice in the dance, and the young men and the old, together; for I will turn their mourning to joy, will comfort them, and make them rejoice rather than sorrow."

JEREMIAH 31:11-13

Today's beautiful reading reminds us once again that God has a way of turning sorrow into joy. Turn the pages of the Bible, and time after time you'll find God rescuing His people. The sorrows of attacking armies, lions' dens, fiery furnaces, and menacing giants have never kept Him from bringing His people out of trouble and into blessing.

In the verses we just read, God was promising to deliver His people who were taken into captivity. Although the name mentioned here is Jacob, the actual reference is to the people of Israel. I love the part in verse 11 that speaks of God ransoming "him from the hand of one stronger than he."

Are you dealing with anything right now that feels too strong for you? It's good to know that the problems too big for us are never too big for our God.

Dear Lord, help me to remember that no situation is so dark that You can't overcome. Amen.

Everyday Joy and Peace

God's Hand of Provision

"O LORD our God, all this abundance that we have prepared to build You a house for Your holy name is from Your hand, and is all Your own. I know also, my God, that You test the heart and have pleasure in uprightness. As for me, in the uprightness of my heart I have willingly offered all these things; and now with joy I have seen Your people, who are present here to offer willingly to You. O LORD God of Abraham, Isaac, and Israel, our fathers, keep this forever in the intent of the thoughts of the heart of Your people, and fix their heart toward You."

1 CHRONICLES 29:16–18

King David was planning and promoting the construction of the temple. He used his resources to fund the project. He also challenged the people to give. Yet, he confessed that everything came from the hand of God. God is our provider.

David acknowledged the Lord as the God of Abraham, Isaac, and Israel. In Abraham He is the God of the sovereign covenant. His promise in Genesis 17 was to make Abraham the father of many. And He did! In Isaac He is the God of miracle provision. His promise in Genesis 18 was to give a son. And He did! In Israel (Jacob) He is the God of divine patience. In Genesis 28 He promised to give the land to Jacob. And He did!

Whatever your situation is today, God has a promise for you. And He will keep it. Today's scripture deals with sacrificial giving. Be certain you are being faithful in your stewardship. God will make a way.

....

Lord, thank You for Your faithful hand of provision. Give me guidance and strength as I open my hand back to You in giving. Amen.

Dr. Ted H. Traylor, Olive Baptist Church, Pensacola, FL

The God of Victory

They returned, every man of Judah and Jerusalem, with Jehoshaphat in front of them, to go back to Jerusalem with joy, for the LORD had made them rejoice over their enemies. So they came to Jerusalem, with stringed instruments and harps and trumpets, to the house of the LORD. And the fear of God was on all the kingdoms of those countries when they heard that the LORD had fought against the enemies of Israel. Then the realm of Jehoshaphat was quiet, for his God gave him rest all around.

2 CHRONICLES 20:27-30

Second Chronicles 20 tells the story of a miracle victory. Moab and Ammon combined to make war against Jehoshaphat. In that context, one of the great Bible statements of faith was made: "O our God . . . we know [not] what to do, but our eyes are upon You" (v. 12). The people were not dismayed and did not walk in fear. God gave a miracle victory.

Today's text teaches us how to respond when God gives a victory. First, there was great rejoicing with instruments and praise. We cannot forget to rejoice. Sing His praise; lift your voice. Dare not sit in public or private worship without a song. Let the redeemed of the Lord say so (Psalm 107:2)!

Second, there was quiet rest. Learn to rest in the Lord. Soak in His sovereign action. He is good. Take His yoke on you and learn from Him (Matthew 11:29). Rest and trust the Prince of Peace.

. . . .

Father, thank You for Your faithfulness in my battles. You never fail. Today I rejoice in Your victory. Forgive me when I am not thankful and try to win the day myself. Teach me when to act and when to simply watch You. In Jesus' name, amen.

God Bless Our Nation

The keeper of the prison reported these words to Paul, saying, "The magistrates have sent to let you go. Now therefore depart, and go in peace." But Paul said to them, "They have beaten us openly, uncondemned Romans, and have thrown us into prison. And now do they put us out secretly? No indeed! Let them come themselves and get us out."

ACTS 16:36-37

Today's text brings to mind the idea we often call the separation of church and state. I live in the United States, where freedom of religion is written into our Constitution. I am also a Southern Baptist. Our *Baptist Faith and Message 2000* includes a strong article on religious liberty. It states, "God alone is Lord of the conscience, and He has left it free from the doctrines and commandments of men which are contrary to His word or not contained in it."[2]

Paul was a gospel preacher and Roman citizen. As a citizen he had certain rights to claim. According to our citizenship, we also have rights and protections. And we have a responsibility to the law when it does not violate God's law.

Let us be reminded by today's text to pray for our elected officials. It is also a reminder to intercede for those living in regions of religious persecution.

As a high school student, I earned a college scholarship in a speech contest. The message focused on the Statue of Liberty and the message engraved on this symbol of liberty: "Give me your tired, your poor, your huddled masses yearning to breathe free." May we never take for granted what God has given us. His blessing and freedom lead to peace and joy.

· ·

God, I ask for you to bless our nation and those living in it.

Dr. Ted H. Traylor, Olive Baptist Church, Pensacola, FL

The Discipline of the Lord

They indeed for a few days chastened us as seemed best to them, but He for our profit, that we may be partakers of His holiness. Now no chastening seems to be joyful for the present, but painful; nevertheless, afterward it yields the peaceable fruit of righteousness to those who have been trained by it.

HEBREWS 12:10-11

When I was a grade school boy, I was excited about a fishing trip with my father. The morning of the special adventure I committed a grievous sin of the tongue. My parents told me I would not go one step until I confessed and apologized. A whipping would have been easier! However, here I am more than fifty years later remembering that discipline. They loved me enough to care.

Our heavenly Father also disciplines His children. Hebrews 12 lists five reasons He does this:

1. He proves He loves us (v. 6).
2. He is training us for obedience (v. 9).
3. He educates us for holiness (v. 10).
4. He provides the path for the fruit of righteousness to be yielded (v. 11).
5. He teaches us endurance (v. 12).

A good earthly father applies discipline, seeking to mold and shape a child's character out of love. I know I'm grateful for everything my father did to lead me on the right path. Yet, how much more does my heavenly Father love me! And oh, how He loves you too! Let us accept his discipline as a sign of His love.

Father, thank You for reproving me when I need it. Thank You for showing such gracious love to me. Mold me, Father, into the image of Your Son.

The Absence of Fear

All your children shall be taught by the Lord, *and great shall be the peace of your children. In righteousness you shall be established; you shall be far from oppression, for you shall not fear; and from terror, for it shall not come near you.*

ISAIAH 54:13–14

In today's verses, the prophet Isaiah speaks of the promises of the millennium. These are great words from a great man about our great God in a coming great age. But we are not in that future age today. The promise stated is this: You will not fear!

Yet today we must face this emotion by faith. Fear can paralyze us. It leads us to isolation from fellowship of God's people. Scripture tells us often not to fear.

As you begin to replace fear with faith, turn to God's promises in His Word:

- "Be strong and of good courage, do not fear nor be afraid of them; for the Lord your God, He is the One who goes with you. He will not leave you nor forsake you." (Deuteronomy 31:6)
- "The Lord, He is the One who goes before you. He will be with you, He will not leave you nor forsake you; do not fear nor be dismayed." (Deuteronomy 31:8)
- "Have I not commanded you? Be strong and of good courage; do not be afraid, nor be dismayed, for the Lord your God is with you wherever you go." (Joshua 1:9)

Need more encouragement? The Bible is full of it (see also Joshua 8:1; 10:8; 10:25; 11:6). Never forget who has brought you through your storms of life thus far. Stand on the Bible promises of God's faithfulness, and fear not.

Father, thank You for Your faithful promises and actions in my life.

Dr. Ted H. Traylor, Olive Baptist Church, Pensacola, FL

The Eyes of Faith

After eight days His disciples were again inside, and Thomas with them. Jesus came, the doors being shut, and stood in the midst, and said, "Peace to you!" Then He said to Thomas, "Reach your finger here, and look at My hands; and reach your hand here, and put it into My side. Do not be unbelieving, but believing." And Thomas answered and said to Him, "My Lord and my God!" Jesus said to him, "Thomas, because you have seen Me, you have believed. Blessed are those who have not seen and yet have believed."

JOHN 20:26-29

Thomas confessed he would not believe Jesus was alive until he saw the nail prints in His hands and placed his finger in that wound in His side. Because of this, he is known as Doubting Thomas.

How are you known? Do you live by sight or by faith?

As a young preacher I met evangelist Manley Beasley. He stated his definition of faith as "counting something as if it were so in order that it might be so." You can be sure that challenged and confused me as a young man. I learned he was far from a name-it-and-claim-it preacher. He taught me and countless others that God gives the promise, not us. God initiates, and we must believe.

In 2 Corinthians 4:18 Paul stated, "We do not look at the things which are seen, but the things which are not seen." This moves us from the temporal to the eternal. Make an appointment today with the Eternal Optimist. Allow the Lord to focus your eyes in faith; then take the steps of faith rather than those of sight.

Lord, sharpen my eyes of faith. Help me see Your promises and walk in them even when I cannot see the future.

Everyday Joy and Peace

Opposition Does Not Prevent

We wanted to come to you—even I, Paul, time and again—but Satan hindered us. For what is our hope, or joy, or crown of rejoicing? Is it not even you in the presence of our Lord Jesus Christ at His coming? For you are our glory and joy.

1 THESSALONIANS 2:18-20

We often think of Satan as being dressed in a red suit and holding a pitchfork. But he is real, and his sole intent is to try to confound believers and prevent followers of Christ from accomplishing their God-given assignments. From the beginning, he has always tried to take God's place and steal God's glory. Today's verses remind us that spiritual warfare is real; and while it's real, it can be won. Paul attributes his inability to go to Thessalonica to an attack by the Enemy—an attack by Satan. Satan weaponizes everyday circumstances to interfere with the work of God in your life. Just as God was working in Paul's life, so too He is working in your life; Satan attacks where God is moving. But no matter how lethal the attack, Satan is powerless against the almighty God. Scripture reminds us that faithful followers of Christ will receive their reward when Jesus comes—a crown. For Paul, he had already received his crown, the Thessalonian church. Even though Satan tried to destroy it, God still prevailed. And even though Satan may try to destroy your purpose, the God in you will always prevail.

....

Kind God, may I remember that Satan's sole purpose is to hinder me. May I trust in Your promise to be with me always, and be ever mindful that where You are at work, so too is Satan. Help me to rest in and rely on You more. Amen.

Gregory Perkins, The View Church, Menifee, CA

Godly Wisdom

The wisdom that is from above is first pure, then peaceable, gentle, willing to yield, full of mercy and good fruits, without partiality and without hypocrisy. Now the fruit of righteousness is sown in peace by those who make peace.

JAMES 3:17-18

T he world has drifted further and further from God. As society wrestles today with what is wise and what is wisdom, so too did the children of Israel. In Judges 21, Joshua had died and the nation had lost its moral compass. The result was selfishness and an abundance of carnality. In essence, a lack of wise living. This behavior, James said, does not come from God. He then provided an illustration of how godly wisdom could be identified. It is pure, peaceable, gentle, willing to yield, full of mercy, and good fruit springs from it. This kind of wisdom is what God has called us to pursue. It is impartial and has no favorites. Pursuing God-centered wisdom allows you to live in peace with all men. This is the ultimate fruit of God's righteousness.

Kind God, may I pursue Your wisdom. May I pursue peace anchored in God-centered principles. May I be pure in my motives, gentle in my encounters with others, willing to yield, a purveyor of Your mercy. And may I reap the benefits of Your good fruit. Help me not to show partiality, or be hypocritical. May my life be an example for others of sowing peace and living in peace with all. Amen.

Abiding in God

"If you abide in Me, and My words abide in you, you will ask what you desire, and it shall be done for you. By this My Father is glorified, that you bear much fruit; so you will be My disciples. As the Father loved Me, I also have loved you; abide in My love."

JOHN 15:7-9

We often engage with God in a transactional fashion, as if He is a vending machine. We say a prayer, push a button, and out comes what we desire. But God is not seeking a transactional relationship. Rather, He is seeking a relationship rooted in abiding in Him. To abide denotes a deep level of intimacy, engagement, and trust. It requires trusting in Jesus, communing with Jesus, and resting in Jesus. Living a fruitful life as a follower of Christ requires rejecting transactional engagement and abiding in Him. Abiding in Him changes your desires and shifts your prayer focus. Forging an intimate relationship with God transforms your heart and mind. Your desires become not what you want but what God desires. This allows God to answer your prayers because your prayers are His desires for you. Abiding in Christ requires the believer to hide the Word of God in his or her heart. To have the heart of God means to understand the desires of God, and it requires submission and obedience to the Word of God.

....

Kind God, You are my lifeline. I cannot live a life of faith without Your help, and I need Your power. Often I pursue my desires and not Yours. Would You forgive me for not trusting You? For not believing that You know what is best for me? Forgive me for engaging with You in a transactional way, and help me pursue loving relationship with You. In Jesus' name, amen.

Gregory Perkins, The View Church, Menifee, CA

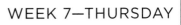
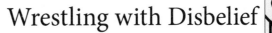

Wrestling with Disbelief

Gideon perceived that He was the Angel of the Lord. So Gideon said, "Alas, O Lord God! For I have seen the Angel of the Lord face to face." Then the Lord said to him, "Peace be with you; do not fear, you shall not die." So Gideon built an altar there to the Lord, and called it The-Lord-Is-Peace. To this day it is still in Ophrah of the Abiezrites.

JUDGES 6:22–24

We often pray to experience God, yet when He moves in our midst, we are ill prepared to receive it. Rather than rejoicing, we become anxious, fearful, or even sad. We may even question if it is really God at work. Although faithful, Gideon wrestled with believing God. If we are honest, there are seasons of life when we all wrestle with believing God. Even in Gideon's disbelief, God remained ever faithful. Rather than condemnation, Gideon was given affirmation. "Peace be with you; do not fear, you shall not die." God had done the miraculous. Gideon's fear had robbed him of fully embracing it. Perhaps you have asked God to move in your situation; but when He does, will you be ready to receive it? Take guidance from the example of Gideon in today's verses, who finally recognized that it was truly God moving in his midst and worshiped Him with peace in his heart.

Kind God, help me to not operate in fear. Help me rest in my faith in You. When I am unsure, may I look to You. May I seek You and discover You. Amen.

Walking in Faith

The seventy returned with joy, saying, "Lord, even the demons are subject to us in Your name." And He said to them, "I saw Satan fall like lightning from heaven. Behold, I give you the authority to trample on serpents and scorpions, and over all the power of the enemy, and nothing shall by any means hurt you. Nevertheless do not rejoice in this, that the spirits are subject to you, but rather rejoice because your names are written in heaven."

LUKE 10:17-20

O ur covenant relationship with Jesus gives believers access to His supernatural power. While this power illustrates itself differently today, His power yet prevails. Demons then and demonic forces now are subject to Jesus. The seventy rejoiced because they operated in faith and attained faithful results. Satan is defeated. He is powerless against a believer who walks in faith. Just as Jesus told them that through faith in Him they had the authority to trample serpents and overpower the Enemy, so too, today, when we walk in faith, we are able to overcome the demonic forces and obstacles placed in our way. But our joy is not in the outcome; our joy is anchored in the promise.

Kind God, help me not think more highly of myself than I ought to. Help me not to forfeit experiencing Your supernatural power in my circumstances because I have lived a life of faithlessness. Give me the grace to trust You more. May my faith be greater than a mustard seed, and may my resolve be to trample the serpents in my life. Not by my power but through Yours. Amen.

Gregory Perkins, The View Church, Menifee, CA

Remaining Faithful

Then those who feared the LORD spoke to one another, and the LORD listened and heard them; so a book of remembrance was written before Him for those who fear the LORD and who meditate on His name. "They shall be Mine," says the LORD of hosts, "on the day that I make them My jewels. And I will spare them as a man spares his own son who serves him."

MALACHI 3:16-17

Sin and rebellion against God was rampant in the people Malachi was talking to in today's verses. It was the heart of God for His people to return to Him. They were not created to live this way. God wanted better for them even if they desired less for themselves. In the midst of wickedness, there remained those who feared God. The character of God is in full view as His heart opened for those who remained faithful to Him. He used words like "Mine," "My," and "own." His own are those who faithfully follow Him. They remained faithful, and in return He remained faithful despite the circumstances. No matter how dire the situation, remain faithful to God. No matter how difficult the circumstance, God will always remain faithful to you. It is who He is, and it is who you are destined to become.

....

Kind God, may I remain faithful even when everyone around me has become faithless. May I choose You over relationships, insecurities, and fears. May I choose You. Help me trust that I am Yours and that You will always be faithful. Amen.

The Joy of Restoration

For Zion's sake I will not hold My peace, and for Jerusalem's sake I will not rest,
until her righteousness goes forth as brightness, and her salvation as a lamp that
burns. The Gentiles shall see your righteousness, and all kings your glory. You
shall be called by a new name, which the mouth of the LORD will name. You shall
also be a crown of glory in the hand of the LORD, and a royal diadem in the hand
of your God.

ISAIAH 62:1-3

I saiah prophesied about the redeeming power of God. Israel had sinned greatly and would be disciplined severely. Isaiah was moved by God to look past their sin to their future restoration. In today's scripture, we see that redemption is a work of God, grace, and glory.

Redemption is an act of God. Marred by sin, Israel was in no position to restore itself. Thankfully, God would not withhold His peace or rest until they were restored. It would not be a work of self-effort but of divine power. What joy to know that the ability to be restored is as great as the power of God.

Redemption is an act of grace. The once-fallen people would receive a new name. The heavenly Potter would not throw the clay away. Rather, in His grace, He would make them new. God's grace is available despite our worst failures.

Redemption is an act of glory. The reason for Israel's restoration was ultimately the glory of God. Likewise, when we experience God's forgiveness and renewal, all the praise goes to Him alone. Praise him today for His grace and glory.

....

Father, when I have sinned, restore me. Though I do not deserve it, I
ask You to forgive me by Your grace so my life can bring You glory.

Mike Stone, Emmanuel Baptist Church, Blackshear, GA

Peace in Hard Times

My brethren, count it all joy when you fall into various trials, knowing that the testing of your faith produces patience. But let patience have its perfect work, that you may be perfect and complete, lacking nothing.

JAMES 1:2-4

Trials are never enjoyable. But James told us that we are to count our trials as joy. And he went on to tell us how to do that.

First is the matter of perspective. The word *count* in "count it all joy" speaks of consideration. That means we can think about our trials in a way that leads to joy. The transformation of our trials into joy does not happen by God miraculously changing the situation. It happens when we change the way we view the situation in which we find ourselves.

Second is the matter of patience. James said our trials test our faith. And that produces patience. Patience is the ability to endure hardship with quiet faith and childlike trust. And there is no way we would ever learn to trust God patiently in trials if trials never come. The trial is producing in us a greater ability to trust God and to take Him at His Word.

Finally, James spoke of becoming perfect. The Bible does not teach that a Christian can become a sinless person in this life, but it does teach that we can and should become more mature and complete. That is what James meant by the word *perfect*. When we recognize that trials give us an opportunity to grow in our walk with God, we can consider those trials as blessings in disguise.

Heavenly Father, grant me Your perspective in my difficulties. Help me learn to "count it all joy" in my hardships because You are a trust-worthy God. Amen.

Peace from Trusting God

"Where were you when I laid the foundations of the earth? Tell Me, if you have understanding. Who determined its measurements? Surely you know! Or who stretched the line upon it? To what were its foundations fastened? Or who laid its cornerstone, when the morning stars sang together, and all the sons of God shouted for joy?"

JOB 38:4-7

In today's passage, God was responding to a series of stinging questions from Job. Despite Job's initial response of trust and worship, time had taken its toll on the old saint. It could be said that it was the length of Job's trial as well as its depth that finally caused him to question God.

God responded with divine sarcasm, revealing a truth as serious as any in the Bible. God is completely in control.

We might understand Job's questioning of God. We have each asked our own questions in the dark night of our own souls. We question God's wisdom, love, or power. We feel as if we need to inform God of something to motivate His providential intervention.

Rather than directly answering Job, the Lord gave a volley of questions in return. They reveal that God was around long before Job, knew far more than Job, and did not need advice from a mere mortal man or woman.

This invites us to assume a posture of trust. When life does not make sense, the problem is not on God's end but on ours. We can find peace in recognizing that an all-knowing, all-powerful, and all-loving God has acted as He deems best.

....

Lord, help me remember that You don't need help from me. You are in control and You do all things well. I choose to trust You in my circumstances. Amen.

Mike Stone, Emmanuel Baptist Church, Blackshear, GA

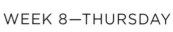

The Joy of Reaching Others

"What man of you, having a hundred sheep, if he loses one of them, does not leave the ninety-nine in the wilderness, and go after the one which is lost until he finds it? And when he has found it, he lays it on his shoulders, rejoicing. And when he comes home, he calls together his friends and neighbors, saying to them, 'Rejoice with me, for I have found my sheep which was lost!' I say to you that likewise there will be more joy in heaven over one sinner who repents than over ninety-nine just persons who need no repentance."

LUKE 15:4–7

In Luke 15, Jesus told three parables about finding something that was lost: the lost sheep, the lost silver, and the lost son. In each case, the discovery brought great joy to the heart.

Joy and peace will never be found in greater measure than when a person tells someone else about the good news of salvation. The psalmist said that those who sow the seed of the gospel in tears shall return with shouts of joy (Psalm 126:5–6). There will be joy in the heart of the person who shares, joy in the person who is reached, and most important, joy in heaven itself.

Do you know Christ as your personal Lord and Savior? Receiving Him will bring joy unspeakable! Do you know someone who needs to hear the gospel? Serving as a faithful witness will bring joy to your heart. And like the shepherd in today's Bible passage, you will call all your friends and ask them to rejoice with you.

....

Dear Father, grant me the privilege of telling someone of Your great love today. And may joy fill the hearts of all involved. Amen.

Be Deeply Rooted

"Hear the parable of the sower: When anyone hears the word of the kingdom, and does not understand it, then the wicked one comes and snatches away what was sown in his heart. This is he who received seed by the wayside. But he who received the seed on stony places, this is he who hears the word and immediately receives it with joy."

MATTHEW 13:18-20

The parable of the sower tells of seed that fell on shallow soil. Because of the lack of the soil's depth, the seed began to grow but the plant quickly succumbed to the hot sun. Jesus describes this person as having received the Word of God "with joy."

Ironically, the thing that made the soil look so good is actually what made it so bad. The plant sprang up because there was not enough soil for the roots to grow in a deep, healthy, downward direction. The tragedy of this parable serves as a warning to us today.

We must make firm commitments to the Lord with all our hearts, souls, minds, and strength. Our devotion must be far deeper than our shallow emotions. God never does His deepest work in our shallowest parts. And our emotions are the most fickle, fleeting, and fruitless part of who we are.

Full surrender to God will sustain us on the sad days as well as the happy days, the hard roads as well as the easy pathways. Today, examine your heart and devotion to ensure that your faith grows beyond a thin layer of emotion; may it become a faith deeply rooted in the power of Christ.

....

Father in heaven, help me follow You with my whole heart. May I love and serve You with every ounce of my being. Amen.

Mike Stone, Emmanuel Baptist Church, Blackshear, GA

Joy Is a By-Product

Let them shout for joy and be glad, who favor my righteous cause; and let them say continually, "Let the Lord be magnified, who has pleasure in the prosperity of His servant." And my tongue shall speak of Your righteousness and of Your praise all the day long.

PSALM 35:27–28

D on't you think God wants me to be happy?" As a pastor, I hear that question in one form or another on a regular basis. I tend to shock my listener with a firm reply. "No. No, God is not interested in your happiness at all." And friend, that is the gospel truth.

The Bible clearly teaches that God can give unspeakable joy and indescribable peace. But what we tend to call happiness is just an emotion that is based on circumstances. God desires to give joy, which is based on obedience. The psalmist called for joy in the hearts of those who favor the righteous cause of God and those who are called God's servants.

Real joy will never be found when it is pursued as a primary goal. Rather, it is a by-product of being right with the Lord and of serving Him faithfully. Wherever there is an absence of joy, there is generally the presence of a problem in the relationship with God.

When we seek joy at the expense of holiness, we end up with neither. But when we pursue holiness, regardless of whether it pleases our emotions, we will end up with holy lives, and joy thrown in for free!

Dear Lord, help me today to walk as Your servant. I want to favor Your righteous cause. As I live for You, may I know what it means to shout for joy and be glad. Amen.

That You May Inherit a Blessing

He who would love life and see good days, let him refrain his tongue from evil, and his lips from speaking deceit. Let him turn away from evil and do good; let him seek peace and pursue it. For the eyes of the LORD are on the righteous, and His ears are open to their prayers; but the face of the LORD is against those who do evil.

1 PETER 3:10–12

The command to love your neighbor as yourself is found in both the Old and New Testaments of the Bible, and it is foundational to the relationship God desires to have with us (Leviticus 19:18; Mark 12:31). God created us out of His love, which then becomes His model of how we should love ourselves and then love the people around us.

Love is the key to unlocking the blessings found in today's scripture: "He who would love life and see good days." This blessing does not happen automatically, but must be coaxed and nurtured throughout every day as we encounter life's challenges. Today's passage is clear about how this should look:

- Do not speak evil or be deceitful.
- Turn away from evil and do good.
- Seek peace and pursue it.

These points must become part of our everyday living if we are to become fully functional in our lives. When we prioritize them, every relationship, every encounter will be flavored with kindness, integrity, peace, and love. It is the blessing we inherit here on earth.

....

Father, help me to "love life and see good days" as Your love flows through my encounters with other people.

Tim DeTellis, New Missions, Orlando, FL

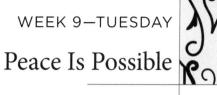

Peace Is Possible

It pleased the Father that in Him all the fullness should dwell, and by Him to reconcile all things to Himself, by Him, whether things on earth or things in heaven, having made peace through the blood of His cross.

COLOSSIANS 1:19-20

P eace in today's world is fleeting, and for many people it is a seemingly impossible, shattered dream. The pressures of life weigh heavily on men and women, boys and girls all over the world as they simply try to make it through another day . . . alive. Hope has given way to despair as the prospect of another day looms before them. Where is peace for these hopeless ones?

The prophet Isaiah wrote, "Unto us a Child is born, unto us a Son is given; and the government will be upon His shoulder. And His name will be called Wonderful, Counselor, Mighty God, Everlasting Father, Prince of Peace. Of the increase of His government and peace there will be no end" (Isaiah 9:6–7).

This Prince of Peace is the same person mentioned in today's passage. His name is Jesus. In other words, God has already sent peace into the world through His Son, Jesus; and by His crucifixion and resurrection, His peace is available to everyone, everywhere—it is a gift.

How do you receive that gift of peace? Believe the gift is yours and then reach out and take it. By simply believing that Jesus is the Son of God and that He gave His life for your life, you receive His gift of eternal life and peace. Ask God to help you believe today that His Peace can be yours.

....

Lord, I ask Your forgiveness for my sins. Help me fully accept it, and show me how to take hold of Your peace today.

Everyday Joy and Peace

Live a Full Life

Go, eat your bread with joy, and drink your wine with a merry heart; for God has already accepted your works. Let your garments always be white, and let your head lack no oil.

ECCLESIASTES 9:7-8

Today's passage encourages us to live in the knowledge that "God has already accepted" our works. We may wonder how that can be since we are still living every day with all the challenges that come our way. How can God have already accepted our works when we still make mistakes and sin?

The key to understanding this is found in our salvation. Yesterday we learned that Christ reconciled all things to Himself and made peace through the shedding of His blood. This vital truth reveals that as we become Christ-followers, that same peace accompanies us no matter where we are or what we do. In other words, God's grace completely covers us through the work of Christ on the cross.

With this assurance, we can greet each day with joy knowing that our debt has been paid in full and Christ reigns in our hearts. This joy comes from the inside of our being, not from anything that may be happening outside. It is a joy and peace that surpasses our understanding, because some days we may feel like utter failures. This is the awesome, unchanging, everlasting love of God shed in our hearts! Therefore, let us shout with joy our praises to God and His Son, Jesus. Let us indeed eat our bread with joy and drink our wine with a merry heart!

....

Keep my focus on You, Lord, so my steps can be sure, my motives are in the right place, and my heart is filled with confident joy.

　　　　　　　　　　Tim DeTellis, New Missions, Orlando, FL

The Mighty Power of God

Break forth into joy, sing together, you waste places of Jerusalem! For the LORD has comforted His people, He has redeemed Jerusalem. The LORD has made bare His holy arm in the eyes of all the nations; and all the ends of the earth shall see the salvation of our God.

ISAIAH 52:9-10

Stop quietly for a few moments and consider today's passage. One phrase declares, "For the LORD has comforted His people." Have you ever needed the comfort that only God can provide? Have you ever felt hemmed in on every side with nowhere to turn and nowhere to go? Have you ever felt as if the only option was to give up and give in to whatever had come against you?

If so, Isaiah 52 should provide you with a welcome dose of "God's got this"! Too often it seems the only thing to do is give up when a prayer hasn't even been prayed yet. Too often the desire to escape is greater than the fortitude to face the giant before you. The entire chapter of Isaiah 52 is a proclamation of the mighty power of God as He redeemed Jerusalem and set it free from captivity. Verse 12 promised that the Lord would go before the people and that "the God of Israel" would be their rear guard. God is willing and ready to bare His holy arm for you as well. When you are standing in the midst of the battle, lift up your eyes, cry out to the Lord, and behold the mighty power of God!

Mighty God, I depend on Your provision, and I crave Your comfort. I will lean wholly on You today.

What Is Your Prayer?

The angel said to him, "Do not be afraid, Zacharias, for your prayer is heard; and your wife Elizabeth will bear you a son, and you shall call his name John. And you will have joy and gladness, and many will rejoice at his birth."

LUKE 1:13-14

You may have wondered whether God truly answers prayer. You may have prayed fervently for something, but it seemed to fall on deaf ears in heaven. Even now, you may have a request before the Lord that is as big as Zacharias's was.

Have you ever wondered what the test of faith is in regard to prayer? Is it how long you wait or how often and fervently you pray for what you need? Jesus had something to say about this:

- "If two of you agree on earth concerning anything that they ask, it will be done for them by My Father in heaven. For where two or three are gathered together in My name, I am there in the midst of them." (Matthew 18:19–20)
- "Whatever things you ask when you pray, believe that you receive them, and you will have them." (Mark 11:24)
- "If you ask anything in My name, I will do it." (John 14:14)

Notice in these passages Jesus talks first about prayer in agreement, then about believing that you will receive what you pray for, and finally, about asking in His name. Jesus does not say to give up after the first attempt or to lose heart if things don't change right away. So keep your requests before the throne of God, asking in faith in Jesus' name, and simply believe that you will receive.

....

Lord, thank You for hearing my prayers. I believe I will receive Your best for my life as I pursue You.

Tim DeTellis, New Missions, Orlando, FL

Love One Another

"These things I have spoken to you, that My joy may remain in you, and that your joy may be full. This is My commandment, that you love one another as I have loved you. Greater love has no one than this, than to lay down one's life for his friends."

JOHN 15:11–13

We began this week talking about how we must love our neighbors as we love ourselves, and we will finish with yet more love. Notice in this passage that Jesus made it clear He wanted the disciples to love one other as He had loved them. Again, God's love for us is the template we must use in our relationships with other people. We must love them.

This call to love is not an easy one to answer. Some people are very difficult to love or to even be around. What about them? Are we supposed to love them too?

Part of our problem is that we equate a person's behavior with who that person is. In other words, we examine what they do and then categorize them into boxes, like "filthy," "angry," "insensitive," "troublemaker," and other labels.

Jesus recognized that people's behavior did not identify them as individuals; it was simply their behavior. He was able to separate the person's behavior from who they were in God's eyes, and He loved them accordingly.

So our challenge is to change our minds about these "unlovable" people and recognize the difference between the behavior and the person. They are still worthy of love as a person, and God empowers us to love them as He does.

Father, help me view every person the way You do. Help me love them despite their behavior, modeling my love on Yours.

The Depths of Peace

I beg you, brethren, through the Lord Jesus Christ, and through the love of the Spirit, that you strive together with me in prayers to God for me . . . that I may come to you with joy by the will of God, and may be refreshed together with you. Now the God of peace be with you all. Amen.

ROMANS 15:30–33

Peace is an elusive thing in our lives. No wonder we write "Rest in Peace" on tombstones. We don't say "rest in joy" or "rest in faith," but rather, "rest in peace." Wouldn't it be wonderful if we could rest in peace while we are alive? Some years ago, my wife and I were vacationing in Mexico and didn't realize a hurricane was bearing down on us. What was a peaceful day of rest soon turned into scenes of people making a mad scramble to get furniture secure and boats anchored, and rushing to buy provisions. When the hurricane hit, the waves crashed and the wind howled. It was eerie. As I reflect on that day, I'm sure that thirty feet below the surface of those turbulent waves, all was calm. For marine life in the depths of the water, it was business as usual.

Where there is depth, there is peace. Could it be there is so little peace in the world because we have so little depth with God? Let's pause today and seek the depth of peace in prayer, in God's Spirit, His Word, and His presence.

....

Lord, show me how to rest in the depths of Your peace, that I may be refreshed. Amen.

Roy G. Mack, Grace Fellowship Church, Niles, OH

His Love Is Better than Life

When I remember You on my bed, I meditate on You in the night watches.
Because You have been my help, therefore in the shadow of Your wings I will
rejoice. My soul follows close behind You; Your right hand upholds me.

PSALM 63:6–8

This psalm is often titled "His Love Is Better than Life." David wrote it while in what should have been one of the most stressful situations of his life. His son Absalom was attempting to overthrow his kingdom. David, once again, was fleeing for his life into the Judaean wilderness, but instead of panicking and crying out in a prayer for God's help, David was going to lay his body down in rest.

While doing so, David rejoiced and worshiped God. The "night watches" refer to how long a night can be when you are sleeplessly burdened. David knew from much experience that night watches are the best times to meditate on God's goodness and His Word. David found the greatest of treasures in these times. David was a poet and musician, and the world has had its share of people who write and sing about finding something or someone they love more than life. That is not what David was referring to. Rather, David found something that was better than his own life: the love of God. David's greatest treasure was not his kingdom, his position of authority, or his wealth. His treasure was to be known and loved by God, to live in the very shadow of His wings and follow God as a sheep follows the shepherd.

. . . .

Dear Father, You are my Great Shepherd. Help me lay all my burdens down and rejoice that I am loved by You.

Our Message Is Peace

"When you go into a household, greet it. If the household is worthy, let your peace come upon it. But if it is not worthy, let your peace return to you. And whoever will not receive you nor hear your words, when you depart from that house or city, shake off the dust from your feet."

MATTHEW 10:12-14

F or many years a member of my church would dress up as Santa Claus and volunteer at schools to ask the children, "What do you want for Christmas?" He said he was heartbroken over a little girl who came three years in a row and said the same thing each year. "All I want for Christmas is for there to be peace in my home."

As Christ's followers, we are to bring God's peace with us, speak peace, and offer peace to all we meet. We are Christ's ambassadors, His representatives of peace. Jesus came to earth for this purpose: to make peace between God and man. That is now our mission as we share the gospel of peace with all who will hear. Our message is the only thing that will bring true peace to any home. We cannot make them hear it, but it is our responsibility to share it and represent it well. No wonder Jesus often said, "He who has ears to hear, let him hear" (Matthew 11:15). In today's verse, Jesus acknowledged that some people won't listen to the message of peace. Shake it off and move on to those who will. It is a gift too precious, too grand, too needed to keep to ourselves. As messengers of peace, let's keep the message spreading.

....

Father, make me a messenger of peace. Grant me patience, and open ears and hearts so Your peace can be known.

Roy G. Mack, Grace Fellowship Church, Niles, OH

The Mighty One

"Whereas you have been forsaken and hated, so that no one went through you, I will make you an eternal excellence, a joy of many generations. You shall drink the milk of the Gentiles and milk the breast of kings; you shall know that I, the LORD, *am your Savior and your Redeemer, the Mighty One of Jacob."*

ISAIAH 60:15–16

A t first glance, this is a bizarre passage of scripture. Its subject is Jerusalem (Zion), and it is a glance ahead to the coming New Testament church of Jesus. When the passage was written, Jerusalem lay desolate, plundered by the Babylonian empire, destroyed and wasted. Its streets were empty, and "no one went through." But the promise remained that one day it would be restored, "an eternal excellence, a joy of many generations." The church, in like manner, will become a generational joy. God uses nations and kings for His good pleasure to sustain the church, like a child nursing its mother. The church will not be sustained by begging or attacking like a monstrous vampire, but rather by drinking like a tender nursing child. God will supply His church. He shows His sovereignty in His promise.

Scripture tells us that Jesus came in "the fullness of the time" (Galatians 4:4). The gospel is for the whole world, so God allowed Rome to absorb the whole world. Rome brought with its rule a time of peace, good roads, effective communication, and law and order. The book of Acts records neutrality and fairness from secular authorities toward the gospel message. Rome was like a ferocious lion, but God had shut her mouth and tamed her for His instrument. We can find peace in the fact that He is our Savior, Redeemer, the Mighty One, and our Provider.

Father, supply us for all You're calling us to do.

Joy in the Church

I wrote this very thing to you, lest, when I came, I should have sorrow over those from whom I ought to have joy, having confidence in you all that my joy is the joy of you all. For out of much affliction and anguish of heart I wrote to you, with many tears, not that you should be grieved, but that you might know the love which I have so abundantly for you.

2 CORINTHIANS 2:3-4

I n today's verses, Paul was writing to the church in Corinth to let them know why he was delayed in returning there. Some in the church were saying Paul was unreliable because he had changed his travel plans. His previous visit had been painful, partly due to a confrontation with someone. He was praying and waiting for God to change that person's heart and the hearts of their supporters. If not, he would have to come and exercise his authority over the situation, and he knew that would cause a strain as well.

Paul's pastoral heart did not want to grieve them, but the situation had to be corrected. Paul wanted this church to be one he could boast about for God's glory. He wanted them to know the love of God and to experience His joy. The way this happened in Corinth is the way it should happen in our church today: Sin must be confronted. The offender needs opportunity and space to repent with a change of heart, and then must be forgiven and restored. This brings joy to the congregation and sets a right example. May we never miss the connection between joy and repentance, in our own hearts and in our communities.

Father, may the world know we are Your disciples by how we love one another.

Roy G. Mack, Grace Fellowship Church, Niles, OH

Hit Songs

It had happened as they were coming home, when David was returning from the slaughter of the Philistine, that the women had come out of all the cities of Israel, singing and dancing, to meet King Saul, with tambourines, with joy, and with musical instruments. So, the women sang as they danced, and said: "Saul has slain his thousands, and David his ten thousands."

1 SAMUEL 18:6-7

A hit song shot straight to number one on all the music charts in Israel. It was about David after he had killed the giant, for which he is still famous. The chorus went something like this: *Saul (the current king) has killed his thousands and David (the upstart) his ten thousands.* I think David was probably flattered to hear that song as he made his way through Israel. He was still enjoying the satisfaction of delivering his people from the oppression of the enemy with one throw of a stone from his sling. But not everyone appreciated the hit song. King Saul surely didn't, and it made him ragingly jealous.

Sadly, often amid celebration and joy, others will be jealous of your success. We cannot control what is happening in the hearts of other people. But we must keep guard in our own hearts for the jealousy we feel when others are joyfully celebrating and they are the center of celebration. Real and lasting joy is found in being able to celebrate with those who are being recognized, singing their hit song, and remembering Jesus' words in Matthew 10:39: "He who finds his life will lose it, and he who loses his life for My sake will find it."

Father, help me celebrate the wins of others with joy in my heart today.

Everyday Joy and Peace

Balance or Bedlam?

If anything is revealed to another who sits by, let the first keep silent. For you can all prophesy one by one, that all may learn and all may be encouraged. And the spirits of the prophets are subject to the prophets. For God is not the author of confusion but of peace, as in all the churches of the saints.

1 CORINTHIANS 14:30-33

What part do you play in the exercise of worship in your church? Today's passage says that our worship should always be fashioned with decency and order. But through the years, many have relegated it to the pages of a bulletin, missing out on the spontaneity of the Spirit of God.

Each of us must exercise our spiritual gifts to encourage the saints and to glorify the Savior in a manner that completes the body of Christ. Some sing, some teach, others preach, and still others share their individual gifts—and it should be done without disruption, with order and peace.

When there is disorder, God is not allowed to work in the lives of the people in the church. As the Lord unfolds His plan for your life, and your spiritual gift is revealed, be careful that your enthusiasm to use that gift does not jump ahead of God's timing and purpose, thus creating confusion and disharmony in the body of Christ. Wait patiently on the Lord for His revelation of "when." Stay in His peace as you keep your mind on Him.

Lord, we pray for complete balance and harmony within Your family of believers. May our worship be blessed by order but also an expectancy of a move of Your Spirit among us. In Jesus' name, amen.

Contributor or Consumer?

The Holy Spirit testifies in every city, saying that chains and tribulations await me. But none of these things move me; nor do I count my life dear to myself, so that I may finish my race with joy, and the ministry which I received from the Lord Jesus, to testify to the gospel of the grace of God.

ACTS 20:23-24

One of life's greatest questions is, "What am I living for?" The fact is, people today live for fame, fortune, and fun. People are more interested in consuming than contributing. They live for themselves, not for God and others.

Paul realized what lay ahead for him if he continued to preach the gospel. But he was not like many today who feel as if they are failing if they don't get a lot in return for what they are giving themselves to. It is not about serving others for gain in return. It is far more important what we contribute to life than what we receive back.

Paul thought that his life meant nothing if he was not doing all he could to serve the Lord. True joy came to him as he followed the example of Christ of pursuing the "joy that was set before Him" (Hebrews 12:2).

Spend some time today analyzing why you do what you do. Ask: *Does it benefit others? What, if anything, do I expect to gain from this? Does it have eternal significance? How is the Lord glorified through it? Did the Lord initiate this in me?*

Father, let me be empty of self so I may be full of You. Live Your life through me as I yield to You. May the good news of the gospel radiate through my life. In Jesus' name, amen.

Everyday Joy and Peace

What Time Is It?

A time to gain, and a time to lose; a time to keep, and a time to throw away; a time to tear, and a time to sew; a time to keep silence, and a time to speak; a time to love, and a time to hate; a time of war, and a time of peace.

ECCLESIASTES 3:6–8

E ver visited the home of a hoarder? Often it is occupied by a spouse who prefers to throw everything away. The conflict in that home can be staggering when one is a keeper and the other a thrower. In today's passage, the wisdom writer refers to "a time to keep, and a time to throw away." Certain things we are to keep, like the faith and purity. But we are to pitch other things from us. It is our responsibility to rid ourselves of things that don't belong.

We are to "tear" our lives open and cry out to God. Then there's a time to "sew," or to mend broken relationships with those we need to forgive and be forgiven by. There's a time for "silence," when it is best to listen. This is a great way to stop an argument. There's a time to "speak" truth, our convictions, and let the world know where we stand. There's also a time to "love" and a time to "hate." Love the things God loves and hate the things that God hates. And finally, there's a time of "war" and a time of "peace." As we war against the things that separate us from God, we will find peace. As we follow God, He will tell us what time it is.

Lord, remind us that it is time to draw closer to You in obedience more than ever before. May Your Holy Spirit guide, empower, and fill us with Your presence. In Jesus' name, amen.

Dr. Mike Whitson, First Baptist Church Indian Trail, Indian Trail, NC

The Power of the Cross

God forbid that I should boast except in the cross of our Lord Jesus Christ, by whom the world has been crucified to me, and I to the world. For in Christ Jesus neither circumcision nor uncircumcision avails anything, but a new creation.

GALATIANS 6:14-15

Have you ever considered the power of the cross? The world views the symbol of the cross as weak and impotent; Paul says it is full of power. The cross has the power to expose sin and God's judgment. The cross has the power to convict sin, the power to break the sway of sin, and the power to forgive sin.

Paul says you can keep all the rules, go through all the ceremonies and liturgies, but there is only one thing that really counts, and that is a new creation made only possible through the cross of the Lord Jesus Christ. Pilate didn't send Jesus to the cross, nor did the Jews, nor did Caesar. Rather, it was God who sent His Son to the cross to give His life that we might have life everlasting. The purpose was to bring about a new creation.

Here is good news: God didn't come to just hammer out the dents in our life or spray some glossy coating over our sinfulness, but to produce a metamorphosis, a new creation in us. No matter how sordid our lives, how wayward from God, the blood of Jesus covers our sin. Oh, the power of the cross!

Friend, if you have never been changed, please pray the following prayer in your heart and really mean it.

....

Heavenly Father, please forgive me of all my sins and save my soul. In Jesus' name I pray, amen.

Kept in Peace

You will keep him in perfect peace, whose mind is stayed on You, because he trusts in You. Trust in the LORD forever, for in YAH, the LORD, is everlasting strength.

ISAIAH 26:3-4

I f we listen to the news of the day and the conversations around us, we can't help but notice how fear has interjected its way into our everyday lives. We focus so much on issues that stimulate fear in our lives. Political unrest across the world. Pandemics, vaccinations, economic gloom and doom. It is no wonder people are filled with doubt, fear, and distrust.

But in spite of all the bad things we see in the world, God never gets tired of giving us His peace. The Word says that peace will be complete and will never fade but will last forever as long as we trust Him.

What do you need to trust Him with today? What are you trying to handle that you need to relinquish to Him? What is keeping you up at night and causing sleeplessness? Have you prayed? Have you focused on the Lord? God saw you through that last episode in your life when you didn't see any way through it. He will see you through this and the next. Trust Him. As the old hymn says,

> Turn your eyes upon Jesus.
> Look full in His wonderful face.
> And the things of this earth will grow strangely dim
> In the light of His glory and grace.[3]

Heavenly Father, thank You in advance for bringing me peace in the midst of my storm. Keep me focused on You, the beginner and completer of my faith. In Jesus' name, amen.

Dr. Mike Whitson, First Baptist Church Indian Trail, Indian Trail, NC

Peace or Worry?

Jesus answered them, "Do you now believe? Indeed the hour is coming, yes, has now come, that you will be scattered, each to his own, and will leave Me alone. And yet I am not alone, because the Father is with Me. These things I have spoken to you, that in Me you may have peace. In the world you will have tribulation; but be of good cheer, I have overcome the world."

JOHN 16:31–33

Everyone we will ever meet desires peace in life. If you are a Christ-follower, you already have peace with God that comes the moment one repents and places their faith in Jesus. But very few people really have the peace of God. They desperately seek peace but spend all their energies in fret and worry.

Peace joins or puts things together. Worry pulls apart. Jesus says that in Him we find personal peace. The world will do nothing but deceive and destroy, but in today's verses Jesus says He has overcome the world already, so there is no need to be afraid or pulled apart.

While we are left here in this world, waiting on the promise of heaven, Jesus said we could expect to have issues, problems, difficulties, and trouble. He didn't say that we should look for peace in education, or yoga, or meditation, drugs, sex, fame, or materialism. He said find your peace "in Me."

Jesus said, *I am the only One who can calm the storm of your life.* Suffering will come, your car may break down, your back may go out, but take heart and rejoice because Jesus has won the battle for you.

....

Heavenly Father, may Your Word be branded in my heart today.
Deliver me from worry. In Jesus' name, amen.

Everyday Joy and Peace

Wonderful Peace

He Himself is our peace, who has made both one, and has broken down the middle wall of separation, having abolished in His flesh the enmity, that is, the law of commandments contained in ordinances, so as to create in Himself one new man from the two, thus making peace, and that He might reconcile them both to God in one body through the cross, thereby putting to death the enmity. And He came and preached peace to you who were afar off and to those who were near. For through Him we both have access by one Spirit to the Father.

EPHESIANS 2:14-18

In this dark and dangerous world in which we live, peace is a little known and rarely experienced concept. People are not at peace with each other, and they are not at peace with God. The reason for this tragedy is because Jesus is not known or has been cast aside by much of the world's population.

Today's text reminds us that Jesus is our peace (v. 14), the maker of our peace (v. 15), and the preacher of peace (v. 17). He is the essence of peace. No one can have peace without Jesus.

Jesus made peace for us through His death on the cross. We were separated from God, the enemies of God, and far from God, but the death of Jesus on the cross changed all of that. When we were saved, we were brought forever near to the Father and given permanent access to Him. Because Christians have peace with God, we can also have peace with one another.

How will you avail yourself of your access to God and His peace today? He welcomes you in to the relationship His Son makes possible for us, and longs to bring you near.

....

Father, thank You for breaking down all the walls that separated us from You and from others. Amen.

Dr. Robert C. Pitman, Bob Pitman Ministries, Muscle Shoals, AL

Hand in Hand for Peace

Hezekiah gave encouragement to all the Levites who taught the good knowledge of the LORD; and they ate throughout the feast seven days, offering peace offerings and making confession to the LORD God of their fathers.

2 CHRONICLES 30:22

H ezekiah was one of only three kings of Judah who were called great and good. The other two were David and Josiah. All the others were self-seeking men who cared nothing for God or the people. Hezekiah recognized the need for government to be rooted in "the good knowledge of the LORD," as we see in today's passage. As king, he was the leader of the government of Judah. He also spent seven days celebrating a feast with the Levites, the pastors and preachers of that day.

It is a good thing when government leaders and spiritual leaders can work together for the benefit of the people they serve. We live in a day when that relationship has become strained. As a result, there is an absence of peace in our land.

As Christians, we should pray for a revival from heaven that will turn all of us back to God and His Word. We may believe today in the separation of church and state, but I would encourage us not to believe in the separation of God and government. Government is ordained by God to be a blessing to people. Governmental leaders need to be men and women who honor God, and pastors and preachers should be examples of godly people. When both groups work together for the glory of God, the results will honor the Lord and bless the people. By working hand in hand, our nation can become spiritually healthy, morally upright, and emotionally strong. Then peace will be experienced in our land.

....

Father, may all those in authority recognize their responsibility in making us one nation under God. Amen.

Come into His Presence

"I will make each of My mountains a road, and My highways shall be elevated. Surely these shall come from afar; look! Those from the north and the west, and these from the land of Sinim." Sing, O heavens! Be joyful, O earth! And break out in singing, O mountains! For the LORD has comforted His people, and will have mercy on His afflicted.

ISAIAH 49:11–13

The greatest place to find joy and experience peace is in the presence of the Lord. As believers we are always welcome into His presence. However, the Christian life is not always a life of ease, and the path is not always smooth. Life is full of mountains and valleys that place obstacles in our way as we seek to come before God. But our heavenly Father has made a promise. He has promised to make a road through the mountains and an elevated highway through the valleys.

Never focus on the roadblocks on the way to God's presence. Remember, the mountains are His mountains and the valleys are His valleys. He uses them in our lives to teach us, strengthen us, and mold us into His likeness. The joy is in the journey!

Once you enter His presence, you can break out in singing, be full of joy, experience His comfort, and rejoice in His mercy.

Father, thank You that Jesus has provided us access to Your presence, and that You always make that access available. Amen.

Dr. Robert C. Pitman, Bob Pitman Ministries, Muscle Shoals, AL

Departing in Peace

[Simeon] came by the Spirit into the temple. And when the parents brought in the Child Jesus, to do for Him according to the custom of the law, he took Him up in his arms and blessed God and said: "Lord, now You are letting Your servant depart in peace, according to Your word; for my eyes have seen Your salvation which You have prepared before the face of all peoples, a light to bring revelation to the Gentiles, and the glory of Your people Israel."

LUKE 2:27-32

These verses give us the testimony of a man named Simeon. The Bible says he was a just and devout man and the Holy Spirit was upon him (Luke 2:25). Simeon lived for some time before Jesus was born, but God had promised him that he would live long enough to see the Messiah.

After Mary had completed her forty days of purification according to Old Testament law, she and Joseph brought Jesus to the temple in Jerusalem to present their firstborn son to the priests. On the day of their arrival, the Holy Spirit also led Simeon to the temple. The moment he saw the infant, he knew the promise of God had been fulfilled. Jesus was and is and always shall be the Christ!

Simeon took the baby in his arms, blessed him, and said, "Lord, let your servant depart in peace, for I have seen [experienced] Your salvation, which is for all people." One day you will depart this earthly residence. If you belong to Jesus, you will depart in peace. And even now—this very day—you can have joy, because of God's gift to us through the Child Jesus.

Father, show us what it means to meet Christ, that we might both live in peace and depart in peace to live with You one day. Amen.

Good Stewardship and Future Joy

"He who had received five talents came and brought five other talents, saying, 'Lord, you delivered to me five talents; look, I have gained five more talents besides them.' His lord said to him, 'Well done, good and faithful servant; you were faithful over a few things, I will make you ruler over many things. Enter into the joy of your lord.'"

MATTHEW 25:20-21

Today's scripture comes from a familiar parable of Jesus. It is about a wealthy man who is going away for an uncertain amount of time. He entrusts his servant with certain goods and responsibilities. He makes it clear that upon his return he will expect an accounting from the servant. The wealthy man is Jesus and the servant is a believer. Jesus is a giver and His servant is a receiver.

All Christians have received much from the Lord. Everything we have comes from Him. He does not give all believers the same gifts, abilities, talents, or opportunities. But every child of God has received some gift, ability, or talent, and we all have some opportunity to contribute. As we await the return of Christ, what we do with what He has given us is known as *stewardship*. We are His servants, and we are His stewards.

Stewardship is not a bad thing; it takes nothing from us. You see, without Jesus we don't have anything. We are to be good stewards with the time, talent, and treasure He has given us. Good stewardship here brings future joy there!

Father, may we be good and faithful servants, looking forward to entering into complete joy when You come for us. Amen.

Free in Him!

When the LORD brought back the captivity of Zion, we were like those who dream. Then our mouth was filled with laughter, and our tongue with singing. Then they said among the nations, "The LORD has done great things for them." The LORD has done great things for us, and we are glad.

PSALM 126:1-3

Physically speaking, unless you have been in prison, you know little about living in captivity. In America, we are free people who live in a free country. This psalmist knew about captivity. The Babylonian army had taken most of the Jews into captivity. Israel had turned away from God and judgment had come. But then they repented, and God allowed them to go back home to freedom.

Spiritually speaking, though, all of us know about captivity. The Bible teaches that before our salvation we were held in captivity by sin and Satan. We were sinners, and we did what we did because we were what we were. Satan held us in bondage to him. He is a cruel taskmaster. He has never blessed any life or family. He is the author of war, crime, broken homes, and ungodliness. When he has his way, life is a terrifying nightmare.

When Jesus saved you, He set you free from that bondage. The nightmare turned into a beautiful dream. Sobbing turned into laughter and groaning became singing. God had done a great thing in your life, and you were glad. Stay glad, my friend!

....

Father, thank You for setting us free from all that held us captive because of sin. May we never forget that we are free because Jesus brought us out of captivity at Calvary. Amen.

Everyday Joy and Peace

Never Without a Witness

Paul, Silvanus, and Timothy, to the church of the Thessalonians in God the Father and the Lord Jesus Christ: Grace to you and peace from God our Father and the Lord Jesus Christ. We give thanks to God always for you all, making mention of you in our prayers, remembering without ceasing your work of faith, labor of love, and patience of hope in our Lord Jesus Christ in the sight of our God and Father.

1 THESSALONIANS 1:1-3

Isn't it great to have people who care about you? In our passage today, Paul was telling the Thessalonians, his Christian family, how much he was thinking about them. It's wonderful to know that someone is thinking about you despite their hectic schedule and the hustle and bustle of life. Just as Paul was telling the Thessalonians in the ancient church, I am telling you now—the Lord treasures you on this day! No matter what you are facing today, know that the Lord of the universe is in love with you and that you are a precious jewel in His eyes.

As you face today, let obstacles become opportunity. And when you are facing delays, use them as moments for development. Understand this, beloved: You are not doing life by yourself. According to Hebrews 12:1, you have an amazing cloud of witnesses cheering you on to victory. So be encouraged today. You got this. Move ahead in faith and in patience, knowing and believing that this will be a great day.

....

Dear Lord, as we face today's opportunities, let us look to You as our guide and our strength, knowing You love us unconditionally. Amen.

Bishop A.B. Vines Sr., DMin, New Seasons Church, Spring Valley, CA

Never Without a Way

"My heart rejoiced, and my tongue was glad; moreover my flesh also will rest in hope. For You will not leave my soul in Hades, nor will You allow Your Holy One to see corruption. You have made known to me the ways of life; You will make me full of joy in Your presence."

ACTS 2:26-28

In today's passage, Peter was quoting a messianic prophecy from Psalm 16. We can see in this prophecy that Jesus' flesh rested in hope. Jesus was resting in the hope that He would conquer death and be resurrected, seated forever at the right hand of God. His whole life's purpose was to reach that one moment where sin was vanquished and we could be free. And if Jesus the Son could have hope in God the Father to raise Him from the dead, we can have and live in the same hope and promise that despite what we are going through, we will rise! It's with this same confidence we can experience the fullness of joy when we put our faith and conviction in the Lord Jesus Christ. How do we rise? We close the door on the *past* by confession of our sins; we thank the Lord Jesus for opening the door to our *future* by forgiving us of our sins; then we take a deep breath and walk toward our *destiny*, trusting Jesus all the way.

....

Lord Jesus, thank You for "resting" with us on this earth, for going to the cross, and for the hope we have in Your glorious resurrection. We can rise because You did!

The Way of Wisdom

Consider the work of God; for who can make straight what He has made crooked? In the day of prosperity be joyful, but in the day of adversity consider: Surely God has appointed the one as well as the other, so that man can find out nothing that will come after him.

ECCLESIASTES 7:13–14

Today's passage teaches us to trust the sovereign care and control of God. Above all, we should never feel self-sufficient in life—never think we have all the answers. Quite the opposite. We must always rely on God as our source of wisdom and fulfillment. Wisdom helps us accept that we cannot know the future; thus, we must trust God. The future will hold both blessing and lessons. Scripture teaches us in Matthew 6:34, "Give your entire attention to what God is doing right now, and don't get worked up about what may or may not happen tomorrow. God will help you deal with whatever hard things come up when the time comes" (MSG). No matter what your troubles are and no matter what darkness is over your life, don't ever give up hope. Always trust in Jesus, hold on, and look to Him for your way out. He will surely help you.

Dear Lord, give me the strength to trust You in every situation today. Help me understand there will be seasons in my life when I can't see Your hands, but I must learn to trust Your heart. Therefore, because of Your love for me, I know that all things work together for my good, according to Romans 8:28. By Your grace, help me not to lose hope. Amen.

Bishop A.B. Vines Sr., DMin, New Seasons Church, Spring Valley, CA

The Joy of Future Glory

The wilderness and the wasteland shall be glad for them, and the desert shall rejoice and blossom as the rose; it shall blossom abundantly and rejoice, even with joy and singing. The glory of Lebanon shall be given to it, the excellence of Carmel and Sharon. They shall see the glory of the LORD, the excellency of our God.

ISAIAH 35:1-2

I n today's passage, the prophet Isaiah issued a breathtaking, mind-blowing promise: Someday in the future the earth will be transformed, perfected, and bursting with gladness. This is a magnificent portrayal of the Messiah's kingdom, known as the millennial reign of Christ on earth. What a time! What a time it will be to bask in the glory of our wonderful Lord and Savior Jesus Christ. What a time that will be as we live in the land of *no more*! No more worrying, no more weeping, no more hate, no more heartbreak, no more pain, no more pressure, no more suffering, no more sin, and no more dying! Let that bring your heart joy today.

Remember also the words from Romans 8:22–23, "All creation has been groaning as in the pains of childbirth right up to the present time. And we believers also groan, even though we have the Holy Spirit within us as a foretaste of future glory, for we long for our bodies to be released from sin and suffering. We, too, wait with eager hope for the day when God will give us our full rights as His adopted children, including the new bodies He has promised us" (NLT).

....

Dear Lord, thank You for allowing us one day to move from the land of no more to the land of more than enough! Amen.

Our Helper

"What king, going to make war against another king, does not sit down first and consider whether he is able with ten thousand to meet him who comes against him with twenty thousand? Or else, while the other is still a great way off, he sends a delegation and asks for conditions of peace. So likewise, whoever of you does not forsake all that he has cannot be My disciple."

LUKE 14:31-33

I n today's passage, the Lord asked us a very hard question—one that might shake some believers: Are we really ready to follow the Lord Jesus Christ?

False discipleship can cause the world to mock and accuse true believers of being duplicitous. Prospective followers can turn away, and disciples can be hindered in their ministry, which will lead them to becoming doubtful, disappointed, and discouraged about their faith.

Following Jesus will cost you your heart, which means total devotion and duty. It will cost you your mind, requiring that you be saturated and surrendered to Christ. You will need to commit your eyes to Him through what you watch and commit your ears to Him through what you hear and listen to. This commitment will cost you your hands, feet, and mouth as you watch what you touch, the places you go, and the things you say.

You may say, "No way—this is impossible." It is without our Helper! What Helper? The Holy Spirit. Jesus promised in John 14:26, "The Helper, the Holy Spirit, whom the Father will send in My name, He will teach you all things, and bring to your remembrance all things that I said to you." We can expect help from Him with peaceful and joyful hearts.

....

Dear Lord, help us call on the Holy Spirit in our times of confusion and doubt so we can continue to walk by faith. Amen.

Bishop A.B. Vines Sr., DMin, New Seasons Church, Spring Valley, CA

P.U.S.H.

I rise before the dawning of the morning, and cry for help; I hope in Your word.
My eyes are awake through the night watches, that I may meditate on Your word.
Hear my voice according to Your lovingkindness; O LORD, revive me according to
Your justice.

PSALM 119:147–149

Our passage today shows us the comfort and power that come from prayer, and our need for it. The psalmist understood that sometimes our circumstances are so severe that they require special times of prayer. These intense moments cause us to give God our complete attention in prayer. Some burdens are so heavy that we feel compelled to Pray Until Something Happens (P.U.S.H.). We should never waver to sacrifice our time and even our rest, when necessary, to call down God's power through prayer. Occasionally, God gives a special stirring of our hearts, awakening us during the night with a powerful urge to call on the power of His name. Whenever our hearts are heavy, and whenever God's Spirit leads, we should pray, regardless of the time of day.

According to Mark 1:35, even Jesus got up to pray: "Now in the morning, having risen a long while before daylight, He went out and departed to a solitary place; and there He prayed." If the Savior of the world knows the importance of communicating with our heavenly Father, can we truly expect God to act on our behalf if we are unwilling to sacrifice our time and efforts to pray about the burdens of life? When you start to P.U.S.H. in prayer, you will see the difference. God grants supernatural peace to those who seek Him.

Dear Lord, my hope and trust are in You! Lord God, eternity is too
long to get it wrong. Speak, Lord Jesus. Your servant is listening. In
Jesus' name, amen.

Are You Listening to God?

"Listen to Me, you who follow after righteousness, you who seek the LORD: Look to the rock from which you were hewn, and to the hole of the pit from which you were dug. Look to Abraham your father, and to Sarah who bore you; for I called him alone, and blessed him and increased him." For the LORD will comfort Zion, He will comfort all her waste places; He will make her wilderness like Eden, and her desert like the garden of the LORD; joy and gladness will be found in it, thanksgiving and the voice of melody.

ISAIAH 51:1–3

Learning how to listen to God is an important lesson in the Christian life. You make decisions at every life stage. You need to know what God says. Many Old Testament books reveal that God spoke to His people, but they refused to listen. It's a repetitive sin throughout the pages of Scripture. God still speaks. But are you listening? Do you know how to hear God's voice? God speaks through His Word, prayer, the Holy Spirit, circumstances, and other people. If you refuse to listen to God's voice, you'll miss many of His richest blessings. Listening to God comes from spending quality time in His Word, talking with Him in prayer, relying on His Holy Spirit, evaluating your circumstances, and surrounding yourself with godly people. These godly people love the Lord, His Word, and you. Your walk with the Lord matures when you listen to Him and observe all that He commands. Listening to and obeying the Lord brings a joy and peace to your life that can only come from Him.

....

Jesus, equip me to hear Your voice. I want to know You and obey Your will for my life. Lord, help me practice the words of Samuel when he said, "Speak, LORD; for thy servant heareth" (1 Samuel 3:9 KJV).

Dr. Ronny Raines, First Baptist Church Clarksville, Clarksville, TN

A Promise Fulfilled

Jacob made a vow, saying, "If God will be with me, and keep me in this way that I am going, and give me bread to eat and clothing to put on, so that I come back to my father's house in peace, then the LORD shall be my God. And this stone which I have set as a pillar shall be God's house, and of all that You give me I will surely give a tenth to You."

GENESIS 28:20–22

I n today's verses, Jacob made many vows to God. He needed direction, food, and clothing. Have you ever made a commitment to God? "God, here's what I promise to do . . ." Did you fulfill your promise? Solomon, the wisest man to ever live, said we need to be slow to speak. When we make vows to God, we don't need to delay in fulfilling (paying) them (Ecclesiastes 5:2). But a consistent sin for believers is procrastination. You make God a promise in a hospital room, a jail cell, or a workplace office. "God, if You'll heal my body, then I'll go to church" or, "God, if You'll release me from jail, I'll serve You," or even "God, if You'll open another career door for me, I'll give an offering." Have you spoken those promises, only for them to go unfilled for days, weeks, months, or years? Today can be a turning point for you. You can fulfill your promise to God. How do you need to obey Him today? Doing so can fill your heart with His peace and bring you closer to Him.

....

Father, my words matter to You. I promised You that I'd give my life to Jesus, I'd follow You in baptism, I'd join Your church, I'd restore a broken relationship, or I'd tithe my paycheck. Jesus, thank You for forgiving me and giving me another chance to fulfill what I promised.

Everyday Joy and Peace

A Peacemaker, Not a Troublemaker

I, therefore, the prisoner of the Lord, beseech you to walk worthy of the calling with which you were called, with all lowliness and gentleness, with longsuffering, bearing with one another in love, endeavoring to keep the unity of the Spirit in the bond of peace. There is one body and one Spirit, just as you were called in one hope of your calling; one Lord, one faith, one baptism.

EPHESIANS 4:1-5

Paul's opening words in today's passage go against the health-and-wealth preaching that is so pervasive in the church. Paul lived to be just like Jesus. Do you know what that means? As you live the Christian life and study God's Word, you need a local church, and you need to live differently than the world. This means being kind, not harsh. It means operating in love, not hate. It means being a unifier who spreads peace, not a divider. And it means thanking the Lord for your church family and encouraging and praying for your pastor all year round. Life may not always be perfect or comfortable, but living to be like Jesus will fill you with His joy and peace. That is much more valuable than any wealth the world provides.

As God's redeemed child, you have the Holy Spirit living inside you. He is calling you because your life matters to Him. As you walk worthy of the calling with which you were called, allow the Lord to use you today, strengthening other believers and having gospel conversations with nonbelievers. You are called!

Father, thank You for calling me to know You and follow You. I want to walk worthy of Your calling. Help me pray for my church and pastor. Equip me to be kind and patient. Use me to love other people. Allow me to be a peacemaker, not a troublemaker.

Dr. Ronny Raines, First Baptist Church Clarksville, Clarksville, TN

It's Time to Worship

Rejoice in the Lord always. Again I will say, rejoice! Let your gentleness be known to all men. The Lord is at hand.

PHILIPPIANS 4:4–5

W orship is a verb. It's what God's people do. Worship isn't a Sunday-morning behavior only. Paul said we're to rejoice in the Lord always. A sacrifice of praise is to be continually offered up to God (Hebrews 13:15). We're to pray (talk with God) without ceasing (1 Thessalonians 5:17). Is biblical worship a lifestyle for you? Are you rejoicing in the Lord always?

Gentleness is evidence that we've worshiped the Lord. People in the restaurant business say Sunday is their hardest day. Church people tend to be the rudest and stingiest people they serve all week. That should not be! Social media platforms reveal that many believers lack gentleness. God's people are quick to criticize and be harsh with other people on social media. Jesus was firm at times, yet He was gentle and kind too. Worshiping God leads to being gentle with people. A gentle, joyful spirit opens the door for gospel conversations. We share with people that the coming of the Lord is at hand. Now is the time of God's favor. Today is the day of salvation (2 Corinthians 6:2). Is your worship pleasing to God? As you relate with other people, are you gentle and joyful, or harsh? Are you sharing Jesus with people who are without eternal hope and in urgent need of salvation? Biblical worship changes lives, and God uses changed lives to make much of Jesus.

Father, I pray that my participation in worship pleases You. I ask You to help me be gentle and joyful with all people. I pray for You to open a door for me today to have a gospel conversation with someone desperate for Jesus.

Everyday Joy and Peace

Preparing Your Funeral Message

Folly is joy to him who is destitute of discernment, but a man of understanding walks uprightly. . . . A man has joy by the answer of his mouth, and a word spoken in due season, how good it is!

PROVERBS 15:21, 23

The apostle Paul never lost his teachable spirit. Near the end of his physical life, God's servant asked for four things: John Mark, a cloak, his books, and above all, his parchments (2 Timothy 4:13). Paul made the most of his days. His funeral message was powerful and continues to bear fruit. Paul said, "I have fought the good fight, I have finished the race, I have kept the faith" (v. 7). Do you have a teachable heart? That means you desire to live God's way. You guard the words that come out of your mouth. You long for conversations that build up, not tear down. When other people see you approaching them, are they happy or unhappy? Life is like a vapor (James 4:14). It can be seen one moment and then quickly disappears. Death plays no favorites, regardless of age, race, or social status. Are you making the most of your days? This means you're loving your family. You're having gospel conversations. You're speaking the truth in love. God is using you to disciple other believers. What's going to be spoken at your funeral? That's a sobering question. The way you live now makes a difference. As you see Jesus' face in glory, may you hear Him say, "Well done, good and faithful servant" (Matthew 25:21)!

....

Father, I don't want to waste my days. I ask You for a teachable spirit, the ability to live an upright life, and a heart to complete my race well. May the final statement at my funeral be, "All the praise goes to Jesus!"

Dr. Ronny Raines, First Baptist Church Clarksville, Clarksville, TN

Don't Let Stones Take Your Place

As He was now drawing near the descent of the Mount of Olives, the whole multitude of the disciples began to rejoice and praise God with a loud voice for all the mighty works they had seen, saying: "'Blessed is the King who comes in the name of the Lord!' Peace in heaven and glory in the highest!" And some of the Pharisees called to Him from the crowd, "Teacher, rebuke Your disciples." But He answered and said to them, "I tell you that if these should keep silent, the stones would immediately cry out."

LUKE 19:37-40

Can you imagine what is happening in heaven now? Worship is taking place. Residents of the heavenly city are singing, "Holy, holy, holy, is the Lord God Almighty, who was and is and is to come" (Revelation 4:8). Worship happens day and night there. As Jesus and His followers descended the Mount of Olives, loud, joyful worship erupted. Jesus was worthy to be worshiped because of who He was and what He did. He is still worthy to be adored and praised.

But sometimes when authentic, joyful worship happens, opposition isn't far behind. The Pharisees criticized the public's participation in worship. Jesus said, though, that worship was unstoppable. If the disciples stayed silent, stones on that holy hillside would start shouting the Lord's praise.

Are you joyfully worshiping as He desires? Or have you grown silent in your praise? As you finish today's devotion, allow your heart to burst open in joyful worship to the One victorious over death and the grave. Jesus is worthy! Stones can't take your place.

. . . .

Father, I adore You. I offer You praise and glory. My prayer is to worship You in spirit and truth. Lord, I'm preparing today to do what I'll do for eternity, and that's joyfully worship You.

Everyday Joy and Peace

Sharing the Good News

How beautiful upon the mountains are the feet of him who brings good news,
who proclaims peace, who brings glad tidings of good things, who proclaims
salvation, who says to Zion, "Your God reigns!"

ISAIAH 52:7

The Lord put a wonderful friend in my life when I was in seminary. My former classmate, Lang, is from a rural area in northeastern India. Though Lang is a third-generation believer in Jesus, the region where his people are from has been largely unreached with the gospel. But by the grace of God, several years ago a Christian missionary penetrated their region with the glorious news of the gospel—that Jesus Christ, the Son of God, has come to save all people who repent of their sins and believe in His name. Lang's grandfather, one of the leading elders of the village, happened to be among the first to hear the message. Lang told me his grandfather, highly inspired, climbed a large tower in the center of their village. Upon reaching the top of the tower, Lang's grandfather shouted for all the village to hear, "Good news! Good news! We have received good news!"

And what glorious news this is for you, me, and the entire world today. For "the Son of Man has come to seek and to save that which was lost" (Luke 19:10). If we have received the gospel of Jesus and been saved, the most important commitment we can ever make is to intentionally share this good news with our family, friends, neighbors, classmates, and work associates. Let us prioritize this commitment today!

....

Dear Lord, thank You for the faithful messenger who taught me the gospel. Use me today to pass it on to someone else in need. In Jesus' name, amen.

Dr. Jeremy Morton, First Baptist Church Woodstock, Woodstock, GA

The Lord Is with Us

They said, "We have certainly seen that the LORD is with you. So we said,
'Let there now be an oath between us, between you and us; and let us make a
covenant with you, that you will do us no harm, since we have not touched you,
and since we have done nothing to you but good and have sent you away in
peace. You are now the blessed of the LORD.'"

GENESIS 26:28-29

I recently met a young man, Viktor, at church. When I asked him how he came to know the Lord, he described how his neighbor, Babs, would exercise by walking the sidewalks in their neighborhood. But Babs walked with a glowing smile on her face. When Viktor asked her why she was always smiling, she said, "I smile because I have Jesus in my heart. He is everything to me. Won't you come to church with me this Sunday?" Viktor said yes to Babs's invitation, and then he said yes to Jesus for salvation!

The speaker in today's passage, King Abimelech of the Philistines, who was speaking to Isaac, didn't know much about God. But Abimelech did understand that the Lord was present in Isaac's life. Isaac's reputation was a testimony to the living God, and Abimelech found it attractive. In fact, the text indicates that Abimelech wanted some of the Lord's blessing that Isaac possessed.

How we live matters! Today's text is a reminder that unbelievers notice our character. As Paul said, "Walk in wisdom toward those who are outside" (Colossians 4:5). And of course, the Lord Jesus taught us to be the salt of the earth and the light of the world (Matthew 5:13–16). How can others tell the Lord is with you today?

Dear Father, may my countenance radiate for You. May others see Jesus in me. In Christ's name, amen.

The Church Keeps Going

Being sent on their way by the church, they passed through Phoenicia and
Samaria, describing the conversion of the Gentiles; and they caused great joy to
all the brethren. And when they had come to Jerusalem, they were received by the
church and the apostles and the elders; and they reported all things that God had
done with them.

ACTS 15:3-4

When the Holy Spirit filled the disciples, He enabled them to be witnesses for Christ to the ends of the earth (Acts 1:8). Every sinner the disciples met was a candidate for the salvation offered by Jesus. And the final picture of salvation shown in scripture is a beautiful, diverse gathering of redeemed saints around the throne of God (Revelation 7:9).

But unfortunately, between God's promise of the Spirit's filling and the eternal glimpse of the nations represented in heaven, there is tremendous opposition. In fact, the church should not be surprised when she encounters adversity and difficulty. Jesus taught His disciples that they would face persecution, just as the prophets faced it before them (Matthew 5:12).

Nevertheless, the story of Acts is the church's permanent reminder that God is always working. His Spirit is alive. His Spirit will prevail. The Lord's church has marched on for two thousand years, and she will do so until Christ returns—we can have peace in that fact no matter what occurs.

Today in your community, God can save any person, anytime, in any place. Lost people are still on His heart. The Holy Spirit wants to fill *you* to continue Christ's mission.

....

Dear Father, thank You for Your promise to build Your church. Use me today to tell someone of Your saving grace. In Jesus' name, amen.

Dr. Jeremy Morton, First Baptist Church Woodstock, Woodstock, GA

An Altar to God

Joshua built an altar to the LORD God of Israel in Mount Ebal, as Moses the servant of the LORD had commanded the children of Israel, as it is written in the Book of the Law of Moses: "an altar of whole stones over which no man has wielded an iron tool." And they offered on it burnt offerings to the LORD, and sacrificed peace offerings.

JOSHUA 8:30-31

Multiple times in Genesis, we see that someone "built an altar to the Lord." For example, after God told Abram to get his wife, livestock, and all his belongings and move to an unknown destination, the Lord appeared to Abram and said, "To your descendants I will give this land. And there he built an *altar* to the LORD, who had appeared to him" (Genesis 12:7; emphasis added).

Today's text reveals that this same pattern of altar building was also practiced by Moses, Joshua, and the Israelites as they consecrated themselves to God. An altar was a prepared place that included stones, sticks, a sacrifice, and fire. It was where worshipers humbled themselves before the Lord and sought His blessing and peace.

Though the altars in our lives look different today, the principle of humbly bowing before the Lord remains the same. Whenever we read about an altar made unto the Lord, we know it symbolized a very special experience that the person had with God.

Do you need direction today? Are you not sure what God wants to do next? Is your faith being tested, and you desire a spirit of obedience? Let's prepare to meet God at the altar, wherever we are! I believe He will meet us there.

....

Dear God, may my heart be in a constant state of humility before You.
I desperately need You! In Jesus' name, amen.

Everyday Joy and Peace

The Joy of Forgiveness

*Nehemiah, who was the governor, Ezra the priest and scribe, and the Levites who taught the people said to all the people, "This day is holy to the L*ORD *your God; do not mourn nor weep." For all the people wept, when they heard the words of the Law. Then he said to them, "Go your way, eat the fat, drink the sweet, and send portions to those for whom nothing is prepared; for this day is holy to our Lord. Do not sorrow, for the joy of the L*ORD *is your strength."*

NEHEMIAH 8:9-10

I vividly recall my father's discipline of my poor behavior. My dad is a wonderful man of God. He has impeccable integrity and a heart of compassion. My brother and I have never doubted his love. But Dad was rather direct when it came time for his sons to be rebuked. You could say that he wholeheartedly affirmed Solomon's words, "He who spares his rod hates his son, but he who loves him disciplines him promptly" (Proverbs 13:24).

Though I remember Dad's stern rebuke, even more I remember his immediate, loving embrace after the discipline took place. Dad would scoop me up in his arms and say something like, "Son, I love you very much. My love is the reason I must discipline you. But the discipline is over. I forgive you and still rejoice that you are my son."

Today's text acknowledges that our tears are real. Sin brings brokenness to our hearts. But forgiveness is equally real. Like Ezra and Nehemiah, let us rejoice at the fresh start God brings. "Blessed is he whose transgression is forgiven, whose sin is covered" (Psalm 32:1).

Dear Lord, thank You that Your mercy is new every morning. Renew my heart today! In Christ's name, amen.

Dr. Jeremy Morton, First Baptist Church Woodstock, Woodstock, GA

Let Us Sing to the Lord

Sing to Him a new song; play skillfully with a shout of joy. For the word of the LORD is right, and all His work is done in truth. He loves righteousness and justice; the earth is full of the goodness of the LORD.

PSALM 33:3-5

One of my favorite episodes on *The Andy Griffith Show* is when Barney Fife unexpectedly fills in as guest soloist for the Mayberry choir. To everyone's surprise, poor Barney "just can't sing a lick." As the choir searches for answers, all while trying not to embarrass Barney, Sherriff Andy comes up with a solution. He tells Barney that the microphone system will amplify his voice a thousand times more, so Barney must sing softly. The more quietly Barney sings, the better! Amazingly, Barney follows instructions and hardly makes an audible sound, while a talented singer backstage sings into a live mic on Barney's behalf. The concert goes off without a hitch!

Everyone appreciates quality singing. Whether the opera, a concert, a high school chorus, a church choir, or even a child singing while playing with toys, there's something remarkably powerful about singing.

As followers of Jesus, we have every reason to sing. We sing because of *who* saved us—we've been saved by Jesus Himself. We sing because of *what* we're saved from. We were bound for eternal hell, but Christ has redeemed and rescued us. We sing because it's a *testimony* to the listening world. Our King is deserving of all the glad songs we can sing. We sing with great joy because Jesus is worthy!

....

Dear Lord, may I lift my voice to You today in heartfelt worship. You are worthy of every praise! Thank You, King Jesus, for giving me a song. Amen.

Everyday Joy and Peace

Peace with God

Surely He has borne our griefs and carried our sorrows; yet we esteemed
Him stricken, smitten by God, and afflicted. But He was wounded for our
transgressions, He was bruised for our iniquities; the chastisement for our peace
was upon Him, and by His stripes we are healed. All we like sheep have gone
astray; we have turned, every one, to his own way; and the LORD has laid on
Him the iniquity of us all.

ISAIAH 53:4-6

What is stealing your peace today? If you really think about it, whatever it is can be traced back to the presence of sin in this world. Because of sin, there is death; maybe you are in a season of grief. Because of sin, people are selfish; maybe you are in a frustrating conflict. Because of sin, we worry; maybe you are overwhelmed by unanswered questions.

Ultimately, our own personal sin separates us from God, and that causes the greatest lack of peace we could ever experience. No matter how hard we try, there's nothing we can do to fix our sin problem.

Today's verses from Isaiah provide us with the best news for our greatest need. Jesus suffered on the cross and paid for our peace. The payment for our sin, the punishment we deserve, was placed on Him.

Through Him alone ultimate peace can be found. Jesus' sacrifice on our behalf reconciles us to God and frees us from sin and all the heartache it causes. Jesus, the Prince of Peace, is able to bring peace through anything we face.

....

Jesus, thank You that You paid the ulitmate sacrifice for peace. Knowing I can do nothing by myself to solve sin issues, I trust in You.

Dr. Grant Ethridge, Liberty Live Church, Hampton, VA

Joy in the Future

Since we are surrounded by so great a cloud of witnesses, let us lay aside every weight, and the sin which so easily ensnares us, and let us run with endurance the race that is set before us, looking unto Jesus, the author and finisher of our faith, who for the joy that was set before Him endured the cross, despising the shame, and has sat down at the right hand of the throne of God.

HEBREWS 12:1-2

If you have trusted Jesus as your Savior, there is joy ahead. Reflect on that for a moment. Maybe not tomorrow, maybe not the next day, but one day soon you will be in the presence of the Lord. Everything will be made right in a place where there is no more crying or pain.

Some days we face things on this earth that seem insurmountable. We go through things—pain, failures, days or years without the answer we've been praying for—that can make it difficult to keep going. I have great news for you—there is joy ahead!

The "cloud of witnesses" we read about in Hebrews 11 faced disappointment, delays, failure, loss, grief, and all sorts of other things you and I face, but they endured and are listed in God's Word as heroes in the faith. How did they endure? The same way Jesus endured the cross, for the joy set before them.

Because He lives, you can face tomorrow! Because He is faithful and promises a future hope for us, there is joy ahead. You can make it through!

....

Father, thank You for the hope of heaven. Please help me lay aside my weight today, focus on the future You've promised, and run with endurance the race set before me.

Everyday Joy and Peace

Peace with Others

As the elect of God, holy and beloved, put on tender mercies, kindness, humility, meekness, longsuffering; bearing with one another, and forgiving one another, if anyone has a complaint against another; even as Christ forgave you, so you also must do.

COLOSSIANS 3:12-13

God chose you. In His perfect sovereignty, He has placed you in your family, town, and sphere of influence at this specific time. He has made a way through Jesus for you to be reconciled to Him, and He has a purpose to accomplish through you.

The enemy will do all he can to keep you from what God has called you to. One of his tactics is causing disunity in the church. Is there another Christian you are at odds with? Have you been wronged or have you wronged another?

In today's passage, Paul urges us to be kind, humble, and forgiving. There's no doubt he gives these instructions remembering that Jesus said, "By this all will know that you are My disciples, if you have love for one another" (John 13:35).

God's plan for getting the gospel to the world is you and me. His purpose for your life involves you making Him known. The world around us is full of disagreement, hate, discord, and frustration. When we treat each other with love and respect, and we have peace, the world notices.

We can't control the actions of others, but we can control our own. Paul says, "As far as it depends on you, live at peace with everyone" (Romans 12:18 CSB). No matter what has been done to you, because He has been kind to you and has forgiven you, you can forgive and live in peace.

....

Father, please help me live at peace with others because I have peace with You.

Dr. Grant Ethridge, Liberty Live Church, Hampton, VA

Peace within Ourselves

Grace and peace be multiplied to you in the knowledge of God and of Jesus our Lord, as His divine power has given to us all things that pertain to life and godliness, through the knowledge of Him who called us by glory and virtue, by which have been given to us exceedingly great and precious promises, that through these you may be partakers of the divine nature, having escaped the corruption that is in the world through lust.

2 PETER 1:2-4

We've talked about peace with God and peace with others, but what about personal peace? Peter says through Jesus we can have that too. In fact, our peace is multiplied through our knowledge of God and His Word.

The Bible is full of God's promises to us. Our God is a promise-keeping God! His promises have purpose. Through God's promises, you are able to share in the divine nature. Too many Christians are controlled not by the heavenly nature but by the earthly nature. We are more natural than supernatural. Do you look more like the culture or Christ?[4]

God's promises enable us to escape the corruption in this world. They enable us to think and respond differently to the circumstances around us. God has given us everything we need for a godly life. Every day we are faced with choices. Are you choosing to believe God's promises and to take Him at His Word? Are you partaking in the divine nature available to you? Are you experiencing the peace of God that surpasses all understanding? Or are you letting the world steal your peace? Claim your peace today by standing on God's promises.

....

Father, thank You that You keep Your promises. Help me trust in You and experience Your peace.

Joy over the Past

At that time Solomon held a feast, and all Israel with him, a great assembly from the entrance of Hamath to the Brook of Egypt, before the LORD our God, seven days and seven more days—fourteen days. On the eighth day he sent the people away; and they blessed the king, and went to their tents joyful and glad of heart for all the good that the LORD had done for His servant David, and for Israel His people.

1 KINGS 8:65-66

When was the last time you paused to reflect on God's faithfulness? What about His faithfulness over the past year? The past month? Yesterday?

In today's passage Solomon celebrated all the good things the Lord had done. He didn't just celebrate quickly; it took two weeks!

As we look back over God's faithfulness, we can't help but thank and praise Him for all He's done. Thank Him for the people He has brought into your life. Think about all the ways He has He provided for you. Praise Him for salvation, healing, protection, and all His blessings.

We all have seasons when joy and peace are hard to find. After Solomon's celebration, the people left "joyful and glad of heart." If you need to be encouraged today, take some dedicated, focused time to reflect on the Lord's faithfulness. Verbalize it to a friend or make a list. Really meditate on it, and you will find yourself testifying with David, "You, LORD, are a shield around me, my glory, the One who lifts my head high" (Psalm 3:3 NIV).

Remember, "The joy of the LORD is your strength" (Nehemiah 8:10).

....

Father, thank You for all the ways You've been faithful to me. Help me find joy and strength in remembering Your goodness.

Dr. Grant Ethridge, Liberty Live Church, Hampton, VA

Joy in Heaven

"What woman, having ten silver coins, if she loses one coin, does not light a lamp, sweep the house, and search carefully until she finds it? And when she has found it, she calls her friends and neighbors together, saying, 'Rejoice with me, for I have found the piece which I lost!' Likewise, I say to you, there is joy in the presence of the angels of God over one sinner who repents."

LUKE 15:8-10

I f you lose something valuable, you look and look until you find it. You retrace steps, ask people you were with, call places you've been. A serious pursuit is involved! If you find the item, you celebrate!

In Luke 15, Jesus told of a woman finding a lost coin to illustrate the joy in heaven when a sinner repents. In the same chapter, Jesus described how a man who had one hundred sheep left ninety-nine of them to go after one that was lost. When he found the sheep, he joyfully carried it home and celebrated with his friends. Jesus also told of a son who left his family, squandered everything, and really messed up. But when he came home, his father threw a great feast and celebrated.

Three times Jesus reiterated the joy in heaven when one person turns from their sin. Have you turned your back on God in an area of your life? Are you struggling to come home to Him? If so, be reminded today of His pursuit of you. There is nothing that will make Him happier than you turning back to Him. In fact, there will be a joyful party in heaven!

....

Father, please forgive me for my sin. Thank You for pursuing me. I turn back to You.

The Prospering Word

"As the rain comes down, and the snow from heaven, and do not return there, but water the earth, and make it bring forth and bud, that it may give seed to the sower and bread to the eater, so shall My word be that goes forth from My mouth; it shall not return to Me void, but it shall accomplish what I please, and it shall prosper in the thing for which I sent it. For you shall go out with joy, and be led out with peace; the mountains and the hills shall break forth into singing before you, and all the trees of the field shall clap their hands."

ISAIAH 55:10–12

In today's verse, the prophet Isaiah shows us that everything God does is strategic and has purpose. God sends the rain and snow to replenish the soil, and vegetation growth occurs. As the moisture comes, it causes growth to take place before it evaporates and returns to the heavens. What an ecosystem.

Just as the water is cycled, there is also a system for our spiritual growth. God's Word always hits its mark. As God's Word goes forth, it penetrates our thoughts and our hearts; as it is received, it alters our lives through obedience— and growth occurs. It comes from God to accomplish His will in us, and it will never fail to achieve what God desires. His Word will not return void. For us, we will go out in joy and be led in peace.

Lord, I thirst and hunger for Your Word so that I may know You intimately. May I fulfill Your purpose and achieve Your will. Amen.

Dr. Frank Cox, North Metro Baptist Church, Lawrenceville, GA

The Search for Significance

There was a man named Zacchaeus who was a chief tax collector, and he was
rich. And he sought to see who Jesus was, but could not because of the crowd, for
he was of short stature. So he ran ahead and climbed up into a sycamore tree to
see Him, for He was going to pass that way. And when Jesus came to the place,
He looked up and saw him, and said to him, "Zacchaeus, make haste and come
down, for today I must stay at your house." So he made haste and came down,
and received Him joyfully. But when they saw it, they all complained, saying, "He
has gone to be a guest with a man who is a sinner."

LUKE 19:2-7

The story of Zacchaeus holds a truth for every person: We are all in search of significance.

As a tax collector, Zacchaeus, wealthy and successful by the world's standards, was seen as a traitor by the Jewish people. Making money had become his god. Yet, something was still missing. His life had no *meaning.*

Zacchaeus no doubt kept hearing stories about the One who gave others significance—this Jesus. He heard He was coming to Jericho, so he ran and climbed into a tree just to see Him.

His curiosity led to his encounter with Jesus. Jesus went to his house, and salvation came to Zacchaeus. His life took on meaning as he repented of his sin and followed Jesus. His actions going forward demonstrated his changed life. He now had what he was searching for—significance. And we find our significance in the very same place: in Christ, who knocks on our door today.

....

Jesus may we find our true meaning in our personal relationship with
You! Amen.

The Path to Fulfillment

Blessed are You, O LORD! Teach me Your statutes. With my lips I have declared all the judgments of Your mouth. I have rejoiced in the way of Your testimonies, as much as in all riches. I will meditate on Your precepts, and contemplate Your ways. I will delight myself in Your statutes; I will not forget Your word.

PSALM 119:12-16

The book of Psalms is the pathway to fulfillment for the believer. It is pregnant with devotional material for those who worship God. In the Old Testament, God's people entered the temple and found comfort, strength, and hope as they sang these psalms unto the Lord. The psalms address real life in living color. Whatever triumph or trial one faces, it will be confronted in these pages.

Psalm 119 is the longest chapter in all God's Word—but you won't grow weary in the reading. It sets your course to be fulfilled in this world of temptation, tribulation, and sorrows.

Precepts for life are found here. How can we be fulfilled, happy, and blessed on our journey? First, be willing to listen to God's teachings. Listen with the intent to hear (v. 12). Second, declare His teachings (v. 13). Third, meditate on God's instructions. Focus your mind for a time on His teaching to draw all nourishment from it (v. 15). Last, delight in His commands and hold them in high regard to the point that His Word is absorbed and becomes your life (v. 16)! If you will, you will discover fulfillment in this life.

Lord, I will hide Your Word in my heart so I will not sin against You. I pray I'll find fulfillment as I walk in Your teachings. Amen.

Dr. Frank Cox, North Metro Baptist Church, Lawrenceville, GA

Freedom and Responsibility

Do not let your good be spoken of as evil; for the kingdom of God is not eating and drinking, but righteousness and peace and joy in the Holy Spirit. For he who serves Christ in these things is acceptable to God and approved by men.

ROMANS 14:16–18

The believer is free, liberated by Jesus. That freedom brings great responsibility. Some say, "I am free in Christ" to justify their desire for the things of the world. Paul teaches when we come to Christ, old things pass away, and all things become new (2 Corinthians 5:17). In that same passage, Paul tells us that God has given to us a ministry of reconciliation (v. 18). We must be responsible in how we live, as we bring about peace. As Christians, we are under the microscope of those who are seeking. Our responsibility is to be light to the lost and to build up those already in the faith.

Paul shares, "All things are lawful for me, but all things are not helpful" (1 Corinthians 10:23). When he says, "Do not let your good be spoken of as evil," he is teaching us not to let what is good become the object of misunderstanding. In this case he is dealing with the issue of the early church's diet. Some people did not believe followers should eat certain foods. We are reminded the kingdom life is not about the diet but about righteous living. We must live to a high standard and walk consistently in the Holy Spirit. By doing so we have peace and joy and fulfill our ministry of reconciliation. We are not to be stumbling blocks but to strengthen others in faith.

Lord, help me walk in righteousness to bring in and build up others in the faith. Amen.

Peace: He Is Coming!

You yourselves know perfectly that the day of the Lord so comes as a thief in the night. For when they say, "Peace and safety!" then sudden destruction comes upon them, as labor pains upon a pregnant woman. And they shall not escape. But you, brethren, are not in darkness, so that this Day should overtake you as a thief. You are all sons of light and sons of the day. We are not of the night nor of darkness. Therefore let us not sleep, as others do, but let us watch and be sober.

1 THESSALONIANS 5:2-6

The most exciting event in the world will be when Jesus comes again. Each of us must be ready for when it occurs. Dr. Luke in Acts 1:11 is clear about who is coming. It will be "this same Jesus" who is coming again.

Paul described the event coming like a "thief in the night." Thieves come when you least expect it. So will Jesus. We have been given a heads-up by scripture. Matthew 24:4–14 describes every circumstance that will usher in His coming. We are seeing so many of these clues in the present day. "When you see all these things, know that it is near—at the doors!" (Matthew 24:33).

For some, this brings fear. But for me, it thrills my soul and brings peace. Be aware of the signs and alert to what they mean. Then be sure of three things: You are *saved*, you are *sharing*, and you are *watching*.

Let's be ready for His coming, knowing that if we are His, it will be a fulfillment of joy beyond any other.

....

Lord, I look forward to Your coming. Give me peace as I share with my lost friends so they too will be ready. Amen.

Dr. Frank Cox, North Metro Baptist Church, Lawrenceville, GA

Peace in the Will of God

King Darius wrote: "To all peoples, nations, and languages that dwell in all the earth: Peace be multiplied to you. I make a decree that in every dominion of my kingdom men must tremble and fear before the God of Daniel. For He is the living God, and steadfast forever; His kingdom is the one which shall not be destroyed, and His dominion shall endure to the end. He delivers and rescues, and He works signs and wonders in heaven and on earth, who has delivered Daniel from the power of the lions." So this Daniel prospered in the reign of Darius and in the reign of Cyrus the Persian.

DANIEL 6:25-28

Daniel knew during his trials that God rules in the affairs of men. The Chaldeans despised Daniel because God's hand was on Daniel's life. They used Daniel's prayer life to issue his death sentence in the lion's den (6:1–15). Before they sealed the tomb, King Darius told Daniel, "Your God will deliver you!"

Darius recognized God's faithfulness to Daniel the next morning when he found Daniel alive and well, unharmed by the lions. God is faithful in the darkest of times. He was Daniel's provider, protector, and deliverer. God shielded Daniel in the lion's den and caused him to prosper in the land.

The lesson is that we serve the God who rules in the affairs of men. There is no safer place to be than in the middle of God's will! Like Daniel, we can have peace because He is with us.

....

Lord, in every circumstance I face, allow me peace in the conviction that You rule in the affairs of my life. May I always be in Your will and live in Your peace. Amen.

God's Messengers

Great is my boldness of speech toward you, great is my boasting on your behalf. I am filled with comfort. I am exceedingly joyful in all our tribulation. For indeed, when we came to Macedonia, our bodies had no rest, but we were troubled on every side. Outside were conflicts, inside were fears. Nevertheless God, who comforts the downcast, comforted us by the coming of Titus.

2 CORINTHIANS 7:4-6

Have you had one of those days when trouble followed you and discouragement was your close companion? Some days just start off bad and get worse as they go. If something can go wrong, it does go wrong. Doubt enters our hearts. We start to wonder whether the Lord even cares about how bad we are feeling. It's tough to feel surrounded by fires even when we're spending time in God's Word and praying on a daily basis. Before allowing the evil twins of cynicism and bitterness into your heart, take note: God never promised a trouble-free day.

Today's passage in 2 Corinthians describes a day in the life of the apostle Paul. He said he experienced trouble on every side. Can you identify? Every direction you look, you feel anxiety and struggle. You might ask, *Does God care about me?* Yes, God does! He comes to us through His messengers. And the messengers are not angels; they are just regular people. Titus came to Paul, and the Lord used this encounter to encourage him. God does this today. Sometimes *we* are the messengers sent to encourage. Whenever you are having a bad day, look for the people God has already sent your way, and receive them as messengers of God's peace.

Thank You, God, for always being faithful and reminding me of Your love in so many ways.

Jeff Crook, Christ Place Church, Flowery Branch, GA

A Graceful Exit

*Zadok the priest, Nathan the prophet, Benaiah the son of Jehoiada, the
Cherethites, and the Pelethites went down and had Solomon ride on King
David's mule, and took him to Gihon. Then Zadok the priest took a horn of oil
from the tabernacle and anointed Solomon. And they blew the horn, and all the
people said, "Long live King Solomon!" And all the people went up after him; and
the people played the flutes and rejoiced with great joy, so that the earth seemed
to split with their sound.*

1 KINGS 1:38-40

Every public building has exit signs, which are great to recognize in case of
emergency. They also remind us about life—everyone walks through an exit
now and then. Life is all about change, and it's constant. We change positions or
jobs, move houses, adjust to new crises or ways of life, and respond with a "new
normal"—these days perhaps more often than not. What does God's Word say
about these moments in life?

In 1 Kings, David was making an exit. Solomon, his son, was making an
entrance. This new beginning was exciting, and King Solomon's reign brought
such celebration that it felt as if the joyful noise split the earth in two! The message
for us is: Don't forget to recognize the exit signs—and exit gracefully. We can't
hold on to things forever. We can't stop change. And for every ending, there is a
new beginning. Let's be thankful in every season, embrace the present, and refuse
to live in the past. Perhaps there is an exit today that you can celebrate with great
joy. Whatever it is, know that the Lord is constant through all the change.

....

May I trust You, God, in all the changes of life. I rejoice that You are
always the same.

Everyday Joy and Peace   107

The Church at Her Best

The churches throughout all Judea, Galilee, and Samaria had peace and were edified. And walking in the fear of the Lord and in the comfort of the Holy Spirit, they were multiplied.

ACTS 9:31

The Lord refers to the church as His bride. What a beautiful metaphor. We can never doubt Christ's love for the church. He gave His best—His very life—for us, His bride. When are we, the church, at our best? The book of Acts is somewhat of a progress report from Luke, the physician. He recorded the early history of the church, its ups and downs, and how the church prevailed in all circumstances. In today's verse, Luke gave us a picture of the church at her best.

• **The church experienced peace.** It is true we can have inner peace during outer turmoil. This church was unified in mission. Discord in the church is never acceptable. Unity is expected.

• **The church was edified.** The word *edified* means built up. We are at our best when we are building one another up with love and encouragement.

• **The Holy Spirit was moving.** The Spirit-filled church is a place where the people are stirred to live out God's truth. This may result in persecution, but the Spirit brings comfort and affirmation.

• **The church was multiplied.** Living things always grow. When people are being reached with the gospel, the church is at her best. What a joy to be part of a church like this! Let us pray that the same will be said of us.

....

Thank You, Father, that You have united Your children into the body of Christ, the church. I lift up my local church family and Your church around the world.

Jeff Crook, Christ Place Church, Flowery Branch, GA

We All Have Marks

As many as walk according to this rule, peace and mercy be upon them, and upon the Israel of God. From now on let no one trouble me, for I bear in my body the marks of the Lord Jesus. Brethren, the grace of our Lord Jesus Christ be with your spirit. Amen.

GALATIANS 6:16–18

I t is impossible to get through life without some marks. We all have a few scars that can vividly remind us of the experiences that caused them. Pain in life is unavoidable; that's true for physical pain and our internal mental and spiritual struggles. Sometimes these wounds are self-inflicted. There's grace for this. I have often said this as a pastor: Bring your wounds to Jesus; use your scars for Jesus. Sometimes, our greatest ministry flows out of our past failures that God has redeemed.

Wounds can also come from living a godly life. The apostle Paul reminded us, "All who desire to live godly in Christ Jesus will suffer persecution" (2 Timothy 3:12). Paul wrote this from experience. He was completely devoted to God, and it caused him some trouble. He was persecuted for his boldness, and he suffered for the gospel. Paul considered it an honor. There's no hint of a victim mentality. He's clear-eyed when he says, "I bear in my body the marks of the Lord Jesus." Paul believed that his marks branded him as a servant of Christ. What a great perspective when we view the hurts in life as helps to identify us with Jesus Christ. Anything that helps us become more like Christ is a good mile marker on life's journey.

Lord, use my hurts and marks for Your glory and for my good. May I welcome all things (even the bad stuff) to make me more like Christ.

Everyday Joy and Peace

The Comfort of God

Thus says the LORD: "Behold, I will extend peace to her like a river, and the glory of the Gentiles like a flowing stream. Then you shall feed; on her sides you shall be carried and be dandled on her knees. As one whom his mother comforts, so I will comfort you; and you shall be comforted in Jerusalem."

ISAIAH 66:12–13

Where does trouble come from? If we trace it back far enough, we find that the curse of sin in the garden resulted in weeds and thorns, pain and problems. Because of that curse, a trouble-free existence will never be found in this life. There is, however, a land of no trouble. We found trouble in the first garden in Genesis; we will not find it in the last garden described in Revelation. "No longer will there be anything accursed, but the throne of God and of the Lamb will be in it, and His servants will worship Him" (Revelation 22:3 ESV). God will redeem all things, and trouble will be no more.

The God of all comfort promises this in heaven. But in the present life, we also have these sure promises from God:

- He will never leave us or forsake us (Hebrews 13:5).
- We have an open invitation to unload our cares on the Lord (1 Peter 5:7).
- God will use our trouble for His great purposes and our growth (Romans 8:28–29).
- Peace will flood our hearts and bring a calmness on the inside even while there is chaos on the outside (Philippians 4:7).
- The Holy Spirit will come alongside us to be our Comforter (John 14:26).

Thank You, God, for Your comfort in this life and for the promise of eternal rest from all trouble that awaits me.

Jeff Crook, Christ Place Church, Flowery Branch, GA

Gloom to Joy

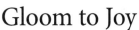

Thus says the LORD: "Again there shall be heard in this place . . . in the cities of Judah, in the streets of Jerusalem that are desolate, without man and without inhabitant and without beast, the voice of joy and the voice of gladness, the voice of the bridegroom and the voice of the bride, the voice of those who will say: 'Praise the LORD of hosts, for the LORD is good, for His mercy endures forever'— and of those who will bring the sacrifice of praise into the house of the LORD."

JEREMIAH 33:10-11

Try saying the word *gloom* right now. Doesn't it force your face into a frown and make such a sad, ominous sound? The prophet Jeremiah describes a season of profound sadness for God's people. Their beloved streets had become empty, but the worst feeling of emptiness was in their hearts. We can call it gloom—the spiritual result of rebellion in their hearts. Just as night follows day, suffering follows sin. Choose to sin, choose to suffer.

But God in His mercy is a restoring God. He turns gloom to joy. He gives beauty for ashes. That which is broken, He restores. Restoration follows repentance. When we return to the Lord and walk in obedience, our joy is restored. When it comes to the choice between gloom and joy, we will go with joy every time. God's people, Israel, returned to God, and God brought them back to joy. The streets were no longer empty, nor did gloom surround them. Joy and worshipful praise were everywhere. Don't waste your gloomy days. They are an opportunity to seek God, the source of lasting joy.

....

God, thank You for Your restoration. May my experiences of gloom be used to bring me close to You. You are my joy.

Don't Forget Your Purpose

Thus says the LORD, your Redeemer, the Holy One of Israel: "I am the LORD your God, who teaches you to profit, who leads you by the way you should go. Oh, that you had heeded My commandments! Then your peace would have been like a river, and your righteousness like the waves of the sea. Your descendants also would have been like the sand, and the offspring of your body like the grains of sand; his name would not have been cut off nor destroyed from before Me."

ISAIAH 48:17-19

Israel had become so complacent while in their Babylonian captivity that they did not want to leave. They had obeyed Jeremiah's voice and had built houses, planted gardens, and raised their families (Jeremiah 29:5–14). So it would not be easy to walk away from it all and go back to Israel. But that was where they belonged, and that was where their next assignment would be. They were stubborn and were not excited about the new things God was doing for them. And in today's passage, the Lord grieved their disobedience.

The Lord had even promised them that they had nothing to fear, but they still rebelled. They had grown so used to being in captivity that the freedom the Lord offered seemed frightening and strange. Their faithlessness in God's provision for where He would lead them next kept them from seeing all the possibilities and benefits that their newfound chance at a new life would provide.

While this is a sad story, it serves as a reminder to us to avoid personal complacency. Could God be beckoning you to move on to a new stage of life? To leave behind some kind of captivity, and move toward the peace like a river He describes?

....

Lord, I pray that I will never forget my purpose. Please guide me in obedience. In Jesus' name, amen!

Tim Anderson, Clements Baptist Church, Athens, AL

Remembering the Past

"You shall observe the Feast of Tabernacles seven days, when you have gathered from your threshing floor and from your winepress. And you shall rejoice in your feast, you and your son and your daughter, your male servant and your female servant and the Levite, the stranger and the fatherless and the widow, who are within your gates. Seven days you shall keep a sacred feast to the LORD your God in the place which the LORD chooses, because the LORD your God will bless you in all your produce and in all the work of your hands, so that you surely rejoice."

DEUTERONOMY 16:13-15

After Israel moved into the promised land, God wanted them to remember that life had not always been easy and that their ancestors lived in tents and booths after they left Egypt. Today, the younger generation never wants to hear the older generation talk about the difficulties of "the good old days." Still, the Lord wrote the memory of Israel's past into the feasts of Passover and Tabernacles. Yes, it is true that the church cannot live in the past, but the church must always be learning from her past as well.

I have had the privilege of pastoring Clements Baptist Church for twenty-eight years. I remember our humble beginnings in a cotton field as we worshiped in a double-wide trailer. And today, by God's grace, we have wonderful facilities and ministry tools that enable us to reach the lost and disciple the saved. Younger generations learn much from older generations and what they've built. Someone has well said, "The church isn't a parking lot for the present; it's a launching pad for the future."

....

Thank You, Jesus, for the stories of our past, and for our hope of a joyful future.

Peace and Unity

Finally, brethren, farewell. Become complete. Be of good comfort, be of one mind, live in peace; and the God of love and peace will be with you. Greet one another with a holy kiss. All the saints greet you. The grace of the Lord Jesus Christ, and the love of God, and the communion of the Holy Spirit be with you all.

2 CORINTHIANS 13:11–14

Without a doubt, all churches have problems. The Corinthian church was certainly no exception to the rule. On the contrary, they were known for divisions, jealousy, fussing, and fighting. Still, the apostle Paul saw beyond all the division in Corinth to the basic unity of the church. God created that unity, and it was there even though there was great divisiveness.

We are part of the family of God, and we ought to act that way, Paul says. Beyond the Corinthians' outward rebellion, he saw the grace and power of God at work, which was able to heal and bring them unity and peace.

Balanced Christian growth and ministry are impossible in isolation. Christians belong to one other and desperately need each other. COVID-19 brought an emphasis on "individual Christianity" rather than in-person public gatherings. But isolation is very dangerous. We are sheep, and we must flock together. We are members of the same body, and we must minister to one another so much more as we see the Lord's Day approaching. As you read today's verses, envision the comfort, peace, and communion Paul wanted for the people. May we experience the same as we seek God's grace in unity, together, as the church.

Thank You, Lord, for Your church. Show us how to live in peace, complete, as Your body here on earth. Amen.

Tim Anderson, Clements Baptist Church, Athens, AL

The Blessing of a Good Memory

"These things I have spoken to you while being present with you. But the Helper, the Holy Spirit, whom the Father will send in My name, He will teach you all things, and bring to your remembrance all things that I said to you. Peace I leave with you, my peace I give to you; not as the world gives do I give to you. Let not your heart be troubled, neither let it be afraid."

JOHN 14:25-27

A *lzheimer's.* Just the mention of the word brings fear to our hearts. "With no cure and an average life span of 10 years after diagnosis, Alzheimer's disease is devastating. People with Alzheimer's struggle to accept and plan for the inexorable loss of their most precious assets—the thoughts, memories, relationships and personality traits that define who they are."[5] Alzheimer's disease is the most common cause of dementia, afflicting some 6 million Americans. Because the population is aging, by 2050 that number could reach 12.7 million.[6]

Now, what does that have to do with Jesus and His disciples? Simply this: Life is full of anxieties for us all. Thanks to a sin-cursed world, none of us is immune to trouble, sickness, or disease. In today's passage, the disciples were afraid because they knew the Lord was in the process of leaving them. They were devastated. But He responded with a great truth that we all need to remember: The Holy Spirit has the power to bring back to human recollection everything Jesus has ever said. Yes, life can sometimes take our physical memory, but the Holy Spirit gives inward peace through life's most difficult storms.

....

Thank You, Jesus, for the Holy Spirit, who speaks to us not as the world speaks, but in pure remembrance of You.

The Blessings of Discipleship

He lifted up His eyes toward His disciples, and said: "Blessed are you poor, for yours is the kingdom of God. Blessed are you who hunger now, for you shall be filled. Blessed are you who weep now, for you shall laugh. Blessed are you when men hate you, and when they exclude you, and revile you, and cast out your name as evil, for the Son of Man's sake. Rejoice in that day and leap for joy! For indeed your reward is great in heaven, for in like manner their fathers did to the prophets."

LUKE 6:20-23

What is *discipleship*? In the church, it's the training of disciples. Many Christians have one or more disciple-making mentors to thank for their spiritual growth; I certainly do. The concept of discipleship may have become unclear in the church these days, but it is no less important today than it was in Jesus' time. Jesus commanded His followers to "make disciples" (Matthew 28:19), but not before He chose twelve men and then poured His own life into them for approximately three years. In today's passage we see Him lifting His eyes to His disciples and unloading some of the greatest wisdom the world has ever known.

Growing in Christ is the key to growing a great church. When a church participates in discipleship ministry, her people will grow and will reach out. We will meet others day by day, pouring our lives into each other as Jesus did. What a privilege and joy to participate in discipleship.

So, why should we grow in Christ? Because Jesus lived and died on our behalf, willingly giving up His life by paying the penalty for our sin. When we pass on this good news in discipleship, we find that everyone is blessed.

Dear Jesus, may I always be a disciple who makes disciples. In Your name, amen.

Tim Anderson, Clements Baptist Church, Athens, AL

Freedom to Follow

I will walk at liberty, for I seek Your precepts. I will speak of Your testimonies also before kings and will not be ashamed. And I will delight myself in Your commandments, which I love. My hands also I will lift up to Your commandments, which I love, and I will meditate on Your statutes.

PSALM 119:45-48

A river with no boundaries is a flood. A highway apart from speed restrictions is a death trap. A country without a government would be a terrible place to live. It is a profound truth to realize that freedom is only gained by accepting limitations. Therefore, the idea that freedom is without its boundaries is a lie. The writer of Psalm 119 has discovered a great truth—that living by God's Word produces freedom, and living apart from it produces bondage.

The psalmist also said that he would not be ashamed to speak to kings about the Lord's goodness. I have learned that if my love for Jesus and His Word is what it should be, I cannot be silent when it comes to the things of God. When I delight in God's Word, loving it and obeying it, sharing it becomes very natural. Witnessing means actively telling others what I have seen and heard about Jesus as well. A Spirit-filled disciple is an incredible tool to be used in the hands of almighty God. So let us live with the kind of liberty the psalmist describes here: finding delight and love in God's statutes.

....

Lord Jesus, thank You for the wonderful privilege of being saved. Thank You for Your Word and the impact it has in my life. I will delight myself in Your Word and lift my hands to Your commands. In Jesus' name, amen.

The Wisdom of Holding Your Peace

He who has knowledge spares his words, and a man of understanding is of a calm spirit. Even a fool is counted wise when he holds his peace; when he shuts his lips, he is considered perceptive.

PROVERBS 17:27-28

I n today's world many feel the pressure to have a "hot take" on every issue and event in our culture. They have to make known what they think—or feel they are expected to think—on social media and in conversation. These "hot takes" don't turn out to be so hot sometimes.

Still others disseminate their emotions through words or social media posts and in conversations, often to later regret it. The Word of God in today's reading explains that those who are filled with the knowledge God supplies in His Word are reserved with their words. They've been made wise by the Word of God. They hold their peace till it is the right time to speak, promoting peace with their restraint. They trust in God's promises, and they speak His truth when it is appropriate with great effect.

I knew a man of wisdom who was very quiet. He would sit in a room and listen to others talk and he said little. After I commented on how quiet he was, he said, "I listen to everyone. Then I know what they know, and I still know what I know." I laughed, but he was right. We must rest in the Lord and His truth and not be pressured to always speak into every situation that creates anxiety. Make it count when you really need to speak, and live a life of calm and peace.

....

Lord, help me rest in Your wisdom and speak it when You desire it.

Mike Orr, First Baptist Church, Chipley, FL

Joy in Song

How shall we sing the LORD's song in a foreign land? If I forget you, O Jerusalem, let my right hand forget its skill! If I do not remember you, let my tongue cling to the roof of my mouth—if I do not exalt Jerusalem above my chief joy.

PSALM 137:4-6

I n today's reading God's people had been exiled to Babylon. They were deeply grieved by what they had lost with the destruction of the temple and their extraction from their homeland. Their captors were probably mocking them too. How would they sing and rejoice now? The psalmist reminds them that God is their hope. His restoration is to come.

You and I live in a world that to us seems on fire. We often mourn the loss we experience caused by the oppression of an unbelieving world. Other times we mourn at the hurt others have inflicted upon us. Still more, we are grieved by our own failures. How is it we will still sing? How will we have joy? Our God does not leave us. He is in the business of restoration. Victory is around the corner or over the next hill. Praise Him!

....

Lord, may my joy come from the hope of restoration You've promised me.

Joy Despite Circumstances

*"While I was with them in the world, I kept them in Your name. Those whom
You gave Me I have kept; and none of them is lost except the son of perdition,
that the Scripture might be fulfilled. But now I come to You, and these things I
speak in the world, that they may have My joy fulfilled in themselves."*

JOHN 17:12-13

While on the earth, the Lord Jesus kept His disciples guarded from the forces in the world and in the spiritual realm. He enabled them to stay in right standing before God. In today's passage our Lord was praying for His disciples to continue to be "kept" after He went back to the Father. His desire was that they experience the full joy that results from closeness to God through obedience.

We live in a tumultuous world today! Our Lord is still interceding for us, and by His power we are kept in His love. We are protected even when evil people and forces attempting to thwart God's plan are deployed against us.

Our joy is not dependent on our circumstances in this fallen world. No, it comes from obedience to our Savior and Lord, who continually strengthens and helps us, and who will one day return to get us.

Lord, help me remain obedient, joyful, and close to You on the earth.

Mike Orr, First Baptist Church, Chipley, FL

Joy Through Spiritual Growth

I am hard-pressed between the two, having a desire to depart and be with Christ,
which is far better. Nevertheless, to remain in the flesh is more needful for you.
And being confident of this, I know that I shall remain and continue with you
all for your progress and joy of faith, that your rejoicing for me may be more
abundant in Jesus Christ by my coming to you again.

PHILIPPIANS 1:23-26

The text for today describes a necessity to experience true joy. It is a gift that results from the Holy Spirit's presence and from spiritual growth.

Paul was in a dilemma. He had difficulty deciding which he would rather experience, death and being with Christ or being released and continue ministry. Death would mean departure from the world to be with Christ. This would be the best. But Paul also knew that should he be released from captivity he would live for Christ (1:21), and his service would benefit the Philippian Christians. Paul would be joyful in his obedience of serving others.

No one experiences the joy Jesus provides without spiritual growth, which includes obedience. You and I will not be joyous without obedience to our Lord and growth in Him.

....

Lord, help me grow in You, that I may experience Your joy.

Seek His Face

He is gracious to him, and says, "Deliver him from going down to the Pit; I have found a ransom"; His flesh shall be young like a child's, He shall return to the days of his youth. He shall pray to God, and He will delight in him, He shall see His face with joy, for He restores to man His righteousness.

JOB 33:24-26

Job had some friends visit him during his time of suffering. They thought Job's suffering was directly related to some sinful act he had committed, and God was chastening him. In today's passage Elihu lectured Job to repent and he would once again experience the joy of seeing God's face.

Actually, Job was in a trial of spiritual suffering, a test. In such a test one still finds joy, comfort, and peace by seeking the face of God. Job's story teaches us that if we trust God, He uses our trials to produce more of His character in us (Jesus is the ultimate example of this). If you are in difficult times, seek God. His presence will allow joy in suffering. Trust Him, for He is doing something in you that will benefit you and glorify Him.

....

Lord, help me seek Your face even in suffering.

Mike Orr, First Baptist Church, Chipley, FL

Continuing in Hope

Receive one another, just as Christ also received us, to the glory of God. Now I say that Jesus Christ has become a servant to the circumcision for the truth of God, to confirm the promises made to the fathers, and that the Gentiles might glorify God for His mercy, as it is written: "For this reason I will confess to You among the Gentiles and sing to Your name." . . . Now may the God of hope fill you with all joy and peace in believing, that you may abound in hope by the power of the Holy Spirit.

ROMANS 15:7-9, 13

I believe the most sought-after possession and experience in the world is joy. People desire to be happy. No one can be happy without hope. Hope only comes through Jesus.

Today's passage emphasizes God's mercy given to all people through Christ. Those who receive God's mercy through faith (believe the gospel) have hope. We have a sure hope, an eternal inheritance.

Two lessons stand out from the reading today that allow joy to pervade us. One is unity and fellowship in the body of Christ. Paul emphasizes this in Romans 15:7–9. Second is our devoted trust in the Lord in Romans 15:13.

May we place our trust in the God who has promised us an eternal hope in Him, which results in being filled with His joy through continued fellowship with believers.

....

Lord, help me be ever mindful of my promised hope.

Faith, Not Fear

"I, the LORD, keep [the vineyard], I water it every moment; lest any hurt it, I keep it night and day. Fury is not in Me. Who would set briers and thorns against Me in battle? I would go through them, I would burn them together. Or let him take hold of My strength, that he may make peace with Me; and he shall make peace with Me."

ISAIAH 27:3-5

When was the last time you were afraid? I mean, really afraid. The kind of fear that grips your heart and life and won't let go? Fear saps all joy from our lives.

Isaiah was writing today's passage to a nation in the grip of fear. It is a song of hope, and it stands in contrast to an earlier song in Isaiah 17 that was a song of destruction. At that time, God was angry with Israel for their backsliding ways. But in today's verses he celebrated their future and their faithfulness.

This song in Isaiah 27 is a song of expectation and peace. It offers peace for those who place their trust in God. It seeks to arouse faith in God, knowing that faith in God brings ultimate peace to the child of God.

Now, back to your fear. The Bible is clear that when we are afraid, it is our trust in God that vanquishes that fear (Psalm 56:4). You cannot be joyful through your own efforts in every circumstance, but in every circumstance you can choose to place your faith in God. The reward for doing that is joy and peace that comes only from Him.

Dear Lord, though fear may come, I choose to trust You today. I trust You, knowing that You are ultimately in control of all and that You alone can bring joy and peace to my life.

Joel Southerland, Peavine Church, Rock Spring, GA

Joy in Others

In all our affliction and distress we were comforted concerning you by your faith. For now we live, if you stand fast in the Lord. For what thanks can we render to God for you, for all the joy with which we rejoice for your sake before our God?

1 THESSALONIANS 3:7–9

Have you ever been so down it seems no amount of good news could brighten your day? Sure you have. Sometimes you look at your circumstances and you can just tell—hope is not on the horizon. It doesn't mean hope isn't coming; it just means there may be some time left in your current journey. How do you find joy in the midst of that?

Paul could tell you. He had started the church at Thessalonica early in his ministry, and he had a deep love for them. But he had been run out of town. He had to escape in the dead of night and leave his beloved church behind. At the time he wrote today's verses, he was still facing persecution, jail, and trials. His situation wasn't improving anytime soon. So Paul decided to get his joy from others.

His friend Timothy had returned from the church and reported to Paul about their love and faithfulness in difficult times. The church was flourishing and thriving, and in that, Paul found joy.

Maybe that's what you need to do today. Maybe there are people you have invested in—family, friends, coworkers, other believers—and they are flourishing. Your investment is paying off. Find joy there. Your situation may not look great, but you can find joy in others.

....

Dear Lord, open my eyes and let me see the results of the investments
I have made in others. Let their success become my joy today.

Everyday Joy and Peace

The Long Game

You had compassion on me in my chains, and joyfully accepted the plundering of your goods, knowing that you have a better and an enduring possession for yourselves in heaven. Therefore do not cast away your confidence, which has great reward. For you have need of endurance, so that after you have done the will of God, you may receive the promise.

HEBREWS 10:34-36

As you read today's passage, you may have done a double-take at the line, "and joyfully accepted the plundering of your goods." That statement is so against the norm it almost doesn't compute. How could people in a persecuted church sit by and watch their goods being taken away for the gospel's sake and be filled with joy? Anger, for sure! Sorrow, certainly! Revenge, you bet! Joy? It doesn't really seem possible.

Or does it?

That phrase alone doesn't tell the whole story. The very next one explains it all: "knowing that you have a better and enduring possession for yourselves in heaven." They could experience loss on earth knowing that the bad circumstances here lead to better circumstances in the next life. They were playing the long game.

Sometimes in life we are too focused on now. And when we are too focused on now, we miss the bigger picture. Play the long game. Know that whatever we suffer for the gospel's sake here on earth brings "better" in the long run. Because of that promise, we can endure hardship knowing that all the pain here brings better in the next life. We can even face hardships here with joy, knowing we will receive what is promised.

....

Dear Lord, help me go through the pain of now with confidence that the future will bring better things.

Joel Southerland, Peavine Church, Rock Spring, GA

Chaos or Calm?

He arose and rebuked the wind, and said to the sea, "Peace be still!" And the wind ceased and there was a great calm. But He said to them, "Why are you so fearful? How is it that you have no faith?" And they feared exceedingly, and said to one another, "Who can this be, that even the wind and the sea obey Him!"

MARK 4:39-41

*C*haos. When was the last time you used that word to describe something going on in your world? Or heard it used by others? One thing's for sure: We're feeling a lot of disorder and confusion in our culture right now.

You probably have faced chaos in your personal life. In the last few years, many of us have dealt with things we never would have dreamed we would face. There has been political, moral, medical, government, economic, and spiritual chaos. And it has affected us all in many ways on a personal level, which you likely well know.

The opposite of chaos is *calm.* Let me introduce you to the Lord of calm— Jesus! The disciples learned firsthand about the calm that follows Jesus. When they were in the midst of turbulent chaos, they turned to Jesus, and He brought the calm. He ceased the storm and taught them the formula for calm—faith in God.

Whatever chaos you have going on in your life, give it to Jesus. Trust Him. Place your faith in the Lord of calm; He can cease the winds or carry you through the storm. Either way, you win.

....

Dear Lord, You see the chaos in my life right now. I trust You to bring calm and order to my situation and to carry me through the storm.

Everyday Joy and Peace

Seek His Presence

In the time of trouble He shall hide me in His pavilion; in the secret place of His tabernacle He shall hide me; He shall set me high upon a rock. And now my head shall be lifted up above my enemies all around me; therefore I will offer sacrifices of joy in His tabernacle; I will sing, yes, I will sing praises to the LORD.

PSALM 27:5-6

We are always looking for something. We are looking for peace or safety or security or comfort or thrills or—you get the idea. We are always on the search for that one more thing in life that will bring happiness. We rarely find it. Why? Because we're not looking in the right place.

The psalmist in today's passage was writing about times of trouble and what we ought to seek out in those times. He says we are to seek out the secret place of the Most High. We should seek it out personally. We should seek it out in the assembly of saints. We should seek it out in praise.

In our times of trouble, our pursuit should be Jesus. The thing we should seek out is not a thing at all, but a person. And often we can find Him where the saints are assembled—what we call church.

When was the last time you went to church truly seeking God in the assembly? In worship? In the message? This Sunday, go to church determined to seek out the Lord. That's where you'll find joy.

....

Dear Lord, help me make You my pursuit of life and seek out Your presence alone and in the assembly.

Joel Southerland, Peavine Church, Rock Spring, GA

Be Naïve to Evil

Your obedience has become known to all. Therefore I am glad on your behalf; but I want you to be wise in what is good, and simple concerning evil. And the God of peace will crush Satan under your feet shortly. The grace of our Lord Jesus Christ be with you. Amen.

ROMANS 16:19–20

In today's scripture, Paul was writing to a Roman church he had never visited. He wrote from the city of Corinth, where problems with the church were well-known. It's almost as if he was writing a warning letter to those in Rome so they wouldn't have to deal with some of the same moral issues the Corinthian church was currently dealing with. The Christians at Rome were experiencing a time of peace that would evaporate in fewer than ten years when Emperor Nero used the Christian community as a scapegoat. Paul was preparing them.

He was bragging on them because their obedience to the gospel was known to all, but he added a warning with it: When it comes to the good things of God, know them well. When it comes to the sinful things of the world, be naïve. We don't have to know all the world's evils; we need to lean into the goodness of God.

That's good advice for us today. In the media overload we experience every day, we are bombarded with the sinfulness of the world. Children know far too much far too soon. Give yourself permission to be a little naïve about the sinful practices of our culture. You'll find that when you do, you have more joy in your life.

....

Dear Lord, whenever I am tempted to know too much of the broken ways of this world, help me to seek more of You.

The Power of God's Presence

Sing, O daughter of Zion! Shout, O Israel! Be glad and rejoice with all your heart, O daughter of Jerusalem! The Lord has taken away your judgments, He has cast out your enemy. The King of Israel, the Lord, is in your midst; you shall see disaster no more.

ZEPHANIAH 3:14–15

My grandfather was a preacher for more than fifty years. While I was in college, I lived with him for two years. Shortly before I moved in with him, my grandmother passed away unexpectedly. Together, my grandparents had enjoyed more than fifty years of marriage. In his grief, my grandfather once told me, "I find myself reflecting on a verse I preached for many years." The verse was Matthew 28:20, a Scripture in which Jesus said, "I am with you always, even to the end of the age."

The promise of the presence of God is the precious possession of every bewildered believer. In the context of today's verses, Israel learned a lesson concerning this matter during her captivity. Though she was carried off to a strange land, and though she suffered unspeakable horror, the Lord used the prophet Zephaniah to proclaim a message of hope and healing, calling Israel to rejoice. At the heart of the Lord's pronouncement was a promise concerning the presence of God. The prophet announced, "The King of Israel, the Lord, is in your midst."

You may not face the calamity that ancient Israel faced, but you will encounter trials in life. To be strong, you must rely on the presence of the Lord. Remember that Christ dwells in two places—in heaven and in the hearts of His people. Live in the light of God's presence, and rejoice that He is with you always.

....

Lord, give me grace to regularly meditate on Your presence so I might be spiritually strong.

Dr. Patrick Latham, Tabernacle Baptist Church, Cartersville, GA

Remember!

I will remember the works of the LORD; surely I will remember Your wonders of old. I will also meditate on all Your work, and talk of Your deeds. Your way, O God, is in the sanctuary; who is so great a God as our God?

PSALM 77:11-13

Are you good at remembering things? It's easy to forget appointments, names of new acquaintances, or important information. Fortunately, modern technology has provided plenty of memory helps. There are a number of smartphone applications designed to help. Remembering is important!

When it comes to our spiritual lives, spiritual memory is important as well. A cursory reading of Scripture reveals that the Lord is concerned with this matter. In the book of Deuteronomy alone, the Lord admonished the Israelites to remember on thirteen occasions (5:15; 7:18; 8:2, 18; 9:7; 15:15; 16:3, 12; 24:9, 18, 22; 25:17; 32:7)! In the new covenant, remembering is equally important. Paul encouraged Timothy to regularly recall gospel realities, saying, "Remember that Jesus Christ, of the seed of David, was raised from the dead according to my gospel" (2 Timothy 2:8).

Recognizing the importance of spiritual memory, the psalmist said, "I will remember the works of the LORD" (Psalm 77:11). Notice the focus of the psalmist's memory—the *works* of the Lord. Throughout history, the Lord has performed many marvelous works (John 5:17). The greatest of them all is His work of redemption. Scripture teaches that spiritual strength is found in remembering such things. When our minds are fixed on the realities of the Lord, our hearts are transformed, and joy and peace permeate our lives.

Lord, help me remember Your truth so I might love You more and serve You faithfully.

Everyday Joy and Peace

Citizenship in Heaven

Our citizenship is in heaven, from which we also eagerly wait for the Savior, the Lord Jesus Christ, who will transform our lowly body that it may be conformed to His glorious body, according to the working by which He is able even to subdue all things to Himself.

PHILIPPIANS 3:20-21

If you have ever traveled abroad, you know what it is like to experience a different culture. Sights and sounds can seem strange in far-off lands. Homesickness is a real thing. Differences in food, customs, languages, and more can produce a lot of stress.

The Bible uses such things as a metaphor for the Christian experience. As believers live on this earth, they exist as spiritual pilgrims (1 Peter 2:11). They are surrounded by a society that thinks and acts differently.

Paul wanted the Philippians to be mindful of such things, so he reminded them their "citizenship is in heaven." His words had special meaning for his first-century readers, as they lived in a Roman colony. Though they were hundreds of miles away from Rome, they had rights and privileges associated with their citizenship. In the midst of difficulties and distress, residents of Philippi had the privilege of appealing to their emperor in the capital city.

Paul used Roman citizenship as a comparison for Christian living. Spiritual progress is ignited when God's children meditate on their standing in Christ. The act of remembering one's inheritance in an otherworldly kingdom does something to embolden and enliven the believer, bringing great joy. As you live in this strange world, keep your heart joyfully fixed on your citizenship in heaven!

....

Lord, thank You that I am a citizen of Your eternal kingdom. Please help me to live in light of such truth.

Dr. Patrick Latham, Tabernacle Baptist Church, Cartersville, GA

Dealing with Rejection

"Do you suppose that I came to give peace on earth? I tell you, not at all, but rather division. For from now on five in one house will be divided: three against two, and two against three. Father will be divided against son and son against father, mother against daughter and daughter against mother, mother-in-law against her daughter-in-law and daughter-in-law against her mother-in-law."

LUKE 12:51-53

Very few people enjoy rejection. The way of Christ, however, often makes us repulsive to an unbelieving world. Jesus spoke of such things when He said He came to bring division. His point wasn't that He or His followers would create unnecessary conflict with others. Instead, His point was that unbelievers would often despise those who faithfully follow Him.

Jesus Himself was subject to ridicule and rejection. In John's gospel, we read, "He came to His own, and His own did not receive Him" (John 1:11). Since Jesus faced hostility from others, we shouldn't be surprised when our faith invites scorn. Our Lord warned us, "Woe to you when all men speak well of you, for so did their fathers to the false prophets" (Luke 6:26).

The Bible reveals that the world will get progressively worse as the end of time draws near (2 Timothy 3:13). Moral depravity and spiritual deception will reach a fever pitch. To be spiritually strong, you must be prepared to live as a light in the darkness. Remember the words of our Lord—"He who rejects you rejects Me, and he who rejects Me rejects Him who sent Me" (Luke 10:16). There may not be peace in the world, but God's peace will remain in your heart as you lean on His strength.

....

Lord, help me not to be surprised when the world ridicules my faith.
Give me strength to stand strong in Your truth and rest in Your peace.

Everyday Joy and Peace

You Are A Priest!

You shall be named the priests of the LORD, they shall call you the servants of our God. You shall eat the riches of the Gentiles, and in their glory you shall boast. Instead of your shame you shall have double honor, and instead of confusion they shall rejoice in their portion. Therefore in their land they shall possess double; everlasting joy shall be theirs.

ISAIAH 61:6-7

What do you think when you hear the word *priest*? Maybe imagery of a religious man in ceremonial garb comes to mind. Perhaps you are drawn to think of gory animal sacrifices. Despite such connotations, the word *priest* is frequently used in the Bible to refer to average, everyday believers. In prophesying of Christ's work on behalf of sin, Isaiah said, "You shall be named the priests of the LORD."

Aware of Isaiah's prophecy, Peter proclaimed, "But you are a chosen generation, a royal priesthood" (1 Peter 2:9). Peter's words make us ask, *Why is the title priest used of Christians?* In Old Testament times, a priest was part of a unique caste of people who had direct access to the holy places within the temple complex. Such places were sanctified and set apart. They were the abode of God.

Used of God's people in the New Testament, the title *priest* reveals that Christ has provided access to God. Such was signified at His death by the tearing of the temple's veil (Matthew 27:51). Because of Jesus, separation between God and His people has been removed. At any moment, one can talk to God in prayer and hear from God via His Word! This is one reason among many that we have His "everlasting joy."

....

Lord, help me never forget that I am a priest before You. Thank You for the joyful opportunity of direct access to You!

Dr. Patrick Latham, Tabernacle Baptist Church, Cartersville, GA

Trials and Troubles

In this you greatly rejoice, though now for a little while, if need be, you have been grieved by various trials, that the genuineness of your faith, being much more precious than gold that perishes, though it is tested by fire, may be found to praise, honor, and glory at the revelation of Jesus Christ, whom having not seen you love. Though now you do not see Him, yet believing, you rejoice with joy inexpressible and full of glory.

1 PETER 1:6-8

W hen I became a Christian, I was somehow under the impression that life would become easier because of my relationship to Christ. To my surprise, life became tougher. For the first time in my life, I found myself engaged in a war against indwelling sin. Old relationships became awkward, as I no longer operated by the same values as my non-Christian friends. Additionally, I unwittingly entered the cosmic struggle of spiritual warfare (1 Peter 5:8).

I soon became dismayed about the struggles and strains of Christian living. Fortunately, an older believer provided sound counsel. He made me aware that trials are a fact of life for all God's people. He directed me to passages of Scripture like the one from 1 Peter above.

As a part of my spiritual maturity, I had to learn that trials are a common occurrence in the Christian life. However, believers can be joyful in the midst of such things, knowing that the Lord has a purpose and a plan in every hardship (James 1:2–3). Jesus said, "In the world you will have tribulation; but be of good cheer, I have overcome the world" (John 16:33).

....

Lord, through my walk with You, please give me strength to steadfastly endure all life's struggles.

More Than Words

> *Grace to you and peace from God our Father and the Lord Jesus Christ. We give thanks to God always for you all, making mention of you in our prayers, remembering without ceasing your work of faith, labor of love, and patience of hope in our Lord Jesus Christ in the sight of our God and Father, knowing, beloved brethren, your election by God. For our gospel did not come to you in word only, but also in power, and in the Holy Spirit and in much assurance, as you know what kind of men we were among you for your sake.*
>
> 1 THESSALONIANS 1:1–5

The church at Thessalonica was started as a result of Paul's second missionary journey. As he wrote this letter to those Christ-followers, he described the impact they'd made on his life. He remembered them for their unceasing work of faith, their labor of love, and their patient hope in Christ. He then told them that they knew him as well. His ministry to them was "more than words" (ERV).

Too many professing Christ-followers today are known for talk that doesn't match their walk. What are you known for? As you begin this week, ask God to help you be known for those things that bring Him glory. Did you notice the three things that Paul mentioned in today's passage? Faith; hope; love (also see 1 Corinthians 13:13). When you are diligent in the work of faith, when it's clear your hope is in Jesus Christ, and when you demonstrate a consistent labor of love, you will be known for more than words. And you will display the kind of "grace and peace" Paul wished on his parishoners.

....

Heavenly Father, may I be known for bringing You glory today. In Jesus' name, amen.

Paul S. Purvis, Mission Hill Church, Tampa, FL

The Promise of Peace

"David My servant shall be king over them, and they shall all have one shepherd;
they shall also walk in My judgments and observe My statutes, and do them.
Then they shall dwell in the land that I have given to Jacob My servant,
where your fathers dwelt; and they shall dwell there, they, their children, and
their children's children, forever; and My servant David shall be their prince
forever. Moreover I will make a covenant of peace with them, and it shall be an
everlasting covenant with them; I will establish them and multiply them, and I
will set My sanctuary in their midst forevermore."

EZEKIEL 37:24-26

O ur God is the original Promise Keeper. His Word, the Bible, is full of promises. Sometimes these promises are made in the form of a covenant. In
today's verses, the prophet Ezekiel describes an "everlasting" covenant of peace.
Did God fulfill this promise? Yes! God offers everyone everlasting peace through
His Son Jesus Christ. Read these words of Jesus: "Peace I leave with you, My peace
I give to you; not as the world gives do I give to you. Let not your heart be troubled,
neither let it be afraid" (John 14:27).

When you place your trust in Jesus, entering into a covenant relationship
with God, you receive the promise of everlasting peace. Have you received that
peace? If not, take time now and pray to God. Acknowledge your sinfulness. Trust
that Jesus died and rose again to offer you peace and salvation. Commit to follow
Christ, and enter into a convenant of peace with God.

If you already have a relationship with God through Jesus, renew your commitment, and rest in His peace today.

....

Thank You, Jesus for the promise of peace. Amen.

Everyday Joy and Peace

Peace in the Storm

The righteous perishes, and no man takes it to heart; merciful men are taken away, while no one considers that the righteous is taken away from evil. He shall enter into peace; they shall rest in their beds, each one walking in his uprightness.

ISAIAH 57:1-2

E veryone you know is either in the midst of a storm, coming out of a storm, or headed into a storm, whether they know it or not. So we never cease to ask: How do we find peace in the midst of life's storms?

In today's passage, the prophet was addressing the reality of death—perhaps life's greatest storm. Puritan Matthew Henry wrote that "the righteous are delivered from the sting of death, not from the stroke of it."[7] A friend of mine restates that truth this way: "Death is an appointment we will all keep. No one will be a minute early, and none will be a second late." The writer of Hebrews stated the same thing long ago: "It is appointed for men to die once, but after this the judgment" (9:27).

Death is a reality, but like every other storm, it is a reality the Christ-follower faces with peace. Listen to these earlier words from Isaiah: "You will keep him in perfect peace, whose mind is stayed on You, because he trusts in You" (26:3).

As you navigate life's difficult moments—discouragement, disease, or even death—look for God's presence and peace. While He may not deliver you from life's storms, He will always deliver His peace. Keep your eyes on Him today.

Dear God, help me keep my focus on You today. I know You bring peace amid my storms. Amen.

Paul S. Purvis, Mission Hill Church, Tampa, FL

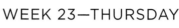

Bloom Where You're Planted

Build houses and dwell in them; plant gardens and eat their fruit. Take wives and beget sons and daughters; . . . that you may be increased there, and not diminished. And seek the peace of the city where I have caused you to be carried away captive, and pray to the LORD for it; for in its peace you will have peace.

JEREMIAH 29:5-7

Jeremiah 29 might seem familiar to you. Verse 11 is often quoted to remind you that God "knows" His plans for you. Today's verses offer context.

The Israelites were in captivity. They wanted out. Right away. God was saying, *Wait. I have plans for you, but they involve perseverance, not immediate deliverance.* In a sense He was saying, *Stop focusing on your circumstances and start focusing on Me.*

Could it be time for you to stop asking for a change of circumstance and start praying for a change of heart? Are you making the difference God intends for you to make, right where you are?

God may not give you a change of venue, but He may be seeking a change within you. Sometimes your peace increases when you seek the peace of those around you. The prophet gives us three ways to seek that peace:

1. Give your best to the place God planted you.
2. Show your love to the people around you.
3. Place your trust in the One who knows you.

Make a decision. Bloom where you're planted today!

Heavenly Father, make me an agent of peace in my little corner of the world today. Amen.

Go in Peace

"I say to you, her sins, which are many, are forgiven, for she loved much. But to whom little is forgiven, the same loves little." Then He said to her, "Your sins are forgiven." And those who sat at the table with Him began to say to themselves, "Who is this who even forgives sins?" Then He said to the woman, "Your faith has saved you. Go in peace."

LUKE 7:47-50

Perhaps you've seen this saying on a bumper sticker or sign: "No Jesus, no peace. Know Jesus, know peace." Though they may be clever, these words are also true. Knowing Jesus is the pathway to peace.

In today's passage we see Jesus comfort a sinful woman with the words, "Go in peace." How is this possible? How does someone known for their sinfulness experience God's comforting peace?

Jesus makes this clear. You'll never have the peace *of* God until you experience peace *with* God. And you can't experience peace with God when unconfessed sin resides in your heart.

In this passage Jesus performed His most amazing and most controversial miracle: the forgiveness of sin. The greatest barrier to personal peace is individual sin. If you are struggling with doubt or discouragement, ask yourself this question: *Is there sin in my life that needs to be confessed?* Not only does sin often come with lasting consequence, sin also prevents God's peace.

Seek God's forgiveness in faith today. When you do, He will allow you to "go in peace."

....

Dear Jesus, thank You for dying for my sins. In faith, I confess my sins and receive Your forgiveness today. As I go throughout this day, I now go in peace, amen.

Paul S. Purvis, Mission Hill Church, Tampa, FL

Worry Less; Pray More

Be anxious for nothing, but in everything by prayer and supplication, with thanksgiving, let your requests be made known to God; and the peace of God, which surpasses all understanding, will guard your hearts and minds through Christ Jesus.

PHILIPPIANS 4:6–7

The lesson from today's verses can be summed up in four words: *worry less; pray more.* This is yet another scriptural command that comes with a promise. When you obey Jesus' command to stop worrying about your daily life (Matthew 6), you experience God's promise and encounter His prevailing peace.

Do you struggle with worry? Anxiety occurs when you feel pulled in multiple directions. Your hopes, dreams, and expectations are pulling you one way, while your fears, worries, and assumptions pull you in another. Eventually you feel pulled apart. You become anxious because you begin to believe life's problems are bigger than God's promises. That is not the case! The apostle Paul reminds us that our God is bigger than our biggest problems.

Are you presenting your worries to the Lord? Notice what happens when you do: "The peace of God, which surpasses all understanding, will guard your hearts and minds through Christ Jesus." When you give your worries to Him through prayer, God's supernatural, incomprehensible peace will post guard around your heart and your mind. That's *big.*

Hold on to this promise. Persistent prayer brings powerful peace. Make the decision to worry less and pray more today.

....

Dear God, I realize You know everything I am facing. As I navigate this day, I give You my concerns, fears, and anxiety. I trust You, and I receive Your peace, in Jesus' name, amen.

Willing to Pay the Price

King David said to Ornan, "No, but I will surely buy it for the full price, for I will not take what is yours for the LORD, nor offer burnt offerings with that which costs me nothing." So David gave Ornan six hundred shekels of gold by weight for the place. And David built there an altar to the LORD, and offered burnt offerings and peace offerings, and called on the LORD; and He answered him from heaven by fire on the altar of burnt offering.

1 CHRONICLES 21:24-26

I s the prize worth the price?" My high school football coach used to yell this during those two-a-day practices in late summer. We practiced hard because we knew the prize of playing well was winning games on Friday nights. The price was long, hard practices that prepared us well. We won two state championships! It was worth the price.

This became a lifelong lesson for me. I ask myself that question before I get involved in anything: *Is the prize worth the price?* I have found that serving God is like this as well. David said it best: "I will surely buy it for the full price, for I will not take . . . that which costs me nothing." David was negotiating for land to build an altar to sacrifice to God. The Bible says David offered burnt offerings and peace offerings, and that God answered him from heaven!

Going on missions, sharing the gospel, discipling others, and studying the Word is going to cost you time, money, and energy—your offerings—but when it comes to serving God, we must be willing to pay the price. Because the prize of peace with God is worth it!

I pray I will see the prize is worth the price of serving You, Lord.

Dr. Kevin C. Williams, First Baptist Church, Villa Rica, GA

Thankful for God's Promises

"This is like the waters of Noah to Me; for as I have sworn that the waters of Noah would no longer cover the earth, so have I sworn that I would not be angry with you, nor rebuke you. For the mountains shall depart and the hills be removed, but My kindness shall not depart from you, nor shall My covenant of peace be removed," says the LORD, *who has mercy on you.*

ISAIAH 54:9-10

One day I came home from work and my youngest son, seven at the time, was hiding from me. Turns out, he had used my hedge trimmers and cut a big hole in one of the bushes in front of our home. My sweet wife had called me and warned me of what had happened. When I found him, he was upset. He said, "I know you're mad and don't love me anymore." I told him that while I didn't like the big hole in the bush, that had nothing to do with whether I loved him. I'd love him no matter what. My son and I laugh about it still today.

In today's passage we read a great promise, "My kindness shall not depart from you, nor shall My covenant of peace be removed." No matter what we do. No matter how big the hole we've managed to cut in our lives.

God has every right to be mad, but He has made a covenant with us through His one and only Son, Jesus Christ, that while we make mistakes and sin, He still loves us! That kindness, that covenant of peace, brings peace to our souls each day. Because we know we can count on His promises.

....

God, please forgive me when I sin and make mistakes. I am thankful for Your forgiveness, grace, and mercy. I am thankful for Your covenant of peace!

Cause and Effect

If they obey and serve Him, they shall spend their days in prosperity, and their years in pleasures. But if they do not obey, they shall perish by the sword, and they shall die without knowledge.

JOB 36:11-12

When I was in the military, I was given an SOP (Standard Operating Procedures) manual. If I followed those procedures, I would keep myself out of trouble; but if I colored outside the lines, I could find myself in a real mess.

I was on duty one day, and some of my peers asked me to go do something with them that I knew was against the SOP. I decided it was best that I not go with them that day. Later, they were caught and disciplined harshly for what they did, and it cost them money, time, and rank. They knew what they were doing was wrong and did it anyway. I was happy I made that decision that day, because going with them could have messed up my future. This is a prime example of cause and effect. For every action, there is a reaction.

When following God, make sure you obey and serve Him. Obedience to God is the key to living a successful and prosperous life, but the opposite is true as well—to disobey God is to bring about calamity in your life. God wants to bless you with good things, like peace and joy, but that will require you following His Word—cause and effect!

....

God, I pray I will obey and serve You with my life. I pray I will continue to hide Your Word in my heart, that I may not sin against You. I pray my life will be a shining example to others to follow Jesus Christ.

Dr. Kevin C. Williams, First Baptist Church, Villa Rica, GA

Blessed

"Blessed are the pure in heart, for they shall see God. Blessed are the peacemakers, for they shall be called sons of God. Blessed are those who are persecuted for righteousness' sake, for theirs is the kingdom of heaven."

MATTHEW 5:8-10

Who here would like to be blessed by God? Everyone, I suspect. In today's passage we find out who God will bless: the pure in heart, the peacemaker, and those persecuted for righteousness' sake.

While in Egypt on a mission trip, I was speaking with pastors from all over the country when one pastor shared with me how he had been persecuted for starting a Christian church in an overwhelmingly Muslim area. The church was vandalized several times, and townspeople placed loudspeakers around the church to interrupt their services. They had done several other things to try and close the church. This pastor had lost his job because of his involvement with the church, and he had been physically threatened. I asked him how he handled all these situations, and he said with a big smile, "I am blessed!"

I thought to myself, *I'm not sure if he understands blessings the way I do.* He quoted some of the passage above, and I thought, *Wow! He is right!*

He said, "They don't like me, but I love them." This pastor truly had a humble, pure heart, and for that he shall see God. He never retaliated because he was a peacemaker, and for that he is called a son of God. He has been persecuted for righteousness' sake, and for that the kingdom of heaven is his. He truly is blessed! May we be such peacemakers where we are today.

....

Lord, I pray I will live my life as a peacemaker—in such a way as to be blessed by You.

Finding Peace

In mercy and truth atonement is provided for iniquity; and by the fear of the
LORD one departs from evil. When a man's ways please the LORD, He makes even
his enemies to be at peace with him.

PROVERBS 16:6–7

Have you ever had someone so mad at you that you thought they were going to physically harm you? This must be how the first-century Christians felt about Saul, who became the apostle Paul. He hated Christians and was on his way to murder some of them when he encountered Jesus on the Damascus Road. I have often thought about how Saul must have felt during that encounter.

Today's passage, I believe, gives us an idea of what he went through. He met mercy and truth that atoned for his sin. The encounter made him fear the Lord, and he departed from his evil ways. He began to please the Lord, and all those who were recently his enemies were now at peace with him. This is how we should all strive to live our lives as well. We need to understand that Jesus died for us and paid our sin debt in full. When this happens, we should have a reverent fear of the Lord that allows us to depart from our evil ways. As we humbly walk with the Lord, people we once viewed as enemies will be at peace with us—because we are at peace with God.

....

Lord, I am thankful for Your mercy and truth. I am thankful that Jesus paid a debt I could never pay. I pray I will walk so closely with You that my enemies are at peace with me.

Dr. Kevin C. Williams, First Baptist Church, Villa Rica, GA

Enduring Trials for Joy

Sing praise to the LORD, you saints of His, and give thanks at the remembrance of His holy name. For His anger is but for a moment, His favor is for life; weeping may endure for a night, but joy comes in the morning.

PSALM 30:4-5

We never truly experience joy until we first endure the trial. In the past year, my wife and I endured a trial like we'd never experienced—we had COVID twice. The first time was hard. My wife, Patrice, was in the hospital nine days, and I was in for twelve days. My wife was in the room next to me. We used Morse code to communicate. She had to have infusions and other medical assistance. I had blood clots and a blood infection along with double pneumonia. They were close to placing me on the ventilator. I ended up on oxygen for two months and blood thinners for eight months. I would love to tell you I wasn't scared, but the truth is I was. I knew that if God took me, I was going to heaven, but I wasn't ready to depart just yet.

While lying in the hospital bed, I prayed and gave thanks to God, and I cried out in remembrance of His holy name. As I read the scriptures, I found peace in today's verses. I kept saying to myself, *I can endure because I know joy is coming. Whether God takes me home to heaven or if I get to go home here on earth, I will have joy!* Thankfully I came home on earth, and I write this today with joy! Are you going through a trial today? Know this: Weeping lasts the night, but joy comes in the morning!

God, help me experience Your joy that comes in the morning by enduring the trials before me.

Grace Beyond Measure

We make known to you the grace of God bestowed on the churches of Macedonia: that in a great trial of affliction the abundance of their joy and their deep poverty abounded in the riches of their liberality.

2 CORINTHIANS 8:1-2

Grace is such a beautiful word! Paul conveyed that beauty as he shared with the believers at Corinth. He challenged them to give out of the abundance of the heart. When we understand this kind of grace, it changes absolutely everything. As God has dealt with us so graciously, we in turn should share that same applied grace with others. The believers in Macedonia were very poor financially, but they were so rich in grace. We can be rich in grace too because of the work of Jesus.

Grace is a picture of what Jesus has done for each of us. He left His throne in heaven to be born as a baby in the flesh in a lowly and humble fashion. He gave up a glorious place in heaven so we could have a place in glory with Him. Jesus' perfect gift is the most beautiful picture of grace. Grace was not meant for us to keep to ourselves. Grace was meant to be given away—in kindness and forgiveness, in generosity toward others. One thing is for sure: We can trust and rest in God's love and grace that goes over and beyond measure. That's where our "abundance of joy" comes from!

....

Jesus, thank You for Your indescribable gift of grace. It is only because of You that I can even comprehend what grace is. Help me share Your grace as You have shared with me. Your grace surely goes above and beyond measure! Amen!

Chip Hannah, Chip Hannah Ministries, Whiteville, NC

Trusting the Process

Those who were scattered went everywhere preaching the word. Then Philip went down to the city of Samaria and preached Christ to them. And the multitudes with one accord heeded the things spoken by Philip, hearing and seeing the miracles which he did. For unclean spirits, crying with a loud voice, came out of many who were possessed; and many who were paralyzed and lame were healed. And there was great joy in that city.

ACTS 8:4-8

I grew up on a farm. In the early days, we planted seed by *broadcasting*—the scattering of seed by a spreader. The drawback to using a spreader and broadcasting is that the wind would sometimes scatter the seed where we did not plan for it to go. But we still had to trust the process. And the seed inevitably grew.

Sometimes God's process is not what we have planned out for our lives, but we must still trust Him and have confidence in His plan. In today's passage, the early Christians were under deep persecution and faced being scattered in every direction. Philip was sent to a people the Jews refused to have anything to do with—the Samarians. For many Jews, it would not have made sense to go and preach to these people. But Philip understood that the message of Christ was for everyone. And consequently, we today know the good news of Jesus.

That same message is to be shared by each and every one of us, everywhere we go. Whether we're going shopping, to work, to a ball game, or on vacation, let us remember we are being scattered to share the beauty of the gospel to our neighbors.

Jesus, use me for Your glory as I am scattered every day, so Your great joy will be experienced by all. Amen!

Excuses and Blessed Assurance

Moses went and returned to Jethro his father-in-law, and said to him, "Please let me go and return to my brethren who are in Egypt, and see whether they are still alive." And Jethro said to Moses, "Go in peace." Now the LORD said to Moses in Midian, "Go, return to Egypt; for all the men who sought your life are dead." Then Moses took his wife and his sons and set them on a donkey, and he returned to the land of Egypt. And Moses took the rod of God in his hand.

EXODUS 4:18-20

M any people are full of excuses. Moses was one of them. God had called Moses and commissioned him for service, but Moses came up with every excuse for why God could not use him. He questioned whether the people would believe the message God wanted him to convey. In Exodus 3:11, "Moses said to God, 'Who am I that I should go to Pharaoh, and that I should bring the children of Israel out of Egypt?'" Then Moses gave the excuse that he lacked the eloquence of speech needed to share God's message (Exodus 4:10). Finally, as we see in today's passage, he took the rod of God in his hand, ready to do God's bidding with blessed assurance that God would be with him.

I don't know about you, but I can identify with Moses and making excuses. When God placed His call on my life, I ran with excuse after excuse. But God's assurance won out. Maybe God has a call on your life and you are running from Him, making every excuse you can think of. One lesson we can learn from Moses is that excuses do not work with God. We don't need them—because we can rest in His assurance that He will be with us every step of the way.

Father, may I give up all my excuses and take Your rod in my hands, walking in Your blessed assurance. Amen!

Chip Hannah, Chip Hannah Ministries, Whiteville, NC

The Highway of Holiness

A highway shall be there, and a road, and it shall be called the Highway of Holiness. The unclean shall not pass over it, but it shall be for others. Whoever walks the road, although a fool, shall not go astray. No lion shall be there, nor shall any ravenous beast go up on it; it shall not be found there. But the redeemed shall walk there, and the ransomed of the LORD shall return, and come to Zion with singing, with everlasting joy on their heads. They shall obtain joy and gladness, and sorrow and sighing shall flee away.

ISAIAH 35:8-10

I have often heard it said that life is about choices. The Bible is clear that there is a choice of a wide road and a narrow road (Matthew 7:13–14). Jesus gives everyone the choice to follow Him because He is the Way, the Truth, and the Life (John 14:6). In today's scripture, Isaiah paints a picture of walking on a Highway of Holiness.

When Isaiah penned these words, travel would have not been safe, but he gave us hope that we can choose to walk this road of holiness—and it will not only be safe, but it will be a blessing to us all. Just as those in Isaiah's day trusted God, you and I can choose to have hope, trust God, and receive His blessing. God has paved the way and given the invitation, but its our choice to respond and worship Him. The question is: What choice will you make? If you choose to walk your own Highway of Holiness in your thoughts, actions, and words today, you can experience joy and gladness too.

Jesus, thank You for providing the Way for me and giving me the choice for a future hope and blessing. May I always choose to do Your will. Amen!

Being a Good Friend

Then Bildad the Shuhite answered and said: "How long will you speak these things, and the words of your mouth be like a strong wind? . . . If you would earnestly seek God and make your supplication to the Almighty, if you were pure and upright, surely now He would awake for you, and prosper your rightful dwelling place."

JOB 8:1-2, 5-6

I am grateful for the friends God has placed in my life and the accountability that comes with our friendship. Some of the worst times in my life were blessed by a dear friend who offered a listening ear, a shoulder to cry on, and wise counsel. Job was not surrounded with friends like this. The words of Job's friends in today's passage were hurtful, damaging, and compassionless. What I do know is that Job needed a true friend to be there for him.

We all need friends to be there for us—but we must also be willing to be a friend as well. No one is an island. We are in this thing called life together, and we were made for relationships. If we only look around us, we'll see so many people who need a true friend. Job prayed for his friends even when they were not so friendly (42:10). Proverbs 27:9 (NIV) says, "Perfume and incense bring joy to the heart, and the pleasantness of a friend springs from their heartfelt advice." What joy we find in having and being a good friend. Jesus was criticized for being a friend to sinners, but I am eternally grateful that He is—for He brings joy unmeasurable.

....

Jesus, may I be a friend not only to my friends but to all. Help me see people the way You see them. Amen!

Chip Hannah, Chip Hannah Ministries, Whiteville, NC

Faithful Promises

He brought out His people with joy, His chosen ones with gladness. He gave them the lands of the Gentiles, and they inherited the labor of the nations, that they might observe His statutes and keep His laws. Praise the LORD!

PSALM 105:43-45

One of God's attributes is that He is faithful. In today's scripture, the psalmist speaks of how God remembered His promises and His faithfulness to His people. In the Old Testament, many times God would seal His promise with a covenant—and once God made a covenant He never broke it. God delivered His people and gave them the land to reap where they had not sown so they could live in obedience and worship Him forever.

There is never a doubt about God's goodness and His faithfulness, but there is an expectation on our part as His people to be faithful in return. Our response to Him should be overflowing joy and gladness because of His never-ending supply of love, mercy, and grace-filled promises. The psalmist ends with "Praise the LORD!" which translates as "Hallelujah!" Our days should be continually filled with praise and worship in our hearts and on our lips. The Israelites could look back and remember all that God had done for them. How can you and I look back at our lives and not be filled with the awe and splendor of who God is and what He has done for us? Remember what He's done for you today, and praise Him!

....

Lord, You are such a good, good Father, and You are so worthy of our praise. Let each day we have be filled with joy, gladness, praise, and worship because of You and Your faithful promises!

Everyday Joy and Peace

Beautiful Feet

How then shall they call on Him in whom they have not believed? And how shall they believe in Him of whom they have not heard? And how shall they hear without a preacher? And how shall they preach unless they are sent? As it is written: "How beautiful are the feet of those who preach the gospel of peace, who bring glad tidings of good things!"

ROMANS 10:14–15

Today's passage is arguably one of the most important passages in the New Testament. Paul talks about the fact that people can only believe the gospel when they have heard the gospel, and that they can only hear the gospel that is preached from those who have been sent. Then there's a phrase that has always grabbed my attention: He talks about the beauty of the feet of those who preach the gospel of peace and bring glad tidings of good things.

We normally think of the intellect or communication skills of those we consider effective preachers of the gospel. But Paul draws attention to their feet. I think that's because they are willing to go where they need to go, to get to those they need to reach, to share the most amazing news anybody could ever hear: that anyone can have peace with God through His Son, Jesus Christ. So, do you have beautiful feet? Will you do what you have to do to get the gospel of peace to those who need to hear it today?

....

Father, help me be faithful in going to and sharing the good news of Your love with those who need to hear it most today. Guide my feet and govern my mouth so I may be a faithful proclaimer of Your good tidings. Amen.

Dr. Brad Whitt, Abilene Baptist Church, Augusta, GA

Celebrate His Mighty Works

Sing aloud to God our strength; make a joyful shout to the God of Jacob. Raise a song and strike the timbrel, the pleasant harp with the lute. Blow the trumpet at the time of the New Moon, at the full moon, on our solemn feast day. For this is a statute for Israel, a law of the God of Jacob.

PSALM 81:1-4

The psalmist's people are a celebrating people. They were called to celebrate their festivals together, corporately. As they would sing and celebrate together, they would remember their amazing, redemptive history—how God brought them out of Egyptian bondage, provided for their needs in the wilderness, and made them a great nation. They were commanded to observe the Feast of Tabernacles to remind them of this. The ram's-horn trumpet that would be blown at the time of the new moon coincided with the time of this important feast. It was the feast they remembered and celebrated as "our feast" because of the great personal impact God's mighty works had on their life.

Do you celebrate the great things God has done in your life? Do you sing about His mercy, grace, and salvation? The psalmist of today's passage wrote these words during a time when Jesus had not yet come. How much more should we celebrate now that He has won the victory over sin and death? Take some time today, and every day, to celebrate what God has done in your life—for His amazing grace, and for the salvation you enjoy because of His mighty works.

Father, today I take time to remember and celebrate Your goodness and grace in my life. Thank You for Your great gift of Your Son, Jesus. Amen.

Everyday Joy and Peace

155

The Joy of Hope

Therefore my heart is glad, and my glory rejoices; my flesh also will rest in hope.
For You will not leave my soul in Sheol, nor will You allow Your Holy One to see
corruption. You will show me the path of life; in Your presence is fullness of joy;
at Your right hand are pleasures forevermore.

PSALM 16:9-11

I was always taught that whenever you see the word *therefore* in the Bible, find out what it's *there for*. The *therefore* at the beginning of today's verse is significant because it marks the confidence the psalmist had in his God. This confidence brought great joy to him—joy that came from his realization of God's sovereignty and blessings. This *therefore* also introduces us to some other reasons for his hope and confidence. The God who had taken care of him in this life would take care of him in the next. He knew his relationship with God would not end at the grave.

Though David, who wrote this psalm, may not have fully understood God's plan for salvation, we do. We know, as the apostles knew, that the joy of hope here is the reality of the resurrection. That's the confidence every believer has. Our relationship with God doesn't end in death, because He has crowned His children with life. Take some time today to rejoice and rest in the fact that God has taken care of you in this life, and He will take care of you in the life to come as well. Forevermore.

....

Father, I thank You today for the gift of life. Not just this life, but the life that is everlasting. Help me to rest in the realization that in Your presence is fullness of joy. Amen.

Dr. Brad Whitt, Abilene Baptist Church, Augusta, GA

Proclaiming Peace

Behold, on the mountains the feet of him who brings good tidings, who proclaims peace! O Judah, keep your appointed feasts, perform your vows. For the wicked one shall no more pass through you; he is utterly cut off.

NAHUM 1:15

Today's scripture is one of my favorite verses in the Old Testament. The picture is vivid and exciting. We read earlier of the "beautiful feet" of those who bring the gospel (Romans 10:14–15). Think of the feet of those who come bringing good news, proclaiming peace, dancing and jumping on the mountains! The background is dark and desperate. That's what makes this verse so special and significant. The proclamation of peace is replete with God's promise of redemption as the prophet paints the picture of the joyful and complete restoration of God's people.

What was real in the Old Testament is reality for us today. We should go forth dancing and jumping, excited to share the good tidings of God's peace to those who desperately need to hear it. When we do, as Nahum said, we cut off the wicked one from those who experience peace with God through salvation in Jesus.

Father, thank You for Your peace! Help me be faithful and excited to share it with those who so desperately need to hear it. Help me to see their need and respond to Your good news. Amen.

Everyday Joy and Peace

God Knows, and It's Good

"I know the thoughts that I think toward you, says the LORD, thoughts of peace and not of evil, to give you a future and a hope. Then you will call upon Me and go and pray to Me, and I will listen to you. And you will seek Me and find Me when you search for Me with all your heart."

JEREMIAH 29:11-13

The Lord, through the prophet Jeremiah, assured His people that all they had encountered and endured wasn't haphazard or without purpose. In fact, the way He words it in the language of today's verse emphasizes His knowledge: "I know." I find that very comforting today when I face situations and circumstances that don't make sense. I may not know why, but He does. He knows; and not only does He know, He has a purpose for my life in everything that happens. And it's good. That may be hard to comprehend or even accept, but the Creator God of the universe says that He knows what I'm going through, He's thinking about me, and everything He thinks will bring peace and hope to my future.

Trust the Lord today. You really can. He is thinking about you. He's planning out your future, and it's a good one, full of hope, not evil. Like the strings on the back of a tapestry, often life seems to be nothing but a bunch of knots and tangles, but from God's vantage point, it's something beautiful.

....

Father, I trust You today, even though I may not understand. Help me rest in the realization that You are thinking of me and planning my steps, and that if I'll search for You, I'll find You and Your plan for my life. Amen.

Dr. Brad Whitt, Abilene Baptist Church, Augusta, GA

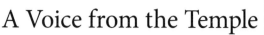

A Voice from the Temple

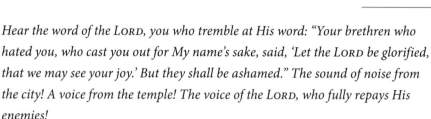

Hear the word of the LORD, you who tremble at His word: "Your brethren who hated you, who cast you out for My name's sake, said, 'Let the LORD be glorified, that we may see your joy.' But they shall be ashamed." The sound of noise from the city! A voice from the temple! The voice of the LORD, who fully repays His enemies!

ISAIAH 66:5-6

I was taught that God's wheel of justice grinds slow, but very fine. I think that's a way to understand today's passage. There is in the context of these verses a great deal of religious persecution and hatred. Also, there is a sense of irony that in the midst of this, God still accepted the temple in Jerusalem as His, for it was from there that He revealed His just and holy wrath against His enemies.

We live in a day when many Christians are persecuted for their faith in Christ. Even in the twenty-first century, Christians are being martyred around the world. We see it today in political and social areas of our culture. We are tempted to huddle and hide, not knowing what to do. Listen for His voice. Today's passage assures that the voice of the Lord will shame those who have shown themselves to be His enemies. Justice will come rolling down like a flood (Amos 5:24). It may be slow, but it's always sure. The Lord *will* be glorified, and we will see His joy.

Father, I know that once I was at war with You. I was far away, but through Your Son, Jesus, I was able to draw near and become Your child. Help me to stand and speak for You, even amid opposition, so You may be glorified. Amen.

Restoring Joy

You shall go out with joy, and be led out with peace; the mountains and the hills shall break forth into singing before you, and all the trees of the field shall clap their hands. Instead of the thorn shall come up the cypress tree, and instead of the brier shall come up the myrtle tree; and it shall be to the LORD for a name, for an everlasting sign that shall not be cut off.

ISAIAH 55:12-13

I have a friend who restores old furniture. From a dining room table to an old, worn-down and wobbly chair, it's amazing what he can accomplish. Give him a call, and in a few weeks, you get back a piece of furniture that looks brand new. My friend's giftedness is restoring something others would just replace.

Our God's very nature is to restore, and when God restores, joy and peace are always the result. In today's verses the prophet Isaiah is inviting God's people to experience the joy of restoration. The word picture of "brier" and "thorns" is the idea of something that seems useless, but before the Lord can become a beautiful tree. The gospel is the continual declaration that while we were at our worst, God gave us His best. God (in Christ) takes away the barren and cursed and brings forth beauty and fruit.

I want to live with joy and peace daily. The "briers" and "thorns" of life don't disqualify me from that joy and peace. Let this passage be an encouragement and a reminder that when the Lord restores, the work is secure.

....

God, You are a restoring God. I choose to trust You with my briers and thorns. I pray that today, I will walk in the joy and the peace of Your restoring touch.

Jason Britt, Bethlehem Church, Bethlehem, GA

The Joy of the Word

O Lord, You know; remember me and visit me, and take vengeance for me on my persecutors. In Your enduring patience, do not take me away. Know that for Your sake I have suffered rebuke. Your words were found, and I ate them, and Your word was to me the joy and rejoicing of my heart; for I am called by Your name, O Lord God of hosts.

JEREMIAH 15:15-16

The prophet Jeremiah endured opposition and persecution for the Lord's sake. Have you ever experienced opposition? Maybe it was someone who opposed you for your beliefs or convictions. Maybe it wasn't a person, but it seemed like life events were opposing you and you tried to remain faithful. In those moments, our emotions, our willpower, and our inner strength aren't enough.

Jeremiah found his strength and joy in focusing on God's Word. The Bible says he "found" God's Word. In the midst of opposition, he didn't forget about it or neglect it; he went and found it. Not only did he find God's Word, he "ate" it. When life gets hard and we face opposition, what we take in matters. Sometimes we look for encouragement from others. Sometimes we try to find something that makes us feel better in the moment. For believers, our source of strength is our active pursuit and consumption of God's Holy Word. A joy comes when God's Word tells us both who we are and whose we are. When you face active opposition, be faithful to actively take in the Word of God, which never changes and isn't dependent on your circumstances.

God, today I am choosing to actively take in Your Word. I want to stand with joy in the face of opposition.

Asking in Jesus' Name

"In that day you will ask Me nothing. Most assuredly, I say to you, whatever you ask the Father in My name He will give you. Until now you have asked nothing in My name. Ask, and you will receive, that your joy may be full."

JOHN 16:23-24

I've been walking with God for almost thirty years now, and it seems like every few months there is something new I learn about prayer. Jesus continually taught His disciples how to pray. In today's verses, at this point in Jesus' ministry the disciples had yet to really pray in Jesus' name, but He was going to teach them how.

There are two things I've learned about praying in Jesus' name. One is that we have power, because of the resurrection, that is hard to fully comprehend. When we place our faith in Jesus, we have unlimited, undeniable, and unending access to our heavenly Father. When I pray in the name of Jesus, I am firmly establishing in myself that I am fully loved by God. My prayers aren't performing for God and they aren't proving that I have faith. My prayers are fueling my faith.

The second thing is praying in Jesus' name also purifies my prayers. I can be self-centered and self-obsessed in what I ask of God at times. Life gets busy; I get distracted. I feel the pressures of life, and my prayers can become more of a religious duty than engaging in a relationship. When I pray in the name of Jesus, purity and clarity of heart bring a joy that is full.

....

Heavenly Father, today I come before You and pray in the powerful and purifying name of Jesus. I ask You to make my joy full today.

Jason Britt, Bethlehem Church, Bethlehem, GA

Fruit Has a Root

The fruit of the Spirit is love, joy, peace, longsuffering, kindness, goodness, faithfulness, gentleness, self-control. Against such there is no law. And those who are Christ's have crucified the flesh with its passions and desires. If we live in the Spirit, let us also walk in the Spirit.

GALATIANS 5:22-25

I don't know if you know much about farming or gardening, but there is a good chance you know more than me. I grew up on a farm where we had various fruit and vegetable gardens growing in the springtime. I wasn't the best student, and I don't have a "green thumb." What I do know for sure is if there is a fruit on the vine, it's because that vine has a root.

The fruits in the believer's life of love, joy, peace, longsuffering, and so forth come from the root of the Holy Spirit of God. Fruits of the Spirit aren't personality traits, nor are they gifts that vary depending on the person. The fruits are evidence of God's Spirit at work in us and through us. The tension for followers of Jesus is that we live in a broken and sinful world and, at the same time, are filled with the presence of God's Spirit. At the moment of salvation, you and I were filled with the Holy Spirit. Crucifying the flesh and its desires is daily dependent on walking in the Spirit. The question that has become most helpful in my life is not, "Do I have all of the Holy Spirit?"; every day the question is, "Does the Holy Spirit have all of me?"

Heavenly Father, today I want to walk fully in the presence and power of Your Holy Spirit. Holy Spirit, You have all of me.

Qualified

That you may walk worthy of the Lord, fully pleasing Him, being fruitful in
every good work and increasing in the knowledge of God; strengthened with
all might, according to His glorious power, for all patience and longsuffering
with joy; giving thanks to the Father who has qualified us to be partakers of the
inheritance of the saints in the light.

COLOSSIANS 1:10–12

When you apply for a job, you submit a résumé. In that résumé, you provide both your work history and personal references. Your work history is a snapshot of what qualifies you to do the job you applied for. The personal references are a list of people who know you and can speak to your qualifications and character. Many times, the criteria for getting a job are about what you've done and who you know.

Today's verses bring great clarity and are an encouraging reminder that it is our heavenly Father who qualifies us to walk worthy and be fruitful in all of our endeavors. We are saved, sanctified, and sustained by God's grace. Our past accomplishments or failures aren't listed on our spiritual résumés. The people who are for us or against us don't determine our qualifications for kingdom impact. God Himself has given us all we could ever need to be both faithful and fruitful. So, as you begin your day, hold on to the truth that you are more than qualified because He is more than enough.

Thank You, Father, that through Christ you have more than qualified me. Today, I pray that by Your power every good work and opportunity that is set before me I will step into with the confidence of someone who is more than qualified.

Jason Britt, Bethlehem Church, Bethlehem, GA

None Like Him

Who is like the LORD our God, who dwells on high, who humbles Himself to behold the things that are in the heavens and in the earth? He raises the poor out of the dust, and lifts the needy out of the ash heap, that He may seat him with princes—with the princes of His people. He grants the barren woman a home, like a joyful mother of children. Praise the LORD!

PSALM 113:5-9

We live in a world of comparison. We are tempted to compare our image, our happiness, and our success with everybody, everywhere, at all times. When we compare ourselves with others, the results are usually pride or discouragement. When we consider ourselves "better" people with greater potential, pride can set in. When we see somebody who has more or greater talent and potential, we get discouraged.

Sometimes the best thing we can do to drop comparison is to meditate on the question, "Who is like our God?" He reigns on high and in power, yet in Christ, He became like us. He does for the poor and broken what they could never do for themselves. He not only rescues them from despair, He also crowns them as royalty.

The gospel is the declaration that He came for us because we couldn't get to Him. Think about that. In a world full of hollow religious systems, none compare to biblical Christianity. Our belief is based on what God has done for us, not what we could ever do for Him. In a world of comparison, there is no love that compares to that.

Heavenly Father, there is nothing that compares to You. Today, I don't have to compare myself to anyone because there is nothing that compares to Your love for me.

The Greatest Invitation

"The sons of the foreigner who join themselves to the LORD, to serve Him, and to love the name of the LORD, to be His servants—everyone who keeps from defiling the Sabbath and holds fast My covenant—even them I will bring to My holy mountain and make them joyful in My house of prayer. Their burnt offerings and their sacrifices will be accepted on My altar; for My house shall be called a house of prayer for all nations." The Lord GOD, who gathers the outcasts of Israel, says, "Yet I will gather to him others besides those who are gathered to him."

ISAIAH 56:6-8

Many of us have likely stood at the end of a church service and sung the "invitational" hymn. The pastor probably preached a message of salvation, sanctification, and service before giving a public invitation. The audience would have been left to ponder how they would respond to the invitation.

The nation of Israel had gone into captivity for many reasons, but one of the primary reasons was their failure to obey the fourth commandment of remembering the Sabbath and keeping it holy. During their forty years of wilderness wandering, and even when they lived in the land of promise, they consistently violated the law of the Sabbath. But in today's passage, Isaiah highlighted an invitation given to non-Jews to join the Israelites in the reverence of the Sabbath. This invitation was given to those who were once excluded from the congregation (Deuteronomy 23). God was opening up the door to anyone and everyone who would worship Him and keep His Sabbath holy. What a beautiful picture of God's grace.

We are invited to celebrate the Sabbath and receive the salvation that is offered by our Lord Jesus. It's the greatest invitation ever given. Receive this gift today through repentance and faith in the finished work of Jesus.

Father, thank You for the greatest invitation ever given—to be saved.

Chad Campbell, Mount Pisgah Baptist Church, Easley, SC

Count Your Blessings

Grace to you and peace from God our Father and the Lord Jesus Christ. Blessed be the God and Father of our Lord Jesus Christ, who has blessed us with every spiritual blessing in the heavenly places in Christ, just as He chose us in Him before the foundation of the world, that we should be holy and without blame before Him in love.

EPHESIANS 1:2–4

I grew up on the Dunean Mill hill in upstate South Carolina. My family and I attended Dunean Baptist Church, a thriving mill town church that was blessed of God. One of my oldest memories is when we would stand and sing the hymn "Count Your Blessings."

In today's passage, Paul's opening words to the church at Ephesus reminded them of the great blessings they possessed in Christ. Those who have experienced biblical salvation have riches untold in Him. Notice with me a couple of things about those blessings.

The *Provider* of our blessings is none other than "the God and Father of our Lord Jesus Christ." His resources are unlimited, and when we entered into relationship with Him, we became rich. Our riches are not in temporal things, but in the eternal. The child of God is rich in Christ Jesus.

Paul then spoke of the *place* of our blessings. Our blessings are "in the heavenly places in Christ." If we are to experience everyday joy and peace, we must realize that our reward is not always in the here and now, but in the day to come. While we operate in the here and now, we realize our ultimate blessings are not temporal but eternal.

....

Lord, may I count my blessings, understanding You are my Provider.

Everyday Joy and Peace

Comfort in Crisis

Grace to you and peace from God our Father and the Lord Jesus Christ. Blessed be the God and Father of our Lord Jesus Christ, the Father of mercies and God of all comfort, who comforts us in all our tribulation, that we may be able to comfort those who are in any trouble, with the comfort with which we ourselves are comforted by God.

2 CORINTHIANS 1:2-4

I n my preaching ministry, I often remind my church of the dangers of the prosperity gospel. The idea, *If I am a believer, God is going to bless me with health and wealth,* is foreign to the Bible. The problem with that idea is that God never promised a life of abundant riches and health. Paul tells us that all who desire to live godly in Christ Jesus will suffer persecution (2 Timothy 3:12). Trials and tribulation are not foreign to the follower of Christ, but He assures us He will be our comfort during those seasons of life.

First of all, notice the source of our comfort. Paul refers to the Father of mercies and God of all comfort. The Greek word for comfort is related to the word *paraclete,* one who comes alongside to help.[8] "The Comforter" is another name for the Holy Spirit (John 14:26 KJV).

Then, notice the sufficiency of our comfort. Paul says He is the God of *all* comfort who comforts us in *all* our tribulation. In this same chapter, Paul speaks of trouble. He speaks of being under such a burden that he despaired even of life. His deliverance would not come by naming it and claiming it, but by trusting in the God of *all* comfort (2 Corinthians 1:8–9). We can rest in that trust and comfort today.

....

Thank You, Lord, that You are my comfort in the midst of my troubles and trials.

　Chad Campbell, Mount Pisgah Baptist Church, Easley, SC

What He Sees

"Once more . . . I will fill this temple with glory," says the Lord of hosts. . . . "The silver is Mine, and the gold is Mine," says the Lord of hosts. "The glory of this latter temple shall be greater than the former," says the Lord of hosts. "And in this place, I will give peace," says the Lord of hosts."

HAGGAI 2:6-9

My family and I have long enjoyed visiting East Tennessee. We have taken our kids to Dollywood countless times. If you've been there, you have seen the detailed carvings of bears they sell in the park. I once heard a guy ask, "How do you make that piece of wood look like a bear?" The artist responded, "I cut everything out that doesn't look like a bear." Where you and I see a tree trunk, the artist sees a beautiful black bear.

In our passage today, the people of God had been working on rebuilding the temple for just over a month. They looked at their work and didn't see what they had hoped. They simply didn't see what God saw. While the first temple was covered in silver, gold, and expensive fabrics, this second temple seemed to be lacking. But this temple would see Christ. He would come there as a baby, as a boy, and they would "[behold] His glory, the glory as of the only begotten of the Father" (John 1:14).

When we look at our lives, we may see the boring piece of wood, but God sees what He is molding us to be.

....

Lord, thank You for building us as You built Your temple. May we be greater than we were formerly, and filled with Your peace.

Peace Is a Person

As they said these things, Jesus Himself stood in the midst of them, and said to them, "Peace to you." But they were terrified and frightened, and supposed they had seen a spirit. And He said to them, "Why are you troubled? And why do doubts arise in your hearts? Behold My hands and My feet, that it is I Myself. Handle Me and see, for a spirit does not have flesh and bones as you see I have."

LUKE 24:36-39

According to a study by Barna in 2017, 37 percent of people admit that their most common prayer is for a "sense of peace."[9] I like to think that the disciples were also praying for a sense of peace in the days after the crucifixion. That is, until the Prince of Peace entered the upper room. Late on Easter Sunday, Jesus stood amid His disciples and brought them peace. How?

Through His words. While the disciples contemplated the resurrection, Jesus spoke to them. His voice was familiar during this time of uncertainty. His words were also recognizable, as He had spoken to them about peace time and time again before He died and rose again. Just as it was for the disciples, His Word is still sufficient to bring peace to your troubled heart.

Jesus also brought them peace through His wounds. His disciples were initially fearful when He stood in their secure room. But what comforted their souls was understanding that He was there in bodily form. He rose to life! How did Jesus prove His resurrection to them? By inviting them to behold His wounds. Those wounds bring healing and peace to a sin-sick world, even today.

Lord, help me to know You are my peace, by Your words and Your wounds.

Chad Campbell, Mount Pisgah Baptist Church, Easley, SC

God's Goodness

Men shall speak of the might of Your awesome acts, and I will declare Your greatness. They shall utter the memory of Your great goodness and shall sing of Your righteousness. The LORD is gracious and full of compassion, slow to anger and great in mercy. The LORD is good to all, and His tender mercies are over all His works.

PSALM 145:6-9

A foundational truth in my Christian development was understanding that God is good. That truth was cultivated each week during the benediction at the church I grew up attending. Our music minister would invite the church body to join hands and sing the old hymn "God Is So Good." Watching a body of believers sing that song taught me about God's goodness. But what makes God good? King David answers that question in today's psalm.

First, he reminds us that God's goodness is connected to His righteousness. Goodness is the quality of being morally virtuous. Righteousness is doing everything morally right. The God we serve is perfect, sinless, and holy. Because of His righteousness, He is good.

While God is good and sinless, we as people are not. This can be quite a troubling thought, but it brings us to our second point: We can celebrate God's goodness because of His response to our sin. In His righteousness, God has every right to punish us all because of our sin. Yet, even in our sinfulness, God responded with goodness. He offers grace, compassion, and mercy through His Son, Jesus. Knowing the amazing grace that our good God offers us through Jesus makes the old hymn I grew up singing so much sweeter. Won't you sing of His goodness today?

Thank You for Your goodness, Lord, and Your mercies toward me.

Everyday Joy and Peace

Joy in Jerusalem's Future

Rejoice with Jerusalem, and be glad with her, all you who love her; rejoice for joy with her, all you who mourn for her; that you may feed and be satisfied with the consolation of her bosom, that you may drink deeply and be delighted with the abundance of her glory.

ISAIAH 66:10-11

In our passage today, Isaiah was reminding Israel that God had not forgotten His promise and that one day Israel would take center stage on the international scene. The Jews of Isaiah's day were a people who went through the motions, but their hearts were full of unbelief. They had turned their backs on God and would suffer for their unbelief in Babylon. They would later reject their Messiah and His offer of the kingdom and crucify Him. They again would be dispersed in AD 70, but God is faithful! In 1948 Israel once again came into their land, but once again they were going through the motions. And no doubt that land will be involved in the millennial kingdom—the second coming of Christ.

In Isaiah 66:7–9, right before today's verse, the prophet gives us the picture of a mother about to give birth. Before delivery there is labor and pain. Then follows the delivery, which will be the millennial kingdom. God will keep His promises, so verse 10 tells us to be joyful and rejoice with Jerusalem! Though the world may be in turmoil, we can be of good cheer. I have read the last chapter, and I can tell you—God wins! Isaiah prophesied it and Revelation confirms it. Christ is coming! The kingdom of heaven is at hand. For all the turmoil of the nation of Israel over these thousands of years, we can rejoice with her—for Jesus is coming.

Even so, come Lord Jesus!

Dr. Rob Zinn, Immanuel Baptist Church, Highland, CA

Faith, Not Works

Paul, an apostle (not from men nor through man, but through Jesus Christ and God the Father who raised Him from the dead), and all the brethren who are with me, to the churches of Galatia: Grace to you and peace from God the Father and our Lord Jesus Christ, who gave Himself for our sins, that He might deliver us from this present evil age, according to the will of our God and Father, to whom be glory forever and ever. Amen.

GALATIANS 1:1-5

P aul founded the church in the Galatian region. He loved the people and he was willing to call out those who opposed the gospel. The central truth of the book of Galatians is justification by faith. We are saved by grace through faith! Period. We cannot work our way to heaven; salvation is the gift of God through the death and resurrection of Christ. If you want the peace of God, you must have a personal relationship with God through Christ. We can't buy our way, work our way, or wish our way into heaven. We must agree with God that we are sinners in need of a Savior. For that reason, God became a man and went to the cross and shed His blood, to die in our place—and three days later, He rose from the dead. We receive Christ and ask Him to forgive us, and we are given new life. After all that, the work was finished. There is no more work we can do. We need only have faith and receive Him. It's faith, not works! That is the truth of the Word of God—that brings us grace and peace.

....

Lord Jesus, thank You for saving me by faith, not by anything I can do.

Great Peace

Seven times a day I praise You, because of Your righteous judgments. Great peace have those who love Your law, and nothing causes them to stumble. LORD, I hope for Your salvation, and I do Your commandments.

PSALM 119:164-166

T he last few years have been a time of turmoil, fear, and uncertainty. One thing, however, is still true: God is on His throne. In today's text the psalmist gives us an insight to peace. Note what he says: "Seven times a day I praise You." We know that seven is God's perfect number. But it may just be a poetic way of saying, "All day long I praise God." Before you ask, "What is there to praise God about all day long?" think about this: Has not God been faithful? In the midst of trials, has not the Lord been there? Are you not a child of God? Is there not a future? Are we not possessors of eternal life? I don't necessarily have to praise God for what I see or feel, but I can praise Him for what I know! He is faithful, He loves me, He will never leave me, and one day I will be with Him and the family of God forever.

Those who can praise will have peace. Inner peace and joy cannot be taken. Today, try it for yourself: Seven times (at least), praise the Lord for what He has done. Spend time studying His Law. Do His commandments. Love the Lord and His Word. Abide in Him, and rejoice in His presence. Then you will find great peace.

....

Thank You, Lord, for Your hand and Your Word. Seven times—all day long—I will praise You.

Dr. Rob Zinn, Immanuel Baptist Church, Highland, CA

Victim or Victor?

Repay no one evil for evil. Have regard for good things in the sight of all men. If it is possible, as much as depends on you, live peaceably with all men. Beloved, do not avenge yourselves, but rather give place to wrath; for it is written, "Vengeance is Mine, I will repay," says the Lord. Therefore "If your enemy is hungry, feed him; if he is thirsty, give him a drink; for in so doing you will heap coals of fire on his head." Do not be overcome by evil, but overcome evil with good.

ROMANS 12:17-21

A s a Christian you are no longer what you used to be. When Christ came into your life, He began to change you, to conform you to His image (Romans 8:23–30). The love of God now abides in you, and it's no longer about *me, myself, and I.* It is about living your life to glorify God. So we begin to walk and live life differently. We are called to walk in love. A Christian is a person in whom the Holy Spirit of God dwells and is living a supernatural life.

A Christian is someone who has been transformed from spiritual death to spiritual life, and people can see the difference. As you grow in your walk with the Lord, His joy, love, and peace will spill out to your family and all those around you. These are the fruits of His Spirit in your life. So, in verses 17–18 of today's scripture we see the principle. In verses 19–20, the promise. It's not hate; it's help (v. 21). Don't be a victim but a victor. Overcome evil with good.

....

God, help us to live in such a way that others see Jesus in us.

Everyday Joy and Peace

A Sacrifice of Praise

By Him let us continually offer the sacrifice of praise to God, that is, the fruit of our lips, giving thanks to His name. But do not forget to do good and to share, for with such sacrifices God is well pleased. Obey those who rule over you, and be submissive, for they watch out for your souls, as those who must give account. Let them do so with joy and not with grief, for that would be unprofitable for you.

HEBREWS 13:15-17

Our text today is almost opposite of our passage yesterday. Instead of telling us what *not* to do (don't repay evil for evil), we are told *what* to do. Instead of being vengeful, hateful, and negative, we are to praise the Lord, do good, and obey those in authority over us. Because of who we are, we can and should be people of praise, be positive, and promote goodwill to others and those in authority. We are to be the salt of the earth and the light of the world, and people ought to notice that we are different than others who do not know the Lord by the way we talk and the things we do and don't do (Matthew 28:18–20). We're not saved by works, but we are saved to do good works for the glory of God—and do them with joy, not with grief. What would it look like today for you to fill your day with thanks and praise? If, when you want to complain, you choose praise instead? Try it and see how much joy it brings to your circumstance.

....

Lord, fill me with Your love and joy and help me to share it with others. Amen.

Dr. Rob Zinn, Immanuel Baptist Church, Highland, CA

A Call to Praise

Let the rivers clap their hands; let the hills be joyful together before the LORD,
for He is coming to judge the earth. With righteousness He shall judge the world,
and the peoples with equity.

PSALM 98:8-9

T oday's text is taken from a psalm of praise. It begins, "Oh, sing to the LORD a new song, for He has done marvelous things" (v. 1). Not *will* do, but *has* done. He has done wonderful things, and the whole earth is called to rejoice. All of nature is called on to praise the Lord—the earth (v. 4), the sea (v. 7), and the world of those who dwell in it (v. 7). The rivers and the mountains all are called to praise the Lord. Why? Because we have a God who is worthy of our praise.

Everything may not be going your way today, but never forget who is in control! He is the Lord of glory, and Romans 8:28 reminds us that He works all things together for our good! We are rapidly heading to the coming of the Lord, and He will judge the earth and rule the world in righteousness. This is not the time to be negative but to have a positive spirit and thank the Lord you're in His family. Praise the Lord! Thank Him for His love, salvation, care, faithfulness, security, and for so much more. Remember, this world is not our home, but He is coming to take us home. Praise the Lord!

....

Father, let me be found faithful. Thank You for Your love and power.
Use me for Your glory. In Jesus' name, amen.

Rejoice, Serve, Know, and Rest

Make a joyful shout to the LORD, all you lands! Serve the LORD with gladness; come before His presence with singing. Know that the LORD, He is God; it is He who has made us, and not we ourselves; we are His people and the sheep of His pasture.

PSALM 100:1–3

Life for an ancient Israelite was often hard, unpredictable, fragile, and fraught with many reasons to fear. It was filled with enemies without, anxieties within, and daily hardships of surviving in a hostile world. Sounds like the twenty-first century, doesn't it?

The realities and responses that held the hearts of ancient Israelites still hold our hearts today. God's people have always relied on His view of things. So, Psalm 100 challenges us with four responses to life's uncertainties and harsh realities.

First, we *rejoice*! Because of Jesus and the gospel, we start every day with new mercies and new reasons to celebrate our Savior with abundant joy. This begins as a choice of the will, by faith, but emotions always follow eventually. Second, we *serve*. The gospel graces us with abundant love and blessing—enough to give away every day. God has someone in mind for you to serve today in His name. Third, we *know*. We resolve and have assurance that even in hard times, God is governing our lives well. He is leading according to His good, eternal purposes. Fourth, we *rest*. We are sheep, He is our Shepherd, and He will always lead us to good pasture.

Rejoice, serve, know, and rest. That's our assignment for today and every day until we see Jesus. Isn't it wonderful to be His sheep?

....

Lord Jesus, I choose today to *rejoice, serve, know,* and *rest*. Thank You for being mine.

Cary Schmidt, Emmanuel Baptist Church, Newington, CT

How Hardship Drives Joy Deeper

O Lord, by these things men live; and in all these things is the life of my spirit;
so You will restore me and make me live. Indeed it was for my own peace that
I had great bitterness; but You have lovingly delivered my soul from the pit of
corruption, for You have cast all my sins behind Your back.

ISAIAH 38:16-17

Hezekiah was a faithful king who honored the Lord. By God's providence, he fell sick and was told by Isaiah that he would soon pass (Isaiah 38). Upon receiving this news, Hezekiah wept and requested that God extend his life.

In grace, God responded, *Hezekiah, you will live for fifteen more years* (v. 5). Imagine the joy and relief that Hezekiah felt! He responded in praise.

The point of today's passage is this: Deathly experiences, suffering, and hardship in this brief life can cause us to live more abundantly. Suffering is used by God's Spirit to awaken us to real life. In verse 17, Hezekiah explains that his bitter experience served to bring about a greater peace within him. Through his trial he had been delivered from not only sickness of body, but sickness of soul. His joy went deeper and became more complete in his forgiven standing with God (what we call the gospel).

When God permits hardship, He is enlarging our living, increasing our peace, and deepening our joy. He is delivering us from a greater kind of bondage—the oppression of the losable, fragile, and unstable things of life. He is, in a sense, using the *temporarily bitter* to deliver us from the *ultimately and eternally bitter.*

....

Lord Jesus, I choose to trust and thank You that You use short-term trials for my ultimate, eternal blessing.

Everyday Joy and Peace

When Bad Advice Sounds Good

"Behold, happy is the man whom God corrects; therefore do not despise the chastening of the Almighty. . . . For you shall have a covenant with the stones of the field, and the beasts of the field shall be at peace with you. You shall know that your tent is in peace; you shall visit your dwelling and find nothing amiss."

JOB 5:17, 23–24

Job's life had fallen apart. In ancient times, many believed that bad things happened to bad people and good things to good people. Religion reduced God to a conditionally loving force—a being who loves the lovable. To Job's friends, he must have deserved his suffering and needed to repent. They assumed that God was withholding blessings until Job earned them.

Today's passage is bad advice that sounds good. Eliphaz was telling Job to strike a deal with God to leverage blessings. Eliphaz was essentially saying, "Job, if you repent and shape up, God will restore you." This is bad advice based on bad theology.

Why? Because God's love is unconditional through Jesus. He relates to us based on Jesus' goodness, not our own. We can never be deserving, and God's blessings cannot be leveraged.

Might God have been chastening Job? In terms of growth, yes. Was Job's suffering a result of sin? No. The point is simply this: Trust God's heart even when He makes no sense. Don't try to understand His reasons or strike deals with His mercy. Eliphaz's good-sounding advice is a performance-based trap that leaves us disappointed and doubting God's heart. Through Jesus, all the goodness of God is already yours, and you never have to earn the favor of your Father.

....

Lord, let my repentance be motivated by Your generous love, not my desire to get something out of You. Your love is enough.

       Cary Schmidt, Emmanuel Baptist Church, Newington, CT

Live Fearlessly

Behold, an angel of the Lord stood before them, and the glory of the Lord shone around them, and they were greatly afraid. Then the angel said to them, "Do not be afraid, for behold, I bring you good tidings of great joy which will be to all people. For there is born to you this day in the city of David a Savior, who is Christ the Lord. And this will be the sign to you: You will find a Babe wrapped in swaddling cloths, lying in a manger."

LUKE 2:9-12

The story of God's Word is not how humanity can climb to God, but rather how God came to fallen humanity. From Genesis to Revelation, the Bible is God's historical, redemptive narrative—beginning with a perfect creation and ending with a perfect *new* creation. In between is the fall of that creation into sinfulness (raw, ugly, and deadly) as well as God's promised redemption through a Savior.

The Old Testament essentially says, "Things are very bad, but hope is on the way—have faith." It all points to Jesus. The New Testament essentially says, "Help has arrived, and Hope is alive—place your faith in Him and follow Him."

God punched a hole in the universe to be with us. The King came first to suffer, conquering sin and death. Then He promised to come again as vindicating King and Judge—consummating His eternal kingdom.

For now, we live out His purposes in the "in-between." We wait in Him—hopefully, faithfully, and fearlessly. Do not be afraid. Our lives are right on schedule in God's universe, and His kingdom is growing. God's good tidings of great joy sustain our hopes and purposes today.

....

Lord Jesus, thank You for coming for me. Help me live fearlessly until You return.

Everyday Joy and Peace

True Spiritual Armor

Stand therefore, having girded your waist with truth, having put on the breastplate of righteousness, and having shod your feet with the preparation of the gospel of peace; above all, taking the shield of faith with which you will be able to quench all the fiery darts of the wicked one. And take the helmet of salvation, and the sword of the Spirit, which is the word of God.

EPHESIANS 6:14–17

The book of Ephesians is a letter Paul wrote from prison in Rome to his friends at Ephesus. For three chapters he expounded the beauty of the gospel, and then for his final three chapters he explained what the gospel looks like when it is lived out. As he closed the letter, he considered the spiritual battle that surrounds us.

We are engaged, every moment of every day, in a very real spiritual battle. It is bigger than culture wars, political conflict, economic debates, or civil injustice. The real enemy is Satan, and the real war is spiritual. And let's be honest—sometimes we feel weak and exhausted in this battle.

Yet, in the battle, Jesus is our true spiritual armor (Isaiah 59). In today's passage, Paul uses the metaphor of a Roman soldier and Old Testament references to salvation to help us visualize what Jesus does.

Jesus helps us stand in this battle of the ages because He is the *truth* that holds us, the *righteousness* we wear, and the *gospel* that grounds us and guides us. He is the source of *faith* that shields us and neutralizes Satan's worst lies, the *salvation* that crowns our heads, and the *living Word* that God's Spirit uses as our primary offensive weapon. Though we may be in a battle, we can still have peace in His protection.

....

Lord Jesus, I choose to trust in You as You lead me victoriously through today's battles.

Cary Schmidt, Emmanuel Baptist Church, Newington, CT

The Gift of Repentance

Behold, You desire truth in the inward parts, and in the hidden part You will
make me to know wisdom. Purge me with hyssop, and I shall be clean; wash me,
and I shall be whiter than snow. Make me hear joy and gladness, that the bones
You have broken may rejoice. Hide Your face from my sins, and blot out all my
iniquities.

PSALM 51:6-9

R epentance is confusing to some people. To some it is a work of penance, earning back the favor of God. To others it is emotional sorrow, proving sincerity to God. To still others, repentance is the first step in a series of good works that undo our bad works.

But in reality, repentance is a gift of grace. It is never penance. It may involve emotion or regret; godly sorrow can lead to repentance (2 Corinthians 7:10). It may involve blessing; the goodness of God leads us to repentance (Romans 2:4). But it never involves hard work.

Repentance is reversal of mind and heart—it is to move from disagreement with God into agreement. It is to admit one's sin, acknowledge one's need for salvation, and humbly seek His mercy to grow forward. Repentance does not *earn* God's forgiveness, for that can never be earned. It merely brings a person in proximity to *receiving* it as His gift of grace through Jesus.

As David said in today's verses, God's mercy is always as close as repentance. Jesus did the heavy lifting of redemption—He bore God's wrath so that we could experience His love. But it begins with the humble admission of guilt. Repentance is a great gift that reveals Jesus is always someone you run *to* and never *from*.

Lord Jesus, when You convict me of sin today, help me to run to You
with an honest heart of repentance, falling into Your mercy and grace.

Everyday Joy and Peace

Pilgrim's Peace

Peter, an apostle of Jesus Christ, to the pilgrims of the Dispersion in Pontus, Galatia, Cappadocia, Asia, and Bithynia, elect according to the foreknowledge of God the Father, in sanctification of the Spirit, for obedience and sprinkling of the blood of Jesus Christ: Grace to you and peace be multiplied.

1 PETER 1:1-2

I grew up in the seventies and eighties as a Southern Baptist pastor's kid. It was common for pastors to move around a lot in those days. I was fortunate though for most of my childhood. We lived in the same town from when I was in the first grade until my senior year. I went to school with the same friends my whole life until I moved from Phenix City, Alabama, to Macon, Georgia, the Friday before I started my senior year. To say I was unpleased is a colossal understatement. I clearly remember the anxiety of going to a brand-new school. It was uncharted territory for me, and I didn't handle it well.

When we find ourselves in an unfamiliar land, whether physically, emotionally, relationally, or otherwise, it creates anxiety in us. Jesus came to this earth to bring peace between a holy God and the people who had created enmity with Him through their sins. We don't have to live in anxiety. When we lose the temporary peace of this world, provided by the comfort of familiarity, we can find abundant peace in the grace that He gives us through the covering of His blood. Let's begin our week resting in His peace rather than anything that this world has to offer. Wherever you are now, remember He has a plan for your life and has paid the price.

....

Lord, help me rest in You today. I will find peace in Your plan and provision. Amen.

Tim Sizemore, Lighthouse Baptist Church, Warner Robins, GA

His Mercy, His Law

Let Your tender mercies come to me, that I may live; for Your law is my delight.
Let the proud be ashamed, for they treated me wrongfully with falsehood; but
I will meditate on Your precepts. Let those who fear You turn to me, those who
know Your testimonies. Let my heart be blameless regarding Your statutes, that I
may not be ashamed.

PSALM 119:77-80

In the world we live in today, culture tends to dictate what is suitable and acceptable. The problem with that is that culture changes. What was socially acceptable fifty years ago is no longer that way. I can't even keep up with what is socially acceptable today versus just a few years ago. God never changes though, and neither does His Word. His ways are true, and just as when He established them, they are precisely the same today.

As the psalmist says in today's verses, we must meditate on His procedures of life for us to be able to know them and act accordingly. Think about the statement, "I will meditate on Your precepts." There is a difference between reading God's Word and meditating on it. When preparing for a test, I don't just read the material and take what I like or what is easy to swallow. I pore over the material that I will be tested on and try to digest it so I will recall it when the heat is on. God's Word is instruction for life. If we don't absorb it when things are going well, we won't recall it when things get rough. But if we do absorb His Word and come to Him in prayer, we'll find a peace that passes understanding (Philippians 4:7).

....

Lord, help me love Your Word every day, not just on Sundays. Amen.

Everyday Joy and Peace

Ups and Downs

Behold, seven thin heads, blighted by the east wind, sprang up after them.

GENESIS 41:6

I have only had one kidney stone. I suffered intensely, day and night, for over a week. I didn't sleep more than an hour at the time. When I finally got to see a doctor, he explained that I needed surgery to remove it. I was so weary from the ten-day battle, I asked if we could do it right there, right then, and I offered my pocketknife.

The worst pain came after the surgery. The doctor explained that it was spasms resulting from the long, intense struggle. The surgery was on a Friday afternoon. Saturday night, I lay on my living room floor and begged God to take either the pain or me. I thought the surgery would immediately take the pain from me, but at 2:00 a.m. Sunday, I had no hope for relief. Eventually, though, it ended.

Today's verse comes from a dream of Pharaoh that Joseph interpreted. It was part of a prophecy of God to bring famine to Egypt, immediately following a time of great prosperity. We should recognize that there will be times in our lives filled with abundance. That may not be an abundance of money but of peace and joy. There will also be times of famine from such things, and we must remember the years of prosperity. It helps me when I recognize that the famine in today's passage was set to begin but also to end. There are ebbs and flows in life. God is God during them all. Have faith, and seek Him for peace; even when no end to suffering is in sight, new life will spring up.

Lord, help me praise You on the mountaintop and in the valley. You are good in both places. Amen.

Tim Sizemore, Lighthouse Baptist Church, Warner Robins, GA

Putting in the Work

Live joyfully with the wife whom you love all the days of your vain life which He has given you under the sun, all your days of vanity; for that is your portion in life, and in the labor which you perform under the sun. Whatever your hand finds to do, do it with your might; for there is no work or device or knowledge or wisdom in the grave where you are going.

ECCLESIASTES 9:9-10

Enjoy the life that God has given you. Work hard to do a great job at whatever you do while you can. Because a time is coming when it will be too late—we will all face death. What do you put your effort into? Do you spend as much time reading about how to have a joyful marriage with the one you already have as you do distracting yourself on social media? It is no wonder that relationships fall apart when we fail to live joyfully with one another. We hold accounts of wrongs done to us way too long and charge exorbitant interest on debts created by those wrongs. Our instruction of verse 9 in today's passage is to put in the effort to live joyfully with the one that we married. It is a choice to make, not something that just happens to us. The same goes for excellence in all areas of life, whether married or unmarried.

I am sure that my staff gets tired of hearing me say, "Whatever we do, we do with excellence." But we only have one life here and a limited amount of time to live it. There are no do-overs. Whatever you do today, at work, at home, at church, do it with everything you have.

....

God, help me to forgive and love with all joy today and every day. Amen.

The Timeless Word

The law of the LORD is perfect, converting the soul; the testimony of the LORD is sure, making wise the simple; the statutes of the LORD are right, rejoicing the heart; the commandment of the LORD is pure, enlightening the eyes; the fear of the LORD is clean, enduring forever; the judgments of the LORD are true and righteous altogether. More to be desired are they than gold, yea, than much fine gold; sweeter also than honey and the honeycomb.

PSALM 19:7-10

As a teenager, how many times did I hear my father Hershel Sizemore's instructions and think to myself how antiquated they were? The world tells us every day that the laws of God are out-of-date and stale, no-good, useless, and sometimes downright wrong. The original wording in today's verse for "converting the soul" speaks of restoring something from complete disarray. The world's philosophy assumes that man is basically good and just needs some tweaking here and there. The truth is that humanity is completely wrecked. Only following the Creator's instructions will put things back together as He designed them.

God's Word will set things right with our souls, give us wisdom, help us distinguish truth from danger, and judge what is right and wrong. Everyone desires lots of wealth and great food. Those are timeless desires. The instructions of the Lord are timeless as well and should be much more covetable. We don't need any new revelations from God; we need to fall in love with the words that He has already given us. We'll find they rejoice our hearts and enlighten our eyes.

....

Dear Lord, give me a desire for the words You have spoken. Amen.

Tim Sizemore, Lighthouse Baptist Church, Warner Robins, GA

I Will Rejoice

I will greatly rejoice in the LORD, my soul shall be joyful in my God; for He has clothed me with the garments of salvation, He has covered me with the robe of righteousness, as a bridegroom decks himself with ornaments, and as a bride adorns herself with her jewels. For as the earth brings forth its bud, as the garden causes the things that are sown in it to spring forth, so the Lord GOD will cause righteousness and praise to spring forth before all the nations.

ISAIAH 61:10-11

M any times in my life, I've stood in a church sanctuary, singing praises to God during the worship service. Sometimes while singing, I've felt as if my heart would pound out of my chest. It was not being overcome with an emotional experience created by a "show"; the truth is that singing certain songs reminds me of His greatness. I become overwhelmed with the realization of everything God has done for me. I think of all that He has forgiven me for and the change that He made in me through salvation. He changed my dirty heart to one that longs to please Him; I cannot help but be blown away with appreciation.

I love to be in a room full of other worshipers who recognize the same thing in their lives and choose to express it—not for show, but out of sheer exuberance. One thing is for sure: If the Lord has made your soul joyful and covered you with His righteousness, you will choose to rejoice in Him and make it known. Will you choose the joy and peace of God today and every day?

God, reveal more of Your goodness to me today than ever before. Amen.

Everyday Joy and Peace

Show Me the Light

"You, child, will be called the prophet of the Highest; for you will go before the face of the Lord to prepare His ways, to give knowledge of salvation to His people by the remission of their sins, through the tender mercy of our God, with which the Dayspring from on high has visited us; to give light to those who sit in darkness and the shadow of death, to guide our feet into the way of peace."

LUKE 1:76-79

W hy is the world so dark today? In fact, why has the world always been so dark? According to scripture, there is one primary reason: *sin*. Too many people don't understand the wretchedness of sin. They think it is not that big of a deal. To God, however, it is a big deal. It is such an important matter that God raised up a prophet to point people to the light. John the Baptist, the subject of today's verse, had one primary purpose: to point people to God's salvation.

Have you ever noticed how your eyes can get used to darkness? You sit in a dark room and after a while, you can adjust. That can be handy physically, but it is devastating spiritually. Our world has gotten quite comfortable living in the dark. God, however, in His mercy, sent the Light of the World, His Son, Jesus Christ, into this dark world to guide us to peace and eternal life.

Embrace the light today so your path will be filled with the peace that only God can give.

....

Father, thank You for showing me the light. Help me care enough for others to point them to the light as well.

Brent Snook, First Baptist Church Glen Este, Batavia, OH

God With Us

The ransomed of the LORD shall return, and come to Zion with singing, with everlasting joy on their heads. They shall obtain joy and gladness; sorrow and sighing shall flee away. "I, even I, am He who comforts you. Who are you that you should be afraid of a man who will die, and of the son of a man who will be made like grass?"

ISAIAH 51:11–12

Life can fill us up with sorrow and sighing if we are not careful. It can get overwhelming. So God wants us to focus on Him. He can bring us through the Red Sea experiences of life. God can provide deliverance, joy, and comfort.

God reminds His people of His power in the past to give them hope and comfort for the future. The world may be more powerful than you, but it is not more powerful than God. You belong to God!

I am sure you at times feel like I do: weak, powerless, and fearful. That is okay! We have God in our corner—the omnipotent, omnipresent, all-wise God. So don't be afraid of a person who will one day die or wither like grass. Trust God, who parted the Red Sea when Israel's formidable enemy came after them. When your boss is unreasonable, trust God. When the doctor calls, rest. When you stand at the casket of the one you thought you could never live without, let God comfort you.

Yes, it is easy to let the circumstances of life put us in the pit of fear. Remember that ruthless people can change, and hard circumstances can be altered, but our God remains the same. He is the One who comforts you.

Lord, help me remember that the God who has been with me, will be with me.

Cords of Love

Blessed is he who comes in the name of the LORD! We have blessed you from the house of the LORD. God is the LORD, and He has given us light; bind the sacrifice with cords to the horns of the altar. You are my God, and I will praise You; You are my God, I will exalt You. Oh, give thanks to the LORD, for He is good! For His mercy endures forever.

PSALM 118:26-29

So many good things in life last for just a time, but not God's mercy. His mercy is the same yesterday, today, and forever. I don't know about you, but I need His mercy daily. Jesus, out of mercy, was bound to the cross of Calvary. The cords of love for us kept Him there. He was our ultimate sacrifice for redemption. Shouldn't the cords of love for Jesus cause us to live for Him? Yet we find at times that we are prone to wander.

Robert Robinson wrote the stanza, "Let thy goodness like a fetter, bind my wandering heart to thee. Prone to wander, Lord, I feel it, prone to leave the God I love. Here's my heart, Lord, take and seal it. Seal it for the courts above."[10] May we bind our wandering hearts to God with the cords of His love.

Paul urged us in Romans 12:1 to be a living sacrifice for God. Do you want liberty in life? If so, be bound to the altar of God. When the discouragement of life or temptations of the world come, may the cords of sacrifice keep us bound to the horns of the altar, because His mercy endures forever.

....

Lord, I praise You for Your mercy. Bind my heart to You.

Brent Snook, First Baptist Church Glen Este, Batavia, OH

Greater Tribulation, Greater Hope

Having been justified by faith, we have peace with God through our Lord Jesus Christ, through whom also we have access by faith into this grace in which we stand, and rejoice in hope of the glory of God. And not only that, but we also glory in tribulations, knowing that tribulation produces perseverance; and perseverance, character; and character, hope.

ROMANS 5:1-4

I certainly can rejoice in the peace that comes from being justified by faith in Christ. Praise God for that? Easy! But praise Him for tribulations? That seems to be a whole different level of praise.

Suffering does something *to* us, but it also does something *for* us. It shows us our weakness; and seeing how weak we are reveals anew our need for Jesus. It is like putting a beautiful jewel against the backdrop of a very black canvas. That jewel glistens with radiance.

As I write this devotion, I am experiencing the greatest trial and tribulation of my life: the passing away of my precious wife of forty-three years. It has driven me to a fork in the road. At that fork are two signs. One says, "Give Up" while the other sign says, "Persevere."

Paul tells us that if we persevere in trials, it will build our character in amazing measure, resulting in greater hope. Isn't it amazing that tribulation can produce a more powerful and stable hope in Jesus?

As I heard a well-known preacher say years ago, "No suffering, no intimacy with God." Tribulations will take us out of our comfort zone and put us on one of two roads: failure or great fruit. So, persevere! We will have peace with God.

Oh Lord, help me to persevere as You work to develop me.

What Brings You Joy?

He asked life from You, and You gave it to him—length of days forever and ever. His glory is great in Your salvation; honor and majesty You have placed upon him. For You have made him most blessed forever; You have made him exceedingly glad with Your presence. For the king trusts in the LORD, and through the mercy of the Most High he shall not be moved.

PSALM 21:4-7

W hat brings the greatest joy to you? There are a lot of things that bring enjoyment to life: travel, people, family, entertainment. But the one thing that brings the greatest and most lasting joy is the presence of God.

David wrote many psalms out of the anguish of his soul. In Psalm 21, however, he wrote out of joy for the victory God gave in battle. But whether a victim or a victor, David rested in God's presence in his life. No wonder he was called "a man after [God's] own heart" (1 Samuel 13:14).

Joseph too knew what it was like to be afflicted and abandoned (Genesis 37). Through his trials, he trusted in God's favor. He also knew what it felt like to be promoted and to prosper. One thing that was evident to him and everyone around was that God's presence made him prosper.

May we focus on and rejoice in our omnipresent God, who will never leave us or forsake us. May we be mindful of His moment-by-moment presence. Thank God that whether the Lord gives or He takes away, He will never remove His presence from us. Knowing we have His presence should bring us confidence, comfort, and celebration.

....

Lord, I am so grateful that whether I am on the mountain or in the valley, You are with me.

Brent Snook, First Baptist Church Glen Este, Batavia, OH

Go and Tell

The angel answered and said to the women, "Do not be afraid, for I know that you seek Jesus who was crucified. He is not here; for He is risen, as He said. Come, see the place where the Lord lay. And go quickly and tell His disciples that He is risen from the dead, and indeed He is going before you into Galilee; there you will see Him. Behold, I have told you." So they went out quickly from the tomb with fear and great joy, and ran to bring His disciples word.

MATTHEW 28:5-8

T wo women came to the tomb of Jesus with very sad hearts, but soon things changed. First, they met an angel. That would get anyone's attention. Then they received the news, positive news: *Jesus is not here. He is alive!* Two admonitions followed the angel's report. First, "Come, see." An empty tomb was one of the "many infallible proofs" that He was alive (Acts 1:3). The second command was, "Go quickly and tell." Their sad hearts turned to hearts of excitement and exuberance. To "go and tell" was not hard for them at all.

One phrase in verse 5 shouts out to us. The angel said, "I know that you seek Jesus." These women had this amazing experience only because they were seeking Jesus. If you are like me and want to be where the action is, seek Christ. As you seek Him, you too will "go and tell" with excitement.

The late Adrian Rogers once said, "Life is too short. Eternity is too long. Souls are too precious. The gospel is too wonderful for us to sleep through it all."[11] So let's wake up and go and tell the world the joyful news that He is risen.

....

Lord, as I seek You, stir my heart to "go and tell."

Thy Kingdom Come

Pray for the peace of Jerusalem: "May they prosper who love you. Peace be within your walls, prosperity within your palaces." For the sake of my brethren and companions, I will now say, "Peace be within you." Because of the house of the LORD *our God I will seek your good.*

PSALM 122:6-9

I n his book *Jesus: The God Who Knows Your Name*, Max Lucado writes, "Worship is when you're aware that what you've been given is far greater than what you can give. Worship is the awareness that were it not for his touch, you'd still be hobbling and hurting, bitter and broken. . . . Worship is the 'thank you' that refuses to be silenced."[12]

In today's psalm, we see a joyful pilgrim arriving in Jerusalem to give worship to God during Jerusalem's annual festival. While there, he prays for the peace of Jerusalem so the city may remain the center of worship for his people. His delight in worshiping the Lord prompts his prayer for the generations of worshipers who will follow in his footsteps; he desires that they too may experience the same privilege he is now enjoying.

Today we still pray for the peace of Jerusalem. Biblical prophecy declares there can be no true peace on earth until the Prince of Peace reigns forevermore. Until that day, commit to pray that God's kingdom of peace will come, on earth as it is in heaven (Matthew 6:10).

. . . .

Prince of Peace, I thank You for my redemption. I long for Your return and the peace it will bring. May my life reflect Your glory and goodness today. In Jesus' name I pray, amen.

Dr. Josh Saefkow, Flat Creek Baptist Church, Fayetteville, GA

The Healing Touch

He looked around to see her who had done this thing. But the woman, fearing and trembling, knowing what had happened to her, came and fell down before Him and told Him the whole truth. And He said to her, "Daughter, your faith has made you well. Go in peace, and be healed of your affliction."

MARK 5:32-34

Getting to Jesus through the crowd was almost impossible, yet one woman fought her way forward to touch Him. As soon as she did, she was healed. Notice the contrast of the multitudes of people who are there to see Jesus simply out of curiosity with the one who actually has the faith to reach out and touch Him! Amid the cacophony of noise, we too must make every effort to get to Jesus.

Our own strength and efforts are too weak and useless to make an impact for God's kingdom. But when we reach out in faith, God's power and grace bring healing to our bodies and souls. Jesus is available, His sustaining grace is attainable, and He alone has the power of disease and death. He knew her affliction and knows yours. Reach out to the Great Physician today through prayer.

....

Father, although I may be weak and timid, I reach out to you to be made whole. Grant me the peace that only You can supply through Jesus. By His name I pray, amen.

A Posture of Gratitude

Grace to you and peace from God our Father and the Lord Jesus Christ. I thank my God upon every remembrance of you, always in every prayer of mine making request for you all with joy, for your fellowship in the gospel from the first day until now, being confident of this very thing, that He who has begun a good work in you will complete it until the day of Jesus Christ.

PHILIPPIANS 1:2-6

The apostle Paul was imprisoned when he penned Philippians, yet his writing is filled with cheerful language. As he awaited trial, Paul's mind drifted to the believers in Philippi. Recollecting his church-plant brought him immense joy despite his circumstances. Paul was modeling a posture of gratitude as he reflected on the church.

Today, find a photo of a friend or family member and place it in a location where you'll see it often. Whenever you pass by, pause and give thanks for who the person is, what the person means to you, and who God is maturing that person to be. Remember, there is no way to offer too much gratitude when we communicate with God.

Father, you are a good and gracious God, and my heart is filled with praise for the family and friendships You have brought into my life. Thank You for the many meaningful relationships that bring my heart joy. In Jesus' name I pray, amen.

Dr. Josh Saefkow, Flat Creek Baptist Church, Fayetteville, GA

All Is Well

Speak to him, saying, "Thus says the LORD of hosts, saying: 'Behold, the Man whose name is the BRANCH! From His place He shall branch out, and He shall build the temple of the LORD; yes, He shall build the temple of the LORD. He shall bear the glory, and shall sit and rule on His throne; so He shall be a priest on His throne, and the counsel of peace shall be between them both.'"

ZECHARIAH 6:12-13

God announces that the Messiah will not only build the temple and serve as priest, but that He will also rule and reign as King. Jesus Christ is "the Branch," and the Word of God declares Christ as King and Priest. He will sit on the throne, but also, He serves as the Mediator between God and man. The writer of Hebrews details how Jesus perfectly fulfills this priest-king role as the Messiah (Hebrews 7:26–28).

As priest and king, Jesus intercedes on our behalf and blesses His people. As His followers, we rest knowing that war, injustice, and sin have an expiration date and that the loving, merciful, holy rule of the Son will endure forever.

Today, pray in confidence knowing your Priest and King carries your prayers to the Father. Pray with Hebrews 4:16 in mind, "Let us therefore come boldly to the throne of grace, that we may obtain mercy and find grace to help in time of need."

....

Father, thank You for the Branch, the Lord Jesus Christ. I come boldly to Your throne of grace knowing you are my Priest and King. I trust in You alone with every need in my life. Amen.

Hope in God

My soul thirsts for God, for the living God. When shall I come and appear before God? My tears have been my food day and night, while they continually say to me, "Where is your God?" When I remember these things, I pour out my soul within me. For I used to go with the multitude; I went with them to the house of God, with the voice of joy and praise, with a multitude that kept a pilgrim feast.

PSALM 42:2–4

Hidden and oppressed, the psalmist who wrote today's passage seeks comfort from his external circumstances by calling past experiences to mind. He remembers leading the march to the house of God, participating in godly fellowship, and worshiping with shouts of joy and thanksgiving. His past encounters with God preserve his faith. Despite the darkness, he is reminded to put his hope in God.

When you feel like you have lost hope, remember the times God has been faithful. Recalling God's faithfulness in the past will help carry you through days of turmoil and discouragement.

I am a lifelong Northeast Ohio sports fan. After decades of heartbreaking loss, my love for Northeast Ohio sports never wavers. Why? Because I can remember the thrill of a winning team and I hang on to the hope they will win again. Whatever heartbreak you face today, Jesus is your hope. And unlike the teams we love, He always comes through.

God, You have been faithful, You are faithful, and You will forever be faithful. I will remember and rejoice in Your works. Thank You for being my sure foundation. In Jesus' name I pray, amen.

Dr. Josh Saefkow, Flat Creek Baptist Church, Fayetteville, GA

The End of the Story

"Behold, I create new heavens and a new earth; and the former shall not be remembered or come to mind. But be glad and rejoice forever in what I create; for behold, I create Jerusalem as a rejoicing, and her people a joy. I will rejoice in Jerusalem, and joy in My people; the voice of weeping shall no longer be heard in her, nor the voice of crying."

ISAIAH 65:17-19

This passage paints a beautiful picture of the full restoration of God's creation. Here, God speaks directly through Isaiah to remind His people of the hope they have in the coming of a new heaven and a new earth, a return to paradise lost where God's original design for Jerusalem and the whole earth will finally be fulfilled.

Friend, Jesus is the victor! He is coming back, and there is a glorious future—a new creation free from sin, suffering, pain, and death—for every born-again child of God.

....

Father, I praise You for the day when there will be no more sickness, brokenness, loneliness, or reason for tears. Thank You for making me a new creation in Christ Jesus.

Like a Good Neighbor

He who is devoid of wisdom despises his neighbor, but a man of understanding holds his peace.

PROVERBS 11:12

I have lived in the same neighborhood for more than thirty years. I have watched people move in and move out. I am thankful that the beauty of the neighborhood has remained the same, even though it has transitioned.

Years ago, I visited the place where my family grew up in Oklahoma. Absolutely nothing looked the same. Houses needed to be painted, yards needed to be tended, and cars were up on blocks. It broke my heart. Apparently, as new people came in, the ones who were there to start with made little effort to maintain the place.

The proverb writer of today's verse suggests there is a time to leave some people alone but at other times we need to speak up. My wife and I have made it a habit to go and meet new neighbors as soon as they seemed settled. We make an effort to reach out to them and, if possible, discover their need for a church home and to find out their unique family situations. It's amazing how the Lord has then opened the door to continued friendship, influence, and ministry.

I've often thought, *If my neighbor doesn't care about the weeds in his yard, very soon they'll be in my yard.* On the other hand, if neighbors think of others and realize that maintaining their own property also benefits others, the whole neighborhood is elevated. So keep those lines of communication open. I think part of the Great Commission from Jesus includes our immediate neighborhood. Seek His wisdom to know just when and how to be a good neighbor, promoting peace all around.

....

Lord, help me to see my neighbors today as You see them.

Dr. Jim Phillips, North Greenwood Baptist Church, Greenwood, MS

Large and In Charge

John, to the seven churches which are in Asia: Grace to you and peace from Him who is and who was and who is to come, and from the seven Spirits who are before His throne, and from Jesus Christ, the faithful witness, the firstborn from the dead, and the ruler over the kings of the earth. To Him who loved us and washed us from our sins in His own blood. . . .

REVELATION 1:4-5

Each and every time we open our Bibles to the book of Revelation, we must remember that it is the only book in the Bible that promises a blessing for all who read and meditate upon it (Revelation 1:3). This means that we should never waste an important truth found in this amazing book. Don't neglect it, but rather make an effort to discover it. Your faith and confidence in the Lord will soar as you unlock its truths.

The verses in our reading today make a special effort to include all three persons of the Godhead. Go back and look again. The Father and the Son and the Holy Spirit have always been and always will be working in unison. The supposed forces of this world may try to be worshiped and adored, but no one and no thing stands above the Lord we serve.

Whatever you might be facing today, rest assured that the Creator God of the universe is not caught off guard by your situation. The Father is on His throne. His Son is aware of our needs, and His Holy Spirit stands ready to move across our lives. Call on Him now, and receive His grace and peace.

....

Heavenly Father, may I never underestimate Your power and presence to meet and exceed my needs.

Everyday Joy and Peace

Declare His Works

He sent His word and healed them, and delivered them from their destructions.
Oh, that men would give thanks to the LORD for His goodness, and for His
wonderful works to the children of men! Let them sacrifice the sacrifices of
thanksgiving, and declare His works with rejoicing.

PSALM 107:20-22

L isten around the church on Sunday morning and you'll hear people talk about what's important to them. They may brag about their grandchildren and even produce a video on their smartphone to show evidence of their praiseworthiness. Others may declare their joy about their latest bargain find or garden success. And during football season, many are huddled up discussing their favorite plays or strategies. There's nothing wrong with expressing our joy.

But if we're really experiencing blessings from God, why do we so often fail to declare it to others? Why do we find it difficult to talk about God? Earlier in today's psalm, one translation reads, "Let the redeemed of the LORD say so" (Psalm 107:2 ESV). And I think we should—more than most of us do. When God has answered your prayers, brag about Him. When He has steered you from disaster or accident, tell somebody. When you have received comfort and affirmation from His Spirit in a time of loss, testify. Be found more often than not with praise on your lips out of a heart of gratitude. Somebody in your sphere of influence will benefit from your witness, and God will be worshiped. Don't miss an opportunity to praise Him with joy today.

....

Lord, show me when to praise You in front of someone else today. It may be the best thing they hear all day. Help me declare Your works!

Dr. Jim Phillips, North Greenwood Baptist Church, Greenwood, MS

A Model of Godliness

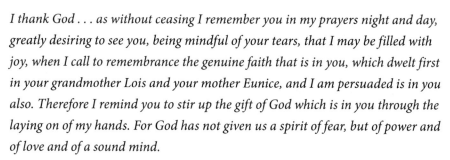

I thank God . . . as without ceasing I remember you in my prayers night and day, greatly desiring to see you, being mindful of your tears, that I may be filled with joy, when I call to remembrance the genuine faith that is in you, which dwelt first in your grandmother Lois and your mother Eunice, and I am persuaded is in you also. Therefore I remind you to stir up the gift of God which is in you through the laying on of my hands. For God has not given us a spirit of fear, but of power and of love and of a sound mind.

2 TIMOTHY 1:3-7

Many of us would agree that when we were infants, we learned to speak and walk by listening to and watching those around us. A baby focusing on her mother's lips will soon be mimicking what she hears. A toddler watching a sibling walk across the room will try and replicate what he sees. We learn by observation.

This is true in the spiritual realm as well. If we discipline ourselves to spend quality time around more mature Christians, we'll more likely be inspired to grow in our faith. In today's passage, Paul credits the salvation and growth of his young disciple Timothy due to the fact he saw godliness lived out in Timothy's own home—a fact that filled Paul with joy.

Still, once we are saved, we are responsible for our own maturity and growth, with power, love, and a sound mind. As we continue to grow, may we be diligent to mature, knowing that others need us to pass along what God teaches us on our own journey.

God, help me to find someone to mentor in the faith as You continue to move me on to maturity. Amen.

Well Pleased

> *Now may the God of peace who brought up our Lord Jesus from the dead, that*
> *great Shepherd of the sheep, through the blood of the everlasting covenant, make*
> *you complete in every good work to do His will, working in you what is well*
> *pleasing in His sight, through Jesus Christ, to whom be glory forever and ever.*
> *Amen.*

HEBREWS 13:20-21

Anyone who has ever competed in sports knows firsthand the feeling of satisfaction that comes when a coach praises your efforts. You've been doing your workouts, studying the playbook, and giving it all you've got on the field, court, or diamond. What you've done in practice proves successful in the game, and the coach is pleased.

The spiritual realm has some similarities. As we study God's Word, we learn more and more what God expects of us out in the world. We come to "the huddle" at church, and God uses our pastor-coach to instruct us in God's playbook (the Bible) so we can apply what we've learned and practiced once we leave the huddle. Though our pastor may never grade our performance, God has a way of affirming our efforts by way of the Holy Spirit in us.

A certain peace is found in the Christian life when our hearts testify that we've given our best to minister to and reach out to others with the opportunities God has given us. Today's passage calls it what is "well pleasing in His sight." As we become more complete in doing His will, may we too hear words of affirmation from the Father. They bring a special kind of joy on earth, and eternal joy in heaven.

....

Oh God, may my life today truly be lived for my good and Your glory.
Amen.

Dr. Jim Phillips, North Greenwood Baptist Church, Greenwood, MS

Finding Your Holy Hum

Blessed are the people who know the joyful sound! They walk, O LORD, in the light of Your countenance. In Your name they rejoice all day long, and in Your righteousness they are exalted. For You are the glory of their strength, and in Your favor our horn is exalted.

PSALM 89:15-17

I am a hummer. I think I learned it from my mom. Growing up, I would hear her go about humming along through the day, doing chores and walking through the house. In time—subconsciously, I presume—I started doing the same. My three sons then learned it from me. On occasion while they were growing up, my wife would declare, "Would you all at least hum the same tune? You're driving me crazy." Without even realizing it, we were each going about humming the tune of our own choosing.

The psalmist today is describing a believer in God simply going about his day walking in the confidence and presence of God. "The joyful sound" could very well have been a hum, or song of praise, being expressed as he went about the day. Knowing the Source of his strength, he simply and quite naturally exhibited a spirit of enthusiasm and peace. Others might have picked up on it, but to him it was his spiritual act of worship.

Knowing I'm saved and serving in the joy of the Lord, I plan to keep doing as I've always done and seek ways to express my gratitude along the way. I would encourage you to do the same. Your whole day might turn out differently when expressing a holy hum.

....

Thank You, Lord, for providing me a heart full of joy and worship.
Amen.

God Keeps His Promises

"Lift up your eyes all around, and see: They all gather together, they come to you; your sons shall come from afar, and your daughters shall be nursed at your side. Then you shall see and become radiant, and your heart shall swell with joy; because the abundance of the sea shall be turned to you, the wealth of the Gentiles shall come to you."

ISAIAH 60:4–5

The people of Israel had seen wicked king after wicked king at the time Isaiah wrote today's verses. They would see a divided kingdom, and they would be conquered and enslaved for many years. They would be scattered all over the world and face many hardships because of their own rebellion and sin. Through it all, God had made a promise to Abraham and the Jewish people. In today's text, the prophet Isaiah shared how God would fulfill His promise to the people of God. They would return to their homeland and they would possess it. Even as you read this, the Hebrew nation is still coming home to Israel.

Throughout scripture, God makes many promises. One of the most profound truths is that if God promised to do something, it will be done. God promised to send His Son to redeem a lost world, and He did. He promised that His Son would return one day, and He will. It would benefit all of us who follow God to get alone in the Word, understand His promises, and even personalize them, meditating on what they mean in our lives and finding joy in them. What has God promised you? Remember that God keeps 100 percent of His promises 100 percent of the time.

Dear Lord, I thank You that You keep Your promises. Help me to know Your promises and to stand on them. Amen.

John Fream, Cypress Baptist Church, Benton, LA

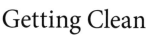

Getting Clean

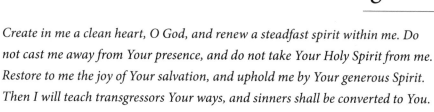

Create in me a clean heart, O God, and renew a steadfast spirit within me. Do not cast me away from Your presence, and do not take Your Holy Spirit from me. Restore to me the joy of Your salvation, and uphold me by Your generous Spirit. Then I will teach transgressors Your ways, and sinners shall be converted to You.

PSALM 51:10–13

Whereas I was a kid, it was so fun to get dirty as I played hard. Perhaps you too remember those childhood days and the fun of mud and dirt. Getting in mud from my head to toes was fun for a little while. But the fun eventually had to end, and the cleanup had to begin. While getting clean was not nearly as fun as getting dirty, it was a must.

David wrote today's psalm of repentance after his affair with Bathsheba and murder of Uriah. It may have been fun for a little while, the "passing pleasures of sin" (Hebrews 11:25), but when he realized that sin had dragged him down and covered him in dirt, David was broken and prayed for repentance. The key to repentance is to be broken about the sin we want to turn from.

David cried out to God to be clean again and to be useful to God for His service. David messed up and got dirty in his sin. But he gives us a good playbook in how to repent in this beautiful psalm. We serve a God who is so good to us that He cleans us up, and He does not give up on us.

....

Dear Lord, please forgive me of my sins and help me to truly repent of them. Cleanse me and use me for Your kingdom work. Amen.

Hold Steady

Beloved, do not think it strange concerning the fiery trial which is to try you, as though some strange thing happened to you; but rejoice to the extent that you partake of Christ's sufferings, that when His glory is revealed, you may also be glad with exceeding joy.

1 PETER 4:12-13

Going through trials is not easy. Sometimes it flat-out stinks. The good news is that those very trials are not in vain, and they do have a purpose for you. In todays' verses, Peter wrote and reminded the tremendously persecuted Christians that God was with them. Nero was the leader of Rome, and he had made it open season on Christians. Christians were persecuted everywhere they turned because of their faith in Christ. Peter wanted them to be enouraged and strong through their trials.

Still today, we live in a fallen world that is opposed to God and His ways. God uses difficulties as a refining fire in our life to make us better and help us know Him deeper. When you go through tough times, remember that God has you. We can rejoice in tough times because God is going to use that difficulty to make us more like Jesus. The world hated Jesus because of who He was (John 15:18–25). The more we are like Him and follow His ways, the more the world will persecute us. Do not let that get you down! Jesus conquered this world, and He will come again to this world. When He does come, and His glory is revealed, we will be glad with exceeding joy.

....

Dear Lord, give me strength for my fiery trial. Use it to bring Yourself glory and to draw me closer to You. Amen.

John Fream, Cypress Baptist Church, Benton, LA

Hate Evil, Love God

You who love the LORD, hate evil! He preserves the souls of His saints; He delivers them out of the hand of the wicked. Light is sown for the righteous, and gladness for the upright in heart. Rejoice in the LORD, you righteous, and give thanks at the remembrance of His holy name.

PSALM 97:10-12

When I was a kid, my mother taught me to not hate anyone. As an adult Christian, that is just as important. We must, however, hate sin and evil. That does not mean we hate people, but it does mean that we hate the sin of people. The world rejects the truth that you can love a sinner and not their sin, but Christians hold it to be the core of who we are.

One thing I hated as a kid was snakes; still do to this day. While I hate snakes in all places, I especially hate snakes on me. In the same way, I take today's verse to mean that I should hate evil, and hate it most on me—in my own life.

As a believer in Christ hates sin and comes to know the Lord, they will experience the blessings and hand of God on their lives. Of course, the promise here is that once a person is saved, they are always saved, preserved. There is also a promise of God's blessing and favor when we seek Him and turn from evil. As a follower of Jesus, I will not be sinless, but I can have a heart that desires to be sinless—to pursue the light "sown for the righteous, and gladness for the upright in heart."

Lord, forgive me of my sins and help me have a heart like Yours toward evil, choosing instead the good. Amen.

Everyday Joy and Peace

Advice, Good and Bad

"Give ear, Job, listen to me; hold your peace, and I will speak. If you have anything to say, answer me; speak, for I desire to justify you. If not, listen to me; hold your peace, and I will teach you wisdom."

JOB 33:31-33

In today's passage, Job was in a bad way and was suffering tremendously. He had three friends, and these friends may have meant well, but they sure proved to not be the best advisors. His friend Elihu was speaking to Job in this chapter and trying to help his suffering friend. Out of all of the friends, Elihu may have given the best advice and may have been the godliest counsel to "hold his peace" and listen. Make sure to get good, godly counsel, and know that God can speak through anyone, but speaks loudest through His Word.

Job's suffering has been a theological wrestling match for most of us. Let's start with a simple truth that is the foundation of our beliefs: God is good, just, and loving. Let's build on that truth: God does nothing evil. Therefore we understand that suffering is either caused by this messed-up world, our own decisions, or because God allows it. Job was being used by God and being taught by God. While it puzzles the world why good people suffer, we as Christians know there are no inherently good people. We also know that we have a good God who will use our sufferings for our own good. So maybe we can use part of Elihu's advice for good: We too can "hold our peace" and listen for God. He will surely be near to us in our suffering (Psalm 34:18).

....

Dear Lord, when the suffering of this world hits, help me to endure it, listen for You, and glorify You. Amen.

John Fream, Cypress Baptist Church, Benton, LA

The Whole Truth

The truthful lip shall be established forever, but a lying tongue is but for a moment. Deceit is in the heart of those who devise evil, but counselors of peace have joy.

PROVERBS 12:19-20

When my daughter was little, one day I found her and her cousin covered in pasty medicine. They had decided to doctor all her dolls in this paste. When I asked what they were doing, it amazed me how quickly my little sweet daughter was ready to lie. Before she could get too far, I asked her to look at her cousin and for him to look at her. They had it in their hair and all over their faces. I asked them if they really wanted to stick with the story of "doing nothing." I think we look like that to our heavenly Father when we lie. Truth is always the best choice!

The concept of truth is an especially important thing. When you are known for being truthful and honest, you gain respect with people. Telling the truth is another way that we as Christians can honor our Lord. We live in a world that does not honor truth the way it once did. Years ago, if someone told a lie, it would ruin their professional life, political life, or just their life in general. Today it seems lies are expected, even rewarded. Jesus Christ was everything opposite of this. His message of love is wrapped around truth—and that truth brings joy. The truth is that He is the Son of God and He came to save this world from sin. I am sure glad that Jesus was not lying about anything—and especially that.

....

Lord, help me to have the character of Christ and not of deceit. Amen.

The God of Creation

You visit the earth and water it, You greatly enrich it; the river of God is full of water; You provide their grain, for so You have prepared it. You water its ridges abundantly, You settle its furrows; You make it soft with showers, You bless its growth. . . . Your paths drip with abundance. They drop on the pastures of the wilderness, and the little hills rejoice on every side. The pastures are clothed with flocks; the valleys also are covered with grain; they shout for joy, they also sing.

PSALM 65:9–13

For twenty-two years, my family prayed for my dad's salvation. At times, I'll admit, it seemed unattainable. But our God of creation got to him! Dad was told that he had less than a year to live. It turned out to be six months. He began paying attention to spiritual things.

Toward the end, he called one afternoon, asking me to come see him. I found him sitting at the end of his dock on the river. He said, "This morning, while it was still dark, I took a walk around my property. I looked up in the sky, and I saw the stars and the moon, and for the first time in my life, I realized there is a God that made it all! I couldn't do that. No man could. So, I got down on my knees and confessed every sin that I could think of, and I asked Jesus Christ to come into my heart and save me. And He did!" Two months later, in glory, he met the God of creation. While we're still on earth, we too can meet Him every day in joy, looking at the wonders He's made.

. . . .

Father, I thank You for Your creation and for the way You reveal Yourself through it. In Jesus' name I pray, amen.

H. Marshall Thompson Jr., Riverstone Community Church, Jacksonville, FL

Doing the Tango

We urge you, brethren, to recognize those who labor among you, and are over you in the Lord and admonish you, and to esteem them very highly in love for their work's sake. Be at peace among yourselves. Now we exhort you, brethren, warn those who are unruly, comfort the fainthearted, uphold the weak, be patient with all.

1 THESSALONIANS 5:12-14

In today's scripture, we find Paul's final instructions to the church at Thessalonica. The church was full of young believers, which is a wonderful thing! Paul constantly assured them of his love for them, and he taught them God's ways. He could never be accused of not letting others know what is expected of them. The instructions in today's passage are expected of us as believers as well. We are expected to recognize those who have the spiritual authority over us, esteem them, and appreciate them as they have taught us the Word of God. We must never take their teaching for granted. We are also to be at peace, speaking truthfully, encouragingly, and patiently to one another.

Now, for many of us that sounds like hard work. And so it is! I have always maintained that to labor in the work of the Lord is to "spiritually sweat." If you think about it, how many people do you know who are truly breaking a spiritual sweat in the work of the Lord? Are you? It's like doing the tango—if we aren't sweating in our work for our Lord, His people, His church, and for precious lost souls, we probably aren't doing it right! But in the end, the result is a beautiful peace.

Dear Lord, I thank You for everything You have given me to do for You and for Your kingdom. Help me to labor well.

What's the Cost?

Grace to you and peace from God our Father and the Lord Jesus Christ. We are bound to thank God always for you, brethren, as it is fitting, because your faith grows exceedingly, and the love of every one of you all abounds toward each other, so that we ourselves boast of you among the churches of God for your patience and faith in all your persecutions and tribulations that you endure.

2 THESSALONIANS 1:2-4

For much of my life, Pastor Rick Baldwin has been my pastor. Over the years he has taught me much, but perhaps nothing has affected me more than this lesson: "Let's be good at the things that don't cost us anything!" Think about it. How much does it cost me to let others know I appreciate them? To let others know the value they bring to my life? To encourage someone else? To build up believers in the faith? Answer: It doesn't cost me anything!

Conversely, when I don't let others know how much I appreciate them, it costs me dearly. When I don't let others know the value they bring to my life, it costs me. When I don't encourage others, it costs me. When I don't build up believers in the faith, it costs me. We do reap what we sow (Galatians 6:7) whether good or bad, and it is more blessed to give than to receive (Acts 20:35).

In today's verses, Paul lifted up the suffering Thessalonians with a kind word. We can lift others up, too! How hard is it to say something nice that brings grace and peace? It's not difficult at all. Try it today and see.

. . . .

Father, I pray that You give me many opportunities to be good at things that don't cost me anything. In Jesus' name I pray, amen.

Run from the Spotlight

The Jews had light and gladness, joy and honor. And in every province and city,
wherever the king's command and decree came, the Jews had joy and gladness,
a feast and a holiday. Then many of the people of the land became Jews, because
fear of the Jews fell upon them.

ESTHER 8:16-17

To me, the book of Esther reads like an action-adventure novel! Faced with death, Esther and Mordecai disregarded their own well-being, forgot about their own fear, and planted themselves in the middle of God's perfect will. Esther put her own life on the line by pleading for King Ahasuerus to have mercy on the Jews. In their place, we may have been tempted to think, *There is no way this is going to turn out well.* But their story shows God in action!

Whether we acknowledge it or not, whether we accept it or not, God is in control. Queen Esther knew our Lord was in control, and because of that fact, she had unfathomable courage—and a whole nation was saved! As for Mordecai, he was appointed to the place of power that the evil Haman once occupied.

Far too many today seek the spotlight. Too many want the praise, accolades, honor, and money that often come with it. But all that is temporal. Our Lord doesn't operate in that manner. Mordecai and Esther took the risk of obeying God and running from the spotlight, and as a result, "the Jews had joy and gladness." May we have the same faith, take risks to follow the Lord, and live in humility too. We certainly won't miss out on the action!

....

Heavenly Father, please give me the courage to run from the spotlight
and to know and do Your perfect will.

Everyday Joy and Peace

How To

I have declared my ways, and You answered me; teach me Your statutes. Make me understand the way of Your precepts; so shall I meditate on Your wonderful works. My soul melts from heaviness; strengthen me according to Your word.

PSALM 119:26-28

You may be old enough to remember the For Dummies book series. I like how one reviewer described it: "The books had bright yellow covers, all promising to explain some difficult subject so plainly that even a doofus can understand it."[13] Well, I confess, I must be a fellow doofus, because I once read *DOS For Dummies* and still had to take several classes to learn it!

Have you ever considered that our how-to book about God's plan for human-kind gives us not only the instructions on how to have a full and meaningful life and how to have eternal life, but access to the Author, second by second, through the person of His Holy Spirit! How awesome is that?

Just try getting some contemporary author to do that for you. Not going to happen! The psalmist writes, "I have declared my ways, and thou heardest me: teach me thy statutes" (119:26 KJV). Should you want to know *how to*, understand our Lord's precepts. Should you want to know how to live out His statutes, how to talk of His wondrous works, read the most wonderful how-to book ever known to man, the Bible. It works for everyone—doofuses and dummies included!

....

Dear Lord, I pray that I may know You and Your Word, and find Your strength and wisdom within it.

H. Marshall Thompson Jr., Riverstone Community Church, Jacksonville, FL

It's Priceless

My son, do not forget my law, but let your heart keep my commands; for length of days and long life and peace they will add to you. Let not mercy and truth forsake you; bind them around your neck, write them on the tablet of your heart, and so find favor and high esteem in the sight of God and man.

PROVERBS 3:1-4

I recently visited the White Oak Plantation in Yulee, Florida, a seventeen-thousand-acre animal conservation center and wildlife refuge. They also have some possessions locked into a trust that are true treasures! One of their stewards placed into my hands just one of several hundred pieces of six-hundred-year-old silk tapestry from China, sewn in 24 karat gold. I asked, "If I put this up for sale tonight on eBay, what dollar amount should I start the bidding at?" He gently took back that tapestry and said, "Well, you couldn't post any price, because it's priceless!" For someone who pays attention to dollars and cents, I could hardly fathom that something could be so valuable that you couldn't put a price on it, but here's the bottom line: There are a few things, seen and unseen, that are absolutely priceless. Wisdom may very well be number one.

Today's passage from Proverbs comes with a heading in my Bible: "Wisdom Is Extremely Valuable." I'd say that's an understatement! If I have learned anything over the thirty-nine years that I have been a Christian, it's simply this: I must have wisdom! It comes from God's Law, His commands, His mercy and truth. It brings long life and peace. And when we ask for wisdom, we get it (James 1:5). Ask today, and you'll gain something truly priceless.

....

Dear Lord, I simply and humbly ask for wisdom from You.

Pray for Others

I exhort first of all that supplications, prayers, intercessions, and giving of thanks be made for all men, for kings and all who are in authority, that we may lead a quiet and peaceable life in all godliness and reverence. For this is good and acceptable in the sight of God our Savior, who desires all men to be saved and to come to the knowledge of the truth.

1 TIMOTHY 2:1-4

I t is easy to get into a prayer rut where we only pray for our family or the ones we love. In today's verse, we are encouraged here to pray for all. It is easy to pray for those we like, but praying for everyone, even those who rule over us, is more difficult. When was the last time you prayed for your boss, teacher, coach, or politicians? We are instructed to do this for a reason, and to even be thankful for them. Praying for your boss means you have a job to be thankful for. Praying for a teacher means you have the opportunity to learn and grow. Praying for a coach means you are part of a team that provides camaraderie. Praying for politicians that they will have wisdom could result in peace and prosperity—that "quiet and peaceable life" today's passage mentions.

When we intercede, we should pray for all of these people to have health, wisdom, and favor of the Lord. Most important, we should be intentional to pray for their salvation. It is God's desire for all to be saved and to come to a knowledge of the truth in Jesus.

Lord, Help me pray for others beyond my family. Put names of others on my heart and give me the desire to lift them up in prayer to You. Amen.

Brian Fossett, Fossett Evangelistic Ministries, Dalton, GA

Precious in His Sight

Peter opened his mouth and said: "In truth I perceive that God shows no partiality. But in every nation whoever fears Him and works righteousness is accepted by Him. The word which God sent to the children of Israel, preaching peace through Jesus Christ—He is Lord of all—that word you know."

ACTS 10:34-37

Red and yellow, black and white, all are precious in His sight." These are words to a song you may have sung as a child, and no truer words were ever spoken. God is not partial. Jesus' nail-scarred hand is extended to every type of person. The ground is level at Calvary! Salvation is extended to all—the weak and the strong, the rich and the poor. All are sinners standing in need of a Savior. Jesus is Lord for all. Under no other name is salvation but Jesus. Call on Jesus, and you will be saved.

Those who accept Jesus experience the favor of God. They understand what it feels like to have a desire to serve God and others. Some people believe if they are good, they will go to heaven, but salvation does not work that way. Salvation comes when one admits a need for a Savior, acknowledging that Jesus is that Savior and asking for forgiveness from sin. Sometimes we mess up by judging others and thinking they are too bad to be saved, but the truth is no one is too far down the road of sin that the nail-scarred hand of grace cannot reach them. Jesus brings the gospel of peace, and salvation is for all!

....

Lord, use me to reach all people for Your kingdom. Help me see others as You see them—hurting sinners in need of a Savior. Amen.

Everyday Joy and Peace

Good Things from Above

There are many who say, "Who will show us any good?" LORD, lift up the light of Your countenance upon us. You have put gladness in my heart, more than in the season that their grain and wine increased. I will both lie down in peace, and sleep; for You alone, O LORD, make me dwell in safety.

PSALM 4:6-8

W ho will show us any good?" is a probing question to get us to think and to be thankful for the One from whom all blessings flow. All that is good in us is Jesus! He provides our daily provisions—peace of mind, protection, and guidance. God shows us good and is gracious even when we do not deserve it. The Lord shines His countenance on us so we may share it with others. He puts gladness in our hearts. When you spend time with God, you come away changed. The Lord does prosper us, His children, but with much more than money and things. He gives us a peace that surpasses all understanding (Philippians 4:7). He does not leave us troubled or conflicted. He brings peace to situations. He assures safety. He allows us rest. We can rest in Him. We are secure in Him. He puts gladness in our hearts and lives, not sadness. He lifts us up—encourages, supports, and inspires us. He shines a light that illuminates our path. So we, like the psalmist, can lie down and sleep in peace and safety, knowing the God of the universe looks out for us.

....

Thank You, Lord, for bringing a calm into my life. Thank You for providing direction. Thank You for smiling on me this day. May You let me share the light of Your countenance with others.

Brian Fossett, Fossett Evangelistic Ministries, Dalton, GA

Praise Springs Forth

I will greatly rejoice in the LORD, my soul shall be joyful in my God; for He has clothed me with the garments of salvation, He has covered me with the robe of righteousness, as a bridegroom decks himself with ornaments, and as a bride adorns herself with her jewels. For as the earth brings forth its bud, as the garden causes the things that are sown in it to spring forth, so the Lord GOD will cause righteousness and praise to spring forth before all the nations.

ISAIAH 61:10-11

From time to time we all need to walk down memory lane and be reminded of what joy flooded our soul when we were saved. Do you remember? We have a reason to celebrate because we are forgiven of our past, present, and future sins. We are given joy and peace like we have never experienced. Our salvation should bring forth praise.

People may ask, "Why praise and worship?" One important reason is that God is worthy of our praise. Another reason is that praise is one form of showing the Lord we are thankful for Him and our salvation. I have heard the expression "get your praise on." The truth is, we should live in a constant state of praise. He should be the first thing on our minds when we wake up and the last thing on our minds when we lie down at night. Our lips should always have a praise for the Lord, and our hands should be lifted high to an amazing Savior.

In today's verses Isaiah gives a wonderful model of what it is to praise. What will your song of praise be today?

....

Lord, help me always be grateful and mindful of my salvation. I want to publicly exude joy, praise, and worship.

Eternal Mercy

Praise the LORD! Oh, give thanks to the LORD, for He is good! For His mercy endures forever. Who can utter the mighty acts of the LORD? Who can declare all His praise? Blessed are those who keep justice, and he who does righteousness at all times!

PSALM 106:1-3

His mercy endures forever. Think about that. His work of mercy, completed in the life of the believer, endures forever. He did a work on and through us at salvation that will pass all of eternity. Therefore, we should always be quick to praise Him and give thanks. We should give testimony of the mighty acts He has done in our lives. Anyone can praise Him who has seen his creation. When we see the beauty and majesty all around us, we should praise Him! We should want to be righteous and just, because He is! He has changed us, and we are His masterpiece. After the Master's hand has touched us with salvation, we are never the same. We see the world and others differently. We see hope instead of despair, joy instead of pain, and light instead of darkness. We find peace in His eternal, unending mercy.

Today's psalm asks, "Who can utter the mighty works of the LORD?" The truth is, words enough don't exist. But we sure can try! How will you attempt it today? Just open your heart and mouth in praise, and begin.

Thank You, Lord, for Your mercy and unconditional love! Help me to be just and righteous. Thank You for touching my life with salvation and changing me forever. Amen.

Brian Fossett, Fossett Evangelistic Ministries, Dalton, GA

Remember Him

"Also in the day of your gladness, in your appointed feasts, and at the beginning of your months, you shall blow the trumpets over your burnt offerings and over the sacrifices of your peace offerings; and they shall be a memorial for you before your God: I am the LORD your God."

NUMBERS 10:10

In Numbers 10, God spoke to Moses and instructed him to make two fine silver trumpets to call the congregation, to sound alarms, and to sound praise to God. These are the trumpets the people heard every month as they remembered God and what He had done for them.

What are your "trumpets"? We should remember the Lord in all things. We should praise Him in the good times and in the bad. He is in control, and just as much God in the desert as He is in the land flowing with milk and honey. We are called to always make a reminder of God's love and power with our thankfulness and acknowledgment of the fact He is worthy. We do not need to forget about God in the good times of our life, or in the days of gladness, because the truth is He made all of those things happen for us. He always works it all out. We can smile and celebrate with joy when we think about His majesty and glory. He loves us so much to call us sons and daughters. Think about that—we are children of the King. Let us be ready and willing to blow a trumpet and celebrate today because of our God!

....

Lord, help me to be mindful of Your worthiness. Help me to always be positive in every season of my life—for You are the Lord my God!

A Day of Rejoicing!

They brought the ark of the LORD, and set it in its place in the midst of the tabernacle that David had erected for it. Then David offered burnt offerings and peace offerings before the LORD. And when David had finished offering burnt offerings and peace offerings, he blessed the people in the name of the LORD of hosts.

2 SAMUEL 6:17-18

In 2 Samuel, David was made king over Israel. All twelve tribes came together once again. Jerusalem, the former stronghold of the Jebusites, was captured and became the city of David, the capital of Israel. But one key piece of the puzzle remained unfinished: bringing the ark of the covenant into Jerusalem.

When the ark arrived, there were shouts of praises, the blasts of a trumpet, and numerous sacrifices offered to honor the God of Israel. David was filled with joy, dancing before the Lord with great fervor. This was a momentous occasion as the ark of God—the visible representation of His presence—came to dwell in Jerusalem.

Can you remember the day the Lord came to dwell within you? For me, it was on a Monday night in January 1980. I was a senior in high school. Although I believed in the "facts and figures" of Jesus, it was just head knowledge. I did not have a personal relationship with Him. But that Monday night, I experienced conviction over my sin and my lost condition. I bowed my knees and in simple faith and true repentance, I asked Jesus to save me. And He did! And my life has never been the same since. How about you? Can you remember your salvation day, your day of rejoicing? Celebrate it today.

God, thank You for saving me. Help me never get over the joy of my salvation! Amen.

Dr. Jeff Schreve, First Baptist Church, Texarkana, TX

When You Doubt Your Salvation

The king shall have joy in Your strength, O LORD; and in Your salvation how greatly shall he rejoice! You have given him his heart's desire, and have not withheld the request of his lips. For You meet him with the blessings of goodness; You set a crown of pure gold upon his head.

PSALM 21:1–3

When I was in college, an evangelist came to our church for a week of services. This man was a great preacher, passionate and fiery. He made the horrors of hell seem so real. The only problem with his sermon was a lack of balance. He caused many Christians to doubt their salvation.

I had only been a believer for two years when this evangelist came. I was hungry for the Word and was growing in my faith. But after hearing his sermons, I began to doubt my salvation. Was I truly born-again? Since I still struggled with sin, maybe I hadn't done something right. Was I going to be told at the judgment, "Depart from Me"? Those frightening thoughts plagued my mind and stole my joy. I was miserable for about a month, wondering if I really even belonged to Christ.

During this time of turmoil, God used Psalm 21 to calm my heart. My heart's sincere desire when I initially called upon His name two years earlier was to be saved. And He did not "[withhold] the request of my lips." He saved me, just as He promised!

Are you struggling with doubts over your salvation? If you have sincerely asked the Lord to save you, find peace and rest on the promise of His Word.

God, thank You that I can rest in You and Your promises. Thank You that You are *the* Savior, and *my* Savior! Amen.

Sold Out for Jesus

Our gospel did not come to you in word only, but also in power, and in the Holy Spirit and in much assurance, as you know what kind of men we were among you for your sake. And you became followers of us and of the Lord, having received the word in much affliction, with joy of the Holy Spirit, so that you became examples to all in Macedonia and Achaia who believe.

1 THESSALONIANS 1:5-7

The church in Thessalonica was a great church. The people were former idol worshipers who heard Paul preach the powerful gospel. Their lives were radically changed as they responded to Christ. The light of God's love and joy replaced the darkness of their idolatry. Regardless of the hardships and affliction that came their way for believing, there was no turning back. They were sold out for the Savior. What a great example to you and me!

How do we know if someone has true salvation? The acid test is a changed life. Paul, Silas, and Timothy exhibited this changed life when they preached the good news of Jesus to the Thessalonians. The Holy Spirit was all over those guys as they told about Jesus' cross and empty tomb. Doubtless, many in Thessalonica wanted what they saw in these missionaries. And just as the Lord transformed Paul, Silas, and Timothy, He transformed those who responded to Christ.

Has He transformed you? Are you sold out for Jesus? If not, why not? Jesus is the only One who can satisfy your heart. The sooner you fully surrender to Him, the sooner you'll experience His love, joy, peace, and power.

....

God, I want to be sold out for Jesus. Give me a passion for You that far exceeds my passion for anything else. Amen.

Dr. Jeff Schreve, First Baptist Church, Texarkana, TX

Balancing the Scales

The humble also shall increase their joy in the LORD, and the poor among men shall rejoice in the Holy One of Israel. For the terrible one is brought to nothing, the scornful one is consumed, and all who watch for iniquity are cut off—who make a man an offender by a word, and lay a snare for him who reproves in the gate, and turn aside the just by empty words.

ISAIAH 29:19–21

Have you ever found yourself wondering why God seems to allow the wicked to prosper? From our limited point of view, it can often appear as if God lets some people get away with murder, so to speak. The righteous struggle and suffer while the unrighteous go unscathed. We can easily lament with the people of Malachi's day and question aloud, "Where is the God of justice?" (Malachi 2:17).

Do not be deceived. The wicked get away with nothing. God is the perfect Judge who always balances the scales and repays evildoers appropriately. As for the person who humbly walks with God, this one will be blessed with great joy in the Lord. Surely, Christ-followers do face great trials and difficulties in this life as we strive to please the Savior in an increasingly anti-Christian world, but God will abundantly reward those who are faithful to Jesus. Let me encourage you to take the long view of life. Cutting corners and compromising with sin may seem to be the easy way to success, but God sees it all and rewards those who do life His way. As today's passage says, the humble increase their joy in the Lord.

....

God, Your ways and Your timing are always right. Thank You that You are faithful to reward Your children and repay Your enemies. Amen.

It's All About Jesus

John answered and said, "A man can receive nothing unless it has been given to him from heaven. You yourselves bear me witness, that I said, 'I am not the Christ,' but, 'I have been sent before Him.' He who has the bride is the bridegroom; but the friend of the bridegroom, who stands and hears him, rejoices greatly because of the bridegroom's voice. Therefore this joy of mine is fulfilled."

JOHN 3:27-29

John the Baptist was a household name in Israel. Many Jewish people came to him for baptism, considering him a powerful prophet of God. Even Jesus Himself said, "Among those born of women, there is not a greater prophet than John" (Luke 7:28). High praise indeed!

Great success in ministry, as John obviously experienced, can easily go to one's head. But that wasn't the case with John. His life's mission was to prepare the way for the Messiah and point the people to the Messiah. When Jesus came on the scene, John had no problem stepping aside and telling his disciples to follow Christ. He had great joy as the friend of the bridegroom.

How well do you do fulfilling the role God has given you? Are the things you do for the Lord really for His glory, or are they secretly for your glory? If your ministry were to diminish suddenly, would you be able to rejoice as John did? If God chose to bless your neighbor with success, could you still be thankful and grateful? Remember, it's all about Jesus. Our only job is to glorify Him. And to see Him glorified is a joy fulfilled.

God, help me to do the things You've called me to do with the right motives, remembering that it is all for the glory of Jesus, my Savior and King. Amen.

Dr. Jeff Schreve, First Baptist Church, Texarkana, TX

Declaring the Truth

It is good to give thanks to the LORD, and to sing praises to Your name, O Most High; to declare Your lovingkindness in the morning, and Your faithfulness every night, on an instrument of ten strings, on the lute, and on the harp, with harmonious sound. For You, LORD, have made me glad through Your work; I will triumph in the works of Your hands.

PSALM 92:1-4

There are three key truths every Christian needs to have carved into his or her heart: (1) *God loves me*, (2) *God is good*, (3) *God works all things together for good to those who love Him.* How do we know those three statements are true and trustworthy? Because our God, who cannot lie, has said so (Romans 8:28).

In Psalm 92, the unnamed psalmist makes a declaration—a strong statement of confession, acknowledgment, and avowal. He gratefully and emphatically speaks of God's great love and unshakable faithfulness. Have you made such a joyful declaration and claimed the promise of God's loyal love and eternal faithfulness? It is so important!

God has called us to walk by faith, not by sight (2 Corinthians 5:7). We are to believe the Word and not our feelings or our circumstances. The truth is that God loves us even when we do not feel His love. He is faithful to us even when we are faithless (2 Timothy 2:13). His love and faithfulness are not conditional. And the more we declare what His Word says is true, the more we expereince the joy and power of the truth. Remember, it is the truth that sets us free; so start declaring the truth today!

....

Lord, help me depend on Your perfect Word every single day. Thank You for being faithful and true. Amen.

A Contrite Heart

Deliver me from the guilt of bloodshed, O God, the God of my salvation, and
my tongue shall sing aloud of Your righteousness. O Lord, open my lips, and
my mouth shall show forth Your praise. For You do not desire sacrifice, or else
I would give it; You do not delight in burnt offering. The sacrifices of God are a
broken spirit, a broken and a contrite heart—these, O God, You will not despise.

PSALM 51:14-17

David began this prayer acknowledging that he deserved death and yet was asking for salvation. Isn't that true for all of us who have sinned and fallen short of the glory of God? When we acknowledge our sin, we are led to *His* righteousness and *His* gift of salvation as the only possible solution. Then, the only proper response to this gift is worship.

David then proceeded to declare what God wants and what He doesn't. The declaration that God is not in need of anything we could offer is both heavy and freeing at the same time. God is interested in our hearts. Repentance and humility are a premium in the economy of God. Does that not bring joy?

Friend, it might pay to try to impress someone in life, whether to get a date or to land a perfect job. But with God, there is no need to impress. Just being who we are is enough. You have captured His imagination fully, and He is interested in you as an individual, regardless of what you've done.

....

Lord, thank You for Your forgiveness and salvation. I come into Your presence with a repentant heart.

Dr. Alex Himaya, BattleCreek Church, Broken Arrow, OK

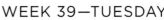

Rejoice in Unity

The whole assembly of Judah rejoiced, also the priests and Levites, all the assembly that came from Israel, the sojourners who came from the land of Israel, and those who dwelt in Judah. So there was great joy in Jerusalem, for since the time of Solomon the son of David, king of Israel, there had been nothing like this in Jerusalem. Then the priests, the Levites, arose and blessed the people, and their voice was heard; and their prayer came up to His holy dwelling place, to heaven.

2 CHRONICLES 30:25-27

After the reign of Solomon, the kingdom was divided into two kingdoms: Judah and Israel. Because no celebration had included both kingdoms since that division, until the one in today's passage, the joy was unmatched!

The priests and Levites arose and blessed the people. Their voice was heard, and their prayers reached heaven. How needed is this in our culture today? May those of us who are called by Christ's name rise above the issues of the day and find common ground with fellow believers. May we join in real praise of our heavenly Father and speak blessing on our land.

I'm sure we could all think of something we would like to take a stand against. But where does that really get us? When we stand together, though, we are an unstoppable army. When you meet another believer, find the common ground on which you stand and stay there. Don't worry about foolish arguments that ultimately divide us.

Indeed, God promises to hear from heaven, forgive our sins, and heal our land. May the whole assembly rejoice—together!

....

Lord, I pray for unity in Your church and among Your believers. Help us stand for what is right and true.

Everyday Joy and Peace

Give Me Passion

How lovely is Your tabernacle, O LORD of hosts! My soul longs, yes, even faints for the courts of the LORD; my heart and my flesh cry out for the living God. Even the sparrow has found a home, and the swallow a nest for herself, where she may lay her young—even Your altars, O LORD of hosts, my King and my God. Blessed are those who dwell in Your house; they will still be praising You.

PSALM 84:1-4

Today's psalm is a Psalm of Ascent, meant for praise on your way up to Jerusalem and the temple for a Jewish festival. The psalmist begins by exclaiming, "How lovely [or how beloved] is your tabernacle, O LORD!" He mentions his soul, heart, and flesh all being involved in this pursuit. Passion for the temple, the God who dwells there, and worship and praise are very evident in this passage. The psalmist is even envious of the birds who live in the temple, raising their young near the altars of God. "My King and my God" could be read, "You are the King who rules over me and the God I worship."

How long has it been since you viewed your corporate worship in this fashion and with this passion? It wasn't too long ago that whenever the church doors were open, families would gather. Now, we are so easily distracted by anything that keeps us away. What if we were as jealous of the birds that hung out on the roof? What would it do to our children if we approached our church and worship services with this kind of anticipation? It would bring incredible joy and passion into our walks with God.

....

God, make me passionate about You and my worship of You today.

234   Dr. Alex Himaya, BattleCreek Church, Broken Arrow, OK

He's Holding the Bag

He said, "Peace be with you, do not be afraid. Your God and the God of your father has given you treasure in your sacks; I had your money." Then he brought Simeon out to them.

This verse comes out of the remarkable story of Joseph and his brothers. At this point in the story, his brothers are not aware that they are dealing with Joseph. The words the servant spoke to them, "Peace be with you, do not be afraid" are eerily similar to the words their God had spoken to Abraham in Genesis 15. He then begins to refer to their God as the God of their father. This is covenant language. He wants them to see that what had happened was indeed the work of their God, the same God their fathers worshiped.

"Then he brought Simeon out to them." Remember the story? In their first encounter, Joseph kept their brother Simeon as collateral and told them to return with their youngest brother. It was only after telling him their money mysteriously appeared back in their sacks of grain that he returned their brother. This was the fulfillment of Joseph's dream about the sun, moon, and stars bowing before him, representing his brothers, father, and mother.

We now know what none of them knew that day: God was bringing this family back together and guiding the needed confession, forgiveness, and peace.

Just as Joseph was overseeing the whole scenario, God is watching the scene play out in your family. There may be strife or tension, but He is the one "holding the bag," so to speak. And He is willing to loosen the purse strings of blessing in your life.

Lord, I pray for Your peace in my family, and for Your provision and deliverance for us.

Everyday Joy and Peace

Righteousness and Peace

The work of righteousness will be peace, and the effect of righteousness, quietness and assurance forever. My people will dwell in a peaceful habitation, in secure dwellings, and in quiet resting places.

ISAIAH 32:17–18

In the messianic vision in today's passage, Isaiah was seeing a coming day when righteousness, peace, quietness, and assurance will be the norm. Make no mistake about it: Peace is the fruit of righteousness. God is not in the business of pasting peace on corruption. We must sow seeds of righteousness if we want to harvest peace and quietness.

That's a word that we haven't heard in a while, isn't it? *Quietness?* What is quietness? How would I find it? Where would I look for it? We've designed our lives to root out every instance of quiet. The constant hum of news and opinion, of sports and entertainment keep us company.

Paul tells Timothy to petition, intercede, and give thanks for kings and all who are in authority so that we can live peaceful and quiet lives marked by godliness and dignity (1 Timothy 2:1–2). Could it be that we have exchanged dignity and humility for hype? The fruit of hype is not peace, and it is certainly not quietness.

Hype will certainly get you noticed, but humility will get you peace. Next time you have the choice to raise a fuss just to get your way, think about what God would have you do instead. Ask Him to shine His light on your heart and to show you any place where the peace of God is not ruling. Then invite Him to bring peace to you today.

....

Father, I want to do the work of righteousness, that peace and quietness would characterize my life. Show me how to find Your peace.

Dr. Alex Himaya, BattleCreek Church, Broken Arrow, OK

Eternal Life

Eternal life to those who by patient continuance in doing good seek for glory, honor, and immortality; but to those who are self-seeking and do not obey the truth, but obey unrighteousness—indignation and wrath, tribulation and anguish, on every soul of man who does evil, of the Jew first and also of the Greek; but glory, honor, and peace to everyone who works what is good, to the Jew first and also to the Greek. For there is no partiality with God.

ROMANS 2:7-11

This is the first mention of "eternal life" by the apostle Paul. He lists three things that are included in that destiny: glory, honor, and immortality. This list of three is found elsewhere in the scriptures and is always attributed to God alone. Why? God alone gives eternal life.

Eternal life is not just marked by longevity, but by the presence of God. We will all spend eternity somewhere, but only those who belong to Jesus will spend it in life with Him.

When Paul moved on to a second category in today's passage, people and their destiny, he only left room for two groups of people: those who do evil and those who are right with God. There is no "partiality" with God because He doesn't play favorites with our destiny.

Glory and honor are not just reserved for our eternal abode after we die. Our eternal lives can start now! When we give God glory each day we live, we show the world where we are going. And when we honor Him and others, we are living as if we're already there—in "glory, honor, and peace."

Father, thank You for the gift of eternal life with You. I honor You, and thank You for my salvation in Christ.

The Joy of Passing Over

They slaughtered the Passover lambs for all the descendants of the captivity, for their brethren the priests, and for themselves. Then the children of Israel who had returned from the captivity ate together with all who had separated themselves from the filth of the nations of the land in order to seek the LORD God of Israel. And they kept the Feast of Unleavened Bread seven days with joy; for the LORD made them joyful, and turned the heart of the king of Assyria toward them, to strengthen their hands in the work of the house of God, the God of Israel.

EZRA 6:20-22

A t the time of this writing, the COVID pandemic has worn out its welcome. I'm ready for the captivity of this pandemic to pass. In Ezra 6, God's people, who had spent seventy years in Babylonian captivity, were back in Jerusalem. It was time to celebrate. What was involved in this celebration?

First, people joined God. Both Jews and Gentiles were separating themselves from the "filth of the nations" in order to join God. God is working, and we must join Him in His work, even in a pandemic.

Second, people were joy-filled by God. Participation in the Passover reminded God's people of His mercy while in Egypt and His deliverance from Egyptian bondage. As a result, God made them joyful. Participation in the local church is essential, even in a pandemic.

Third, people were rejoicing in God. One day all believers will pull up a chair to the marriage supper of the Lamb. There will be no more panic or pandemics, no more disappointments or death, and no more sin or Satan. What a joyful day that will be!

....

Father, help us be a people who join You, are joy-filled by You, and rejoice in You.

Dr. Sam Greer, Red Bank Baptist Church, Chattanooga, TN

Sing Praises

I will sing of Your power; yes, I will sing aloud of Your mercy in the morning; for You have been my defense and refuge in the day of my trouble. To You, O my Strength, I will sing praises; for God is my defense, my God of mercy.

PSALM 59:16–17

We can never praise God too much because we can never praise Him enough. So how do we praise? The psalmist answers these five questions:

What should we sing? By this I don't mean song selection. I mean we sing of God's power, His mercy, and His strength, as Psalm 59 records.

How should we sing? We are to sing aloud. By this I don't mean we always sing *loud*. We want to join others in singing aloud to our God. A choir is a good picture of heaven on earth.

When should we sing? We are to sing morning, noon, and night. By this I don't mean that you have to be a morning person. God's mercies are new every morning because we need them every morning, noon, and night (Lamentations 3:22–23).

To whom do we sing? We are to sing to God. Not merely *about* God, but *to* God. The pronoun "You" indicates that the psalmist is singing to God.

Why should we sing? Because He is more than worthy! Not all of us can sing with skill and talent, but we all should sing joyfully to God. It brings us a little closer to heaven.

....

Father, may our song of worship be ever pleasing in Your sight and an acceptable offering to Your ears.

What Is Truth?

The Elder, to the elect lady and her children, whom I love in truth, and not only I, but also all those who have known the truth, because of the truth which abides in us and will be with us forever: Grace, mercy, and peace will be with you from God the Father and from the Lord Jesus Christ, the Son of the Father, in truth and love.

2 JOHN VV. 1–3

What is truth? When he asked Jesus this question in John 18:38, Pilate was as frustrated as we are when it comes to knowing what is true and what is false. What, if anything, can be believed anymore as truth? But truth is not a *what* but a *who*. In John 14:6, Jesus said, "I am the way, the truth, and the life." Why is it important to know this truth?

The truth loves. John writes to the elect lady "whom I love in the truth." Truth is, Jesus loves to love you and He loves for us to love one another in "grace, mercy, and peace."

The truth links. John's "all who have known the truth" links followers of Jesus of all generations past, present, and future. What connects us is not our politics, preferences, traditions, or religion. Jesus, the truth, connects us to God the Father and one another.

The truth lives. The truth abides, resides, dwells, and umpires in us. Truth is not only alive and well around us, but He lives in us.

The truth lasts. The truth ensures we don't live happily ever after; rather, happily *forever* after. Have you trusted the truth? You can. His name is Jesus. Trust in Him now.

....

Father, may you sanctify us with Your truth. Your Word is truth.

Dr. Sam Greer, Red Bank Baptist Church, Chattanooga, TN

God's Tree House

I am like a green olive tree in the house of God; I trust in the mercy of God forever and ever. I will praise You forever, because You have done it; and in the presence of Your saints I will wait on Your name, for it is good.

PSALM 52:8-9

One of the oldest trees on record is an olive tree, estimated to be four thousand to five thousand years old.[14] No wonder David used an olive tree in today's passage to illustrate something that was rooted, stable, safe, and secure. Notice the tree was in God's house. David's faith was strong because He lived in the presence of the Lord. What does that look like? We discover it in three key words from this scripture.

Trust; don't turn. Stay rooted in God's presence. Don't uproot and go your own way. Trust in the mercy of the Lord in your life. God alone can be trusted even when others can't. God alone can be trusted even when you don't.

Worship; don't worry. The emphasis in "I will praise you . . . because You have done it" is not on the what, but the who. *You* have done it. Done what? Make a list of all God has done. Then you will be more apt to worship Him than worry.

Wait; don't run. Waiting for God doesn't mean we don't move. We move. But we move alongside other believers and behind the Lord, attuned to His Spirit.

Trust, worship, and wait. As you do these things, you will become rooted in the peace of the Lord.

....

Father, may I be like an olive tree rooted in Your presence. Help me trust, worship, and wait on You.

Calling out the Called

Paul, called to be an apostle of Jesus Christ through the will of God, and Sosthenes our brother, to the church of God which is at Corinth, to those who are sanctified in Christ Jesus, called to be saints, with all who in every place call on the name of Jesus Christ our Lord, both theirs and ours: Grace to you and peace from God our Father and the Lord Jesus Christ.

1 CORINTHIANS 1:1-3

Say, "Hey Siri, Lumos" or "Hey Google, Lumos" to your iPhone or Android phone. What happens? The flashlight on your phone turns on. Isn't that cool? But wait—do we have phones to be cool or to be able to make calls? Paul wrote of the importance of being called by God, not being cool before man. He was calling out the called by reminding them:

Christ is *calling* people. Jesus called Saul the assassin, who became Paul the apostle, on the road to Damascus. Jesus called Saul to be saved. Christ is still calling people to be saved. Have you answered His call?

Christ is *calling out* the called people. Paul was not called to be an apostle by man, but by God. Christ called Him.

Christ is *calling out the called people to call people to call on Him.* (It's okay—you can read that again.) Part of being the church is being at church. Yet, the church is not merely a building; it's building up people in "grace and peace," as Paul greeted them. Yes, we should invite people to church, but we must invite people to Christ with that grace and peace. So, how are you called? And how are you calling others today?

....

Father, thank You for your call. Give us boldness, opportunity, and compassion to call people to call on Jesus.

Dr. Sam Greer, Red Bank Baptist Church, Chattanooga, TN

Peace Is Possible

Unto us a Child is born, unto us a Son is given; and the government will be upon His shoulder. And His name will be called Wonderful, Counselor, Mighty God, Everlasting Father, Prince of Peace. Of the increase of His government and peace there will be no end, upon the throne of David and over His kingdom, to order it and establish it with judgment and justice from that time forward, even forever. The zeal of the LORD of hosts will perform this.

ISAIAH 9:6–7

In the opening scene of the movie *The Lion King*, the long-awaited birth announcement of Simba is carried throughout the animal kingdom. The monkey Rafiki lifts the newborn cub into the air and . . . cue the music. For the rest of the day, you will have this tune in your head. You're welcome.

Isn't that the type of reaction every parent envisions when they send out the birth announcement of their newborn? Every birth is announced *after* the baby is born. Except one. The prophet Isaiah announced the birth of Jesus seven hundred years *before* He was born. What does Jesus' birth announcement tell us?

"Unto us" is an interesting opener in today's verse. Most birth announcements will identify the parents of the newborn. Jesus is different. He is the Prince of Peace coming to bring peace *to us.*

Jesus alone makes peace possible. We can live with the peace of God. Peace depends on God, not the government. The government is on Jesus' shoulders. He is in charge. Good news! You can resign as manager of the universe. The Prince of Peace has come. Let's lift Him high!

....

Father, thank You for Your peace. Help us be peacemakers by pointing people to You.

Is God Enough?

Though the fig tree may not blossom, nor fruit be on the vines; though the labor of the olive may fail, and the fields yield no food; though the flock may be cut off from the fold, and there be no herd in the stalls—yet I will rejoice in the LORD, I will joy in the God of my salvation. The LORD God is my strength; He will make my feet like deer's feet, and He will make me walk on my high hills.

HABAKKUK 3:17-19

In today's verses, Habakkuk settles the important question, "Is God enough?" Though the answer seems obvious, careful reflection is necessary. As God's prophet surveyed the wickedness of Judah, he repeatedly peppered the Lord with questions. *How long will this last, God (1:2)? Why won't You do something, Lord (1:3)?*

God was not, as Habakkuk assumed, turning a blind eye to the sinfulness of His people. To the contrary—His plan was to exile them by means of the pagan Babylonians. Strangely, the Lord determined to raise up a wicked people to chasten His sons and daughters. Their lives were engulfed by the hardship of God's justice. All that was left was to plead for mercy in the midst of God's wrath (3:2).

Remarkably, Habakkuk realized that no matter what lay ahead, God was enough to sustain the people of Judah. Without a blossoming fig tree; without fruit on the vines; without oil from the olive; without food in the field; without the strength of the herd—he could still "joy in the God of [his] salvation." Why? God was, and is, *enough.*

He is the source of your strength. He will steady your feet. He will bring you through with rejoicing.

Lord, thank You for being all I need. Give me the faith to believe it. Amen.

Dr. Adam B. Dooley, Englewood Baptist Church, Jackson, TN

Two Ways to Live

The hope of the righteous will be gladness, but the expectation of the wicked will perish.

PROVERBS 10:28

T his section of Proverbs (10–13) carefully contrasts righteousness with wickedness. The righteous love justice, compassion, and truth (12:5; 12:10; 13:5). The wicked celebrate divisions, harmful words, and deceptions (10:2; 11:9; 12:6). These two ways of living bring starkly different ends, just like the kinds of lives they produce.

Ultimately, the Lord secures the eternal outcome for these two paths. The *hope* of the righteous is far more than the wishful expectation that integrity and obedience might be beneficial in eternity. Instead, we are certain God will bring about much *gladness* for those who are steadfast and faithful, as the joys of eternity swallow up the heartache and struggles of life. Sacrifices that give us pause today will be the foundation of our greatest rewards in heaven.

Two times, however, we read that the expectation of the wicked will perish (10:28; 11:7). In other words, the compromised path that seems to lead to happiness and fulfillment will give way to shattered dreams and desires. Jesus later warned about this broad road by forecasting the destruction it brings (Matthew 7:13). God will not ignore the injustices of the wicked forever because the way that seems right to the majority will finally result in eternal death (Proverbs 14:12).

Believers today should find both comfort and motivation in these descriptions. Be encouraged; injustice will not remain forever. Be motivated; righteousness is the greatest reassurance of joy in our heavenly home.

....

God, thank You for putting me on the right path. Help me to endure as a person of righteous faith. Amen.

The Security of the Kingdom

Let Your priests be clothed with righteousness, and let Your saints shout for joy.
For Your servant David's sake, do not turn away the face of Your Anointed. The
LORD has sworn in truth to David; He will not turn from it: "I will set upon
your throne the fruit of your body. If your sons will keep My covenant and My
testimony which I shall teach them, their sons also shall sit upon your throne
forevermore."

PSALM 132:9–12

T oday's psalm centers on the promises God made to King David, with an emphasis on the assurance that a son of David would always sit on the throne in Zion. Because the eternal descendant of David is none other than Jesus Christ, each king in the Davidic line was a reassuring reminder that the Messiah was coming and the kingdom of God's people was secure. Any interruption in their succession, however, seemed to indicate a wavering on the promises made to the man after God's own heart.

Why should we care about these verses today? Simply put, our eternal life is inextricably tied to the Davidic promise. The apostle Paul celebrated Jesus as the fulfillment of God's commitment to Israel's favorite king (Romans 1:2–5). The salvation we enjoy through Christ is a manifestation of the kingdom these promises predict. The security of our eternal life rests in the abiding nature of David's perpetual throne. The heavenly reign of Jesus that we look forward to is the greatest expression of what the psalmists longs for here. That's why the saints are shouting for joy! Our eternal life is part of David's reward!

Thank You, Father, for Your promise to King David. Help me to rest in the security it brings to my life. Increase my faith to trust You more. Amen.

Dr. Adam B. Dooley, Englewood Baptist Church, Jackson, TN

Leadership Matters

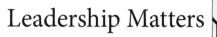

Do not neglect the gift that is in you, which was given to you by prophecy with the laying on of the hands of the eldership. Meditate on these things; give yourself entirely to them, that your progress may be evident to all. Take heed to yourself and to the doctrine. Continue in them, for in doing this you will save both yourself and those who hear you.

1 TIMOTHY 4:14-16

Unfortunately, false doctrine is nothing new. The church must remain alert in order to resist the lies of the devil. Realizing that leaders are the first line of defense for God's flock, Paul admonished Timothy to give himself fully to the call of God. Why should this personal charge matter to us?

The leadership we choose matters. As Christians, we should be discerning about who we follow and learn from. All churches are not the same. All sermons are not trustworthy. All pastors should not be emulated. So what do we look for before placing ourselves under the spiritual leadership of another?

In a word, *consistency.* Paul charged his protégé to meditate on his calling and be fully devoted to the work of the Lord. Not a career. Not building a platform. Not the accumulation of wealth. Not the accolades of men. Serving Jesus and others ought to be the top priority for those who lead the church. In a leader, look for someone whose personal life is consistent with sound doctrine. Remember, "the fruit of the Spirit is love, joy, peace, longsuffering, kindness, goodness, faithfulness, gentleness, self-control" (Galatians 5:22–23). May these things be evident to all—in us and in our leadership.

Father, give me discernment in the church. Surround me with those who love You and Your Word. Strengthen those who lead Your people. Amen.

When the Lord Reigns

He will judge Your people with righteousness, and Your poor with justice. The mountains will bring peace to the people, and the little hills, by righteousness. He will bring justice to the poor of the people; He will save the children of the needy, and will break in pieces the oppressor.

PSALM 72:2-4

The peace and prosperity of Israel under the reign of King Solomon was unlike anything before or since. The words of today's verse were an appropriate petition on the lips of God's wise king who was eager to rule well. Yet, despite his holy ambition, this son of David could not deliver the eternal peace we long for. Solomon's kingdom only pointed to the harvest of blessings ushered in by the arrival of the Messiah. This prayer will one day be fulfilled in the new heaven and earth where another Son of David will reign forever and ever.

In that day, the poor will find justice, peace will abound, and righteousness will cover the land. Needs will be met. Oppression will end. And the name of Jesus will endure forever (72:17) as the whole earth declares His glory (72:19). Can you even begin to imagine how wonderful it will be when God Himself dwells among us, and we are His people? No more tears, or death, or mourning, or crying, or pain as the first things pass away in exchange for eternal glory (Revelation 4:4).

This is the kingdom for which Jesus instructed us to pray, and even now we look for the shadows of its coming (Matthew 6:10). How are you building His kingdom? What signs do you see that it is near?

Lord, come quickly. May Your will be done in my life as I live to build Your kingdom. Amen.

Dr. Adam B. Dooley, Englewood Baptist Church, Jackson, TN

Is There Grace?

Then all the children of Israel, that is, all the people, went up and came to the house of God and wept. They sat there before the LORD and fasted that day until evening; and they offered burnt offerings and peace offerings before the LORD.

JUDGES 20:26

Have you ever wondered how God could possibly forgive you? Consider today's verse, which comes on the heels of one of Israel's darkest moments. Sexual promiscuity within the tribe of Benjamin led a cowardly Levite to toss his concubine aside in order to protect himself (19:22–25). The result was horrific abuse followed by the untimely death of an innocent woman, whose corpse was then defiled (19:25–30). These atrocities led to a civil war among the tribes of Israel who were determined to punish the wicked Benjaminites. Through a series of battles, thousands of Jewish people died (20:19–48). Though the scene is shocking, consequences like these are commonplace when we live as if there is no God (21:26).

And yet, how often do we find ourselves guilty of living for ourselves? Do we chart our own course? Do we allow our impulses to control us? Do the pleasures of the moment blind us to the realities of eternity?

Was there any grace left for Israel? Is there any left for us? Remarkably, the Lord heard their prayers and acknowledged their peace offerings, and He will hear ours too. Repentance is often painful, and forgiveness does not necessarily remove the consequences of our rebellion. Yet, the Lord is attentive to our cries and eager to intercede when we call out to Him.

....

Father, help me humble myself, own my mistakes, and yield to You. Forgive me for my sins. Help me to live in the power and peace of Your grace. Amen.

Worry War(t)

Evildoers shall be cut off; but those who wait on the LORD, they shall inherit the earth. For yet a little while and the wicked shall be no more; indeed, you will look carefully for his place, but it shall be no more. But the meek shall inherit the earth, and shall delight themselves in the abundance of peace.

PSALM 37:9-11

Hi, my name is Doug, and I'm a worrier. Longtime worrier. As in, at the age of fifteen, I was diagnosed with stomach ulcers. When I was growing up, my dad would ask me what I was so worried about. Any worrier knows you can answer that in one of two ways: either, (a) "Here's a list of a thousand things I'm worried about;" or (b) "I have no idea what I'm worried about." Worry became a constant hindrance in my life.

I now can tell you that the Lord used Psalm 37 to show me His path to peace and overcoming worry. David's psalm opens with "Do not fret" and then follows in verses 3–7 and 9 with five keys to avoid fretting—trust in the Lord; delight yourself in the Lord; commit your way to the Lord; rest in the Lord; and wait on the Lord.

No doubt, the path to abundant peace is in the Lord through a personal relationship with Jesus Christ! Worry is mostly our fear of the what-ifs coupled with our desire to control situations over which we have no control. Meekness (see v. 11) means yielding control of your life and the care of your loved ones to the Lord. You can trust Him, and He will give you peace.

....

Lord, help me trust You and delight in the abundance of peace that only You can give. Amen.

Dr. Douglas O. Melton, Southern Hills Baptist Church, Oklahoma City, OK

Family Prayers

Beloved, I pray that you may prosper in all things and be in health, just as your soul prospers. For I rejoiced greatly when brethren came and testified of the truth that is in you, just as you walk in the truth. I have no greater joy than to hear that my children walk in truth.

3 JOHN VV. 2-4

B lessed with a wife, four sons, four daughters-in-law, and ten grandchildren (as of this writing), I'm always looking for scriptural prayers to pray for my family. Ephesians 1:15–19 and 3:14–21 are both strong, beautiful prayers, as is this one in today's passage.

First, notice that John is praying for Gaius, a fact that should not be overlooked. The verb tense indicates he was praying for him then and was continuing to pray for him. Texting our family or calling them or talking to them in person or writing or visiting are all great, but the absolute best communication activity is to pray without ceasing for them. When family conflicts arise, put prayer into practice. It's hard to stay mad at someone for whom you are praying.

Second, don't miss the love. Six times in fifteen verses John talks about agape (godly, unconditional, sacrificial) love. Praying for someone is a beautiful demonstration of the love you have for that person.

But please don't miss that John is just as concerned for his friend's spiritual health as his physical. I too often am guilty of praying far more fervently for others' physical healing than I am their spiritual healing. We have gratitude for the former; we have no greater joy than with the latter.

Our heavenly Father, please bless my family's health both physically and spiritually. May my family and I walk in the truth of Jesus Christ. Amen.

Someone Please Turn on the Light

The people who walked in darkness have seen a great light; those who dwelt in the land of the shadow of death, upon them a light has shined. You have multiplied the nation and increased its joy; they rejoice before You according to the joy of harvest, as men rejoice when they divide the spoil. For You have broken the yoke of his burden and the staff of his shoulder, the rod of his oppressor, as in the day of Midian.

ISAIAH 9:2-4

Y ou may already be thinking of Christmas coming, worried about gift lists and having enough time to complete everything. But in Isaiah's day, people would have been eager for the day to arrive quickly. The prophecy of Jesus' birth would have been met with joy and longing for His arrival as soon as possible.

To understand their elation, let's remember who they were: they were dwelling "in the land of the shadow of death." The valley that David walked through in Psalm 23 was literally their lot in life.

Sounds a lot like us apart from Christ. We too were walking in darkness, burdened by our bondage to sin and the rod of Satan's oppression upon us. What's worse, we were completely helpless to get ourselves out.

In a New Mexico cave one summer, I experienced total darkness. A little of that goes a long way. What was fun for a moment soon evaporated. No sight. No direction. No good.

Can you imagine the people's joy in Isaiah's day when, in Isaiah 9:6, the prophet wrote, "For to us a child is born, to us a son is given" (ESV)? The Light of the World shines in the darkness.

....

Father, may today I share the light of Christ with someone walking in darkness. Amen.

Dr. Douglas O. Melton, Southern Hills Baptist Church, Oklahoma City, OK

Servant and Saint

Paul, a bondservant of Jesus Christ, called to be an apostle, separated to the gospel of God . . . Through Him we have received grace and apostleship for obedience to the faith among all nations for His name, among whom you also are the called of Jesus Christ; to all who are in Rome, beloved of God, called to be saints: Grace to you and peace from God our Father and the Lord Jesus Christ.

ROMANS 1:1, 5–7

Reading the New Testament books in order, the first of Paul's letters we find is the book of Romans. By way of introduction, the first title he gives himself, even before the use of "apostle," is "bondservant of Jesus Christ." What a wonderful first impression of Paul and first reminder of who and whose we are.

Further still, to those who are saved by Christ, he gives a second reminder of who we are—"called to be saints." Servant and saint.

We carry a number of job titles in life—student, husband, wife, mom, dad, teacher, director—but prioritized above all that, Paul would say you are a servant of Jesus Christ and called to be a saint. That's our job, and both are full-time, never part-time positions. Yes, for those in Christ, you are a child of God, a follower of Jesus Christ, but Paul is instructing us to never forget we are servants and saints.

What's interesting is that we are prone to say, "Oh, I'm no saint!" But if you are saved, if you are covered in the righteousness of Jesus Christ, that's exactly who you are. Sainthood is based on His work, not yours. What joy, comfort, and peace that can bring to your heart.

Our heavenly Father, thank you that by your grace and mercy, I can live today as a servant of Jesus Christ and one of His saints. Amen.

Treasure Hidden in Plain Sight

Happy is the man who finds wisdom, and the man who gains understanding; for her proceeds are better than the profits of silver, and her gain than fine gold. She is more precious than rubies, and all the things you may desire cannot compare with her. Length of days is in her right hand, in her left hand riches and honor. Her ways are ways of pleasantness, and all her paths are peace.

PROVERBS 3:13-17

The lottery jackpots are now in the billions. So are the odds of winning one. Well, not quite the billions, but certainly into the hundreds of millions to win the biggest prize. What's worse, for the one or ones who do win, testimonials seem to indicate that, by and large, their overall quality of life and happiness do not improve. That's a real head-scratcher for much of the Western world, who equate wealth with happiness.

The Scripture, as always, paints a whole different picture. There truly is something that brings far greater gain to your life than all the silver, gold, rubies, or the accumulation of anything else you could desire: that one thing is wisdom.

You don't need to go to the local quick-stop market to buy a ticket or join the search for the fountain of youth; you don't need to go deep-sea diving for gold doubloons. The Scripture says just find wisdom.

I tell people that there are passages in the Bible that are extremely hard to understand. This isn't one of them. Find wisdom. Here's the place to start: believe in God and understand that He is the One who created all things, and that life is found only through faith in His Son, Jesus Christ.

....

Dear Lord, please give me wisdom and understanding. Amen.

Dr. Douglas O. Melton, Southern Hills Baptist Church, Oklahoma City, OK

Joining Creation's Celebration

*Let the field be joyful, and all that is in it. Then all the trees of the woods will rejoice before the L*ORD*. For He is coming, for He is coming to judge the earth. He shall judge the world with righteousness, and the peoples with His truth.*

PSALM 96:12–13

What an interesting passage. The fields and all the trees of the woods will rejoice. Why? For the Lord is coming to judge the earth. Why would the Lord's coming make all of creation glad? For that same creation, like all His created beings, is in bondage to corruption. It dies. It withers and fades away.

But that all ends for creation with the coming of the Lord! There will be a new heaven and a new earth! Psalm 96 tells us that the heavens, the sea, the fields, the forest and everything in it rejoices at the coming of the Lord.

You too can have that same joy. If the coming of the Lord is scary to you, that can all be changed. The key is in the last sentence of our passage: you will be judged with righteousness and with *His* truth. That's such good news! Someday you will stand before God in one of two ways—either in your own good works, your own righteousness, which will fall far short, or in the perfect righteousness of Jesus Christ. God will judge you with His truth, and His truth is Jesus. He is the only way. He is the only life. He is the only One who died on the cross for your sins. Trust Him today and rejoice knowing that He's coming soon.

....

Lord, lead me to one today who needs to hear the truth that Jesus is coming soon. Amen.

Set Apart for Honor

In a great house there are not only vessels of gold and silver, but also of wood and clay, some for honor and some for dishonor. Therefore if anyone cleanses himself from the latter, he will be a vessel for honor, sanctified and useful for the Master, prepared for every good work. Flee also youthful lusts; but pursue righteousness, faith, love, peace with those who call on the Lord out of a pure heart.

2 TIMOTHY 2:20-22

I think every boy has some fantasy of being at bat in the bottom of the ninth inning with the winning run in scoring position. In that instant, he sees his chance to change the world as he visualizes a hit over the center-field fence. There is a longing within him to do great things.

As the apostle Paul writes to Timothy in today's verses, he speaks of being prepared to be used for great things using the analogy of common vessels and vessels of honor. The Master chooses honorable vessels for honorable tasks. He doesn't serve a meal to important guests in a dog's dish or on paper plates, but on the family's best china.

If we desire to be used for great things, we must prepare ourselves as vessels of honor. This means that there are things we must flee and things we must pursue. We would be foolish to use a dirty dish to serve a fine meal, or to convince ourselves that an unsanctified life would be chosen by God for His most important and honorable tasks. Choose today to be a vessel of honor. How? Today's verse tells us to "pursue righteousness, faith, love, peace." How will you pursue them today?

Father, point out those things in my life I must forsake to be useful to You as an honorable vessel. Amen.

Dr. Chris Aiken, Englewood Baptist Church, Rocky Mount, NC

Not One Promise Is Forsaken

"Behold, I will bring it health and healing; I will heal them and reveal to them the abundance of peace and truth. And I will cause the captives of Judah and the captives of Israel to return, and will rebuild those places as at the first. I will cleanse them from all their iniquity by which they have sinned against Me, and I will pardon all their iniquities by which they have sinned and by which they have transgressed against Me. Then it shall be to Me a name of joy, a praise, and an honor before all nations of the earth, who shall hear all the good that I do to them; they shall fear and tremble for all the goodness and all the prosperity that I provide for it."

JEREMIAH 33:6–9

As a boy, whenever my parents would discipline me for my rebelliousness, they always told me their actions were for my good. I found that claim to be quite difficult to accept, even if it was true.

God's word to His people in today's passage must have felt incredibly difficult to accept. As they faced judgment for their rebellion, God assured them that the judgment would not be final or fatal. Rather, God Himself would bring healing and restoration once the discipline was completed. God faithfully disciplines our wayward hearts to draw us back to Him. He does this in fulfillment of His promise and for the glory of His name.

If you are a child of God and experiencing His discipline today, take courage. He is not finished with you yet. He will restore you with an abundance of peace and truth as you return to Him in humble and repentant submission.

Father, train my heart to trust You in every circumstance as You glorify Your own name. Amen.

Security in His Sovereignty

The voice of the LORD makes the deer give birth, and strips the forests bare; and in His temple everyone says, "Glory!" The LORD sat enthroned at the Flood, and the LORD sits as King forever. The LORD will give strength to His people; the LORD will bless His people with peace.

PSALM 29:9-11

Abraham Kuyper famously stated, "There is not a square inch in the whole domain of our human existence over which Christ, who is Sovereign over all, does not cry: 'Mine.'"[15] In today's verses, God's sovereign rule and boundless power are at the heart of David's psalm. The voice of God commands the weather, commandeers the winds, crushes the cedars, and causes the vast wilderness to shake. It is God's unrivaled power that causes events both great and small. God is equally sovereign over the seemingly insignificant birth of a single newborn deer as He is in the worldwide prominence of Noah's flood.

The same God who controls these events also guards His promises and fulfills His purpose. Some people fear God's power, and rightly so if it were ever divorced from His character. But God's character, His person, always informs His practices, and He always acts in furtherance of His fame and glory.

Friend, we will face nothing today that is beyond the power of our sovereign King. We need not face anything alone. In fact, God desires that we lean into Him as our firm foundation and strong support. He will bless His people with peace.

....

Father, teach me to trust You as I walk before You in full confidence that if God is for us, no one can stand against us! Amen.

Dr. Chris Aiken, Englewood Baptist Church, Rocky Mount, NC

The Hem of the Garment

Jesus said, "Somebody touched Me, for I perceived power going out from Me."
Now when the woman saw that she was not hidden, she came trembling; and
falling down before Him, she declared to Him in the presence of all the people the
reason she had touched Him and how she was healed immediately. And He said
to her, "Daughter, be of good cheer; your faith has made you well. Go in peace."

LUKE 8:46-48

Have you ever felt unworthy? Maybe you were hesitant to try out for a sports team or to ask someone to a dance. Maybe you chose a lesser job, an easier degree path, or even resisted a gospel invitation at church, all based on a sense of inner unworthiness.

The woman in today's passage felt unworthy. Her infirmity was beyond the reach of contemporary medicine. She was a religious and social outsider. As there is no mention of her husband, her physical condition may have resulted in a life of singleness. Circumstances prompted both desperation and hopelessness within her. Surely even Jesus would not want to bother with her.

But He did minister to her. Though she sought to escape notice, Jesus sought her. He commended her faith, encouraged her, and sent her away in peace. One might think the faith that only seeks to touch the hem of a garment is somehow lacking, yet the Lord affirmed the woman for exercising it. Perhaps you cannot imagine coming boldly to Jesus, but could you muster up the courage to touch the hem of His garment? If so, that's just the faith that leads you to healing, help, hope, and peace at the hands of Jesus.

....

Thank You, Lord, for restoring me when I respond even with "hem of the garment" faith. Amen.

Everyday Joy and Peace

Worship Is a Decision

You shall increase my greatness, and comfort me on every side. Also with the lute I will praise You—and Your faithfulness, O my God! To You I will sing with the harp, O Holy One of Israel. My lips shall greatly rejoice when I sing to You, and my soul, which You have redeemed. My tongue also shall talk of Your righteousness all the day long; for they are confounded, for they are brought to shame who seek my hurt.

PSALM 71:21-24

Today's psalm bears the imprint of an aged man looking back on a life of faith. He can see clearly the hand of God in both good times and bad, in comfort and in calamity, in discipline and deliverance.

Even as his enemies conspire against him and plan his demise, he turns in worship to the firm foundation of his faith. In God he finds security. In God he finds peace. His circumstances are at odds with the deeply rooted truth that he knows regarding God's faithfulness. The outcome of his prayers is not yet known, but his resolve remains the same. *Revive me, Lord, and I will choose to praise You.*

The psalmist ties his worship to God's inherent worth. He promises joyful praise for God's unfailing covenant, His unmitigated compassion, His unlimited power, and His unparalleled glory. Even as the psalmist awaits the Lord's deliverance, He extols the Lord's faithfulness, holiness, redeeming love, righteousness, and perfect judgment. He decides to worship God for who He is because worship is an informed response to the person and character of God, rather than an emotional reaction to circumstances of the worshiper. How will you do the same today?

....

Lord, fix my eyes on You as I praise You for who You are. Amen.

Dr. Chris Aiken, Englewood Baptist Church, Rocky Mount, NC

The Last Word

It shall come to pass in the latter days that the mountain of the LORD's house shall be established on the top of the mountains, and shall be exalted above the hills; and peoples shall flow to it. Many nations shall come and say, "Come, and let us go up to the mountain of the LORD, to the house of the God of Jacob; He will teach us His ways, and we shall walk in His paths." For out of Zion the law shall go forth, and the word of the LORD from Jerusalem.

MICAH 4:1-2

I t is easy enough in the days in which we live to become distracted, disheartened, and even disillusioned. The world can be a cruel place. People abandon their faith in droves and disavow even the existence of God.

God, however, is not defined by the opinions of others. The Word of God is replete with the consistent claims of God that a day is coming when all that is wrong will be made right. History's most ardent atheist will one day bow before Jesus and declare Him as Lord (Philippians 2:10–11). What His people cling to by faith will one day soon become visible by sight.

God's people, regardless of their circumstances, can firmly anchor to the hope that the last word belongs to almighty God. He seeks to release the captive (Luke 4:18), to restore the downtrodden (Psalm 145:14), and to replace that which the locusts have eaten (Joel 2:25). He shall not be denied. This inner peace and confidence exudes from Micah's prophetic word: "It *shall* come to pass in the latter days."

Father, grant me the grace to rest in Your Word as I walk confidently in Your will this day. Amen.

Everyday Joy and Peace

Why Pray?

May the LORD answer you in the day of trouble; may the name of the God of Jacob defend you; may He send you help from the sanctuary, and strengthen you out of Zion; may He remember all your offerings, and accept your burnt sacrifice. May He grant you according to your heart's desire, and fulfill all your purpose. We will rejoice in your salvation, and in the name of our God we will set up our banners! May the LORD fulfill all your petitions.

PSALM 20:1–5

Have you ever prayed for a miracle, and nothing changed? God is unchanging, so why should we even bother to pray? To enjoy the power of prayer, we first must understand the *purpose* of prayer. Prayer is not our way of getting our will done in heaven. Prayer is God's way of getting His will done on earth.

God is not a genie in a bottle. He is an all-knowing, all-powerful, all-good Being who desires to pour His blessings on His people. Prayer doesn't change God, but He changes us. "If we ask anything according to His will, He hears us. And if we know that He hears us, whatever we ask, we know that we have the petitions that we have asked of Him" (1 John 5:14–15).

Is today's passage saying that we can ask God for anything, and He will miraculously give it to us? It's not likely, based on the context. In 1 John 3:22, the conditions for receiving are obedience to God's commands and a willingness to serve God by doing what pleases Him. When our hearts' desires are the same as God's heart's desire, we will find ourselves rejoicing in His provision.[16]

....

Father, in all my prayers, spark in me a relentless pursuit of Your will.

Dr. Stephen G. Cutchins, First Baptist Church, North Augusta, SC

The Power of a Word

They brought the ark of God, and set it in the midst of the tabernacle that David had erected for it. Then they offered burnt offerings and peace offerings before God. And when David had finished offering the burnt offerings and the peace offerings, he blessed the people in the name of the LORD.

1 CHRONICLES 16:1-2

D o you agree with the saying, "Sticks and stones may break my bones, but words will never hurt me"? Unfortunately, this old saying presents a confusing and unbiblical message. Words are powerful because they reflect our hearts' condition. Therefore, our comments carry a lot of weight, with the power to either hurt or heal.

Jesus said, "Not what goes into the mouth defiles a man; but what comes out of the mouth, this defiles a man" (Matthew 15:11).

Our tongues may be tiny, but they are influential. They can set things aflame, and fire feeds on itself. And we all know what happens when a fire burns out of control. The influence of our words can warm like a cheerful fire in a grate, or it can decimate like hellfire. "Out of the same mouth proceed blessing and cursing. My brethren, these things ought not to be so" (James 3:10).

In today's passage, David took the time to bless the people and burn peace offerings. People are starving for affirmation. Chances are, you have never actually encountered someone who asked for *less* encouragement. Positive comments result in powerful change. Perhaps you're asking, "What do I encourage?" Everything! Take every opportunity. Get in the habit of blessing people and catching them doing things you can encourage.

....

Father, use my words to encourage three people today.

Everyday Joy and Peace

Do. Not. Quit.

Oh, send out Your light and Your truth! Let them lead me; let them bring me to Your holy hill and to Your tabernacle. Then I will go to the altar of God, to God my exceeding joy; and on the harp I will praise You, O God, my God. Why are you cast down, O my soul? And why are you disquieted within me? Hope in God; for I shall yet praise Him, the help of my countenance and my God.

PSALM 43:3-5

Sometimes, we all feel like quitting. We all have goals, dreams, and achievements that we meticulously plan out in our lifetimes. But so often, we are discouraged because we haven't yet seen results. We expect things to happen quickly and on our terms. But God doesn't always move at the pace we prefer. Instead, He works strategically, according to His purpose for each of us.

Whatever the Lord has put in front of you, don't back down! Keep moving forward. Say what Nehemiah said: "I am doing a great work, so that I cannot come down" (Nehemiah 6:3). God placed a dream in your heart for a reason. So don't quit. We have all the strength we need to endure through God's Holy Spirit.

Seek inspiration in God's presence, like the psalmist did in today's verses. He took his inner disquiet to the altar and sought God with joyful praise. See, everything God asks you to do is a *great work* for Him. Decide in your heart and mind that you won't give up no matter what. Lean on the Holy Spirit for the encouragement to get back up and keep fighting. Let the Holy Spirit restore your hope; then watch God move as you're working for Him![17]

....

Father, restore my hope today.

Dr. Stephen G. Cutchins, First Baptist Church, North Augusta, SC

Grace Without Holiness

Do not quench the Spirit. Do not despise prophecies. Test all things; hold fast what is good. Abstain from every form of evil. Now may the God of peace Himself sanctify you completely; and may your whole spirit, soul, and body be preserved blameless at the coming of our Lord Jesus Christ.

1 THESSALONIANS 5:19-23

*H*oliness is doing what you ought to do in response to God's grace. Find comfort knowing that "grace" is receiving something you didn't earn or deserve. But accepting His grace without holiness leads to abusing our freedom to do what we selfishly want. What areas of your life need more holiness today?

Ironically, the more we assert self-centered freedom, the more we become enslaved to sin. When we choose to persist in sin, we actually lose control over ourselves. We eventually forfeit any choice entirely. Jesus said, "Most assuredly, I say to you, whoever commits sin is a slave of sin" (John 8:34).

True freedom is not choosing to do whatever you want to do; it is choosing to do what you *ought* to do. Remember, it's not the strength of our faith but the object of our faith that gives us victory. When we make Christ the object of our faith, the Bible says, we experience victory in three specific ways.

First, God removes the penalty of sin, and we move from death to life. Second, God initiates the ongoing process of sanctification, where "the God of peace Himself" conquers the power of sin in our lives. This process allows us to experience holiness and become more like Christ. Finally, He removes the very presence of sin, and we are in heaven. What a thorough victory we have in Him![18]

Father, in response to Your grace, help me abstain from evil. I will seek Your peace.

Trust God with Your Fear

Moses said to the people, "Do not be afraid. Stand still, and see the salvation of the LORD, which He will accomplish for you today. For the Egyptians whom you see today, you shall see again no more forever. The LORD will fight for you, and you shall hold your peace."

EXODUS 14:13-14

W hat are you most afraid of in this world? Fear is so personal and familiar that our fears come with many names. For example, *arachnophobia* is the fear of spiders. *Claustrophobia* is the fear of tight spaces. Perhaps the most ironic fear is *phobophobia*, a fear of phobias.

Being afraid makes us uncomfortable, and sometimes we embrace the illusion that we'll be happy if we're comfortable. But happiness comes from fulfilling God's purposes for us. When He gets involved, things get disrupted. He is the unchanging Changer of all things.

David acknowledged that he dealt with fear. "Whenever I am afraid, I will trust in You" (Psalm 56:3). He met the opposition of Goliath, Saul, his sons, and, when he failed with Bathsheba, even God.

Fear allows us to trust our God more fully. With God's strength, we can outpace our fear with trust. In today's verse, Moses exhorted the people to stand still and witness God's strength in action. We can encourage ourselves the same way: "The LORD will fight for you, and you shall hold your peace."

What fear are you facing today? How will you respond? Let me encourage you to put your trust in God. Then, imagine yourself a year from now. What if you could say that you didn't back down, that you didn't let fear force you to miss out on what God has for you? Hold your peace![19]

Father, when I am afraid, help me put my full trust in You.

Dr. Stephen G. Cutchins, First Baptist Church, North Augusta, SC

He Started It

You, beloved, building yourselves up on your most holy faith, praying in the Holy Spirit, keep yourselves in the love of God, looking for the mercy of our Lord Jesus Christ unto eternal life. And on some have compassion, making a distinction; but others save with fear, pulling them out of the fire, hating even the garment defiled by the flesh. Now to Him who is able to keep you from stumbling, and to present you faultless before the presence of His glory with exceeding joy . . . be glory.

JUDE VV. 20-25

W e all have heard a kid shout, "He started it!" after being caught fighting with another kid. The kid deflects, of course, to excuse bad behavior. Even children can see the importance of who initiates something.

In our relationship with God, He initiates the connection by first loving us. Romans 5:8 says, "God demonstrates His own love toward us, in that while we were still sinners, Christ died for us." Jesus gave us the ultimate object lesson on love when He laid down His life for us. As today's passage says, His sacrifice presents us "faultless before the presence of His glory with exceeding joy." He died and rose again, picking us up, dusting us off, and presenting us as faultless. What an extraordinary act.

When John says, "We love Him because He first loved us" (1 John 4:19), he's not just talking about any kind of love. Instead, this "agape" love is the power that motivates us to respond to someone else's needs with no expectation of reward. This love comes from God alone and expresses itself primarily through sacrifice.

Simply put, He started it, and He sustains it. We can have peace in that.

Father, thank You for loving me first. Teach me to love more like You.

Valuing Your Marriage

To the rest I, not the Lord, say: If any brother has a wife who does not believe, and she is willing to live with him, let him not divorce her. And a woman who has a husband who does not believe, if he is willing to live with her, let her not divorce him. For the unbelieving husband is sanctified by the wife, and the unbelieving wife is sanctified by the husband; otherwise your children would be unclean, but now they are holy. But if the unbeliever departs, let him depart; a brother or a sister is not under bondage in such cases. But God has called us to peace. For how do you know, O wife, whether you will save your husband? Or how do you know, O husband, whether you will save your wife?

1 CORINTHIANS 7:12–16

With renting a venue, decorating, providing food and entertainment for guests, and paying for attire, the average cost of a wedding in America is nearly $30,000. Yet, some couples do not cherish their marriages as highly as they value their wedding ceremonies.

Today's passage shows that God values marriage. Even for Christians married to non-Christians, Paul gives this simple instruction: protect your marriage. Unless an unbeliever insists on leaving, the Christian spouse should seek to stay together. Why? Because "God has called us to peace." Believers are channels of grace, showing the family Christ's sanctifying love. Paul even offers hope that believers may bring their unsaved spouses to Christ! When Christians seek peace in our marriages, God honors us, works in the hearts of our spouses, and blesses our children.

. . . .

Father, help me please You in my marriage. Give me grace to show Christ's love to my spouse and children. Use me as a godly influence in their lives. In Jesus' name, amen.

Dr. Stephen Rummage, Quail Springs Baptist Church, Oklahoma City, OK

Are You Surviving, or Thriving?

Praise the LORD, O Jerusalem! Praise your God, O Zion! For He has strengthened the bars of your gates; He has blessed your children within you. He makes peace in your borders, and fills you with the finest wheat.

PSALM 147:12-14

I f my wife goes out of town during the spring or summer, she usually gives me careful instructions about watering the flowers, with specific directions for how much water and how often for each plant. After three decades of marital experience, I can now be left alone for a few days with her begonias without completely dehydrating them. Still, the flowers always seem to perk up more when she comes back home. With me, they survive. With her, they thrive!

Our text records the praises of God's people as they flourished under His faithful care. After years away in exile, God brought His people back to Jerusalem. There, they praised Him for His past deliverance and looked forward to His faithfulness. In the past, God had "strengthened the bars" of the city gates, repairing what had been broken. He had also blessed their children, showing His goodness to coming generations. In the future, God's people knew that He would restore peace and fill them with the finest wheat, satisfying their emotional and physical needs. Because of God's goodness, His people were thriving. The Lord wants you to thrive and not just survive the challenges you face. He can repair the brokenness in your life, bless your family, and satisfy your deepest needs so you can thrive and flourish.

....

Lord, thank You for being faithful to me in the past. Thank You that I can trust You today and in the future to work in my life for my good and Your glory. In Jesus' name, amen.

Vertical and Horizontal Peace

You shall offer peace offerings, and shall eat there, and rejoice before the LORD your God.

DEUTERONOMY 27:7

Episodes of the spooky 1960s sci-fi series *The Outer Limits* began with the phrase, "There is nothing wrong with your television set. Do not attempt to adjust the picture. We are controlling transmission . . . We will control the horizontal. We will control the vertical." Today, our digital screens no longer have horizontal and vertical hold controls, but old analog televisions did. To get a good picture, the vertical and horizontal adjustments had to be set just right. From a spiritual perspective, that has always been true. Things have to be set right in our vertical relationship with God and our horizontal relationships with other people for the picture of our life to be good.

In Deuteronomy 27, as Israel prepared to enter the promised land, Moses commanded the people to set up large stones on Mount Ebal. The stones were to be inscribed with God's Law. Moses also instructed the people to build an altar for burnt offerings and peace offerings (vv. 6–7). Burnt offerings were completely consumed in the fire and given to God to make things right with Him. Peace offerings were not burned up. Instead, they were shared with other worshipers. The two offerings together show us the importance of making things right with God and with others. When our vertical and horizontal relationships are right, we will experience the deepest joy of the Lord.

....

Father, thank You that through Jesus Christ You made the way for me to be right with You. Cleanse me of sin so my heart will be right in Your sight. Grant me Your power to live in peace with the people You have placed in my life. In Jesus' name, amen.

Dr. Stephen Rummage, Quail Springs Baptist Church, Oklahoma City, OK

Does Sin Pay?

Wait on the LORD, and keep His way, and He shall exalt you to inherit the land;
when the wicked are cut off, you shall see it. I have seen the wicked in great
power, and spreading himself like a native green tree. Yet he passed away, and
behold, he was no more; indeed I sought him, but he could not be found. Mark
the blameless man, and observe the upright; for the future of that man is peace.

PSALM 37:34-37

One of the toughest questions to answer is why evil people succeed. We've all seen examples of wrongdoers winning, whether it's the class valedictorian who cheats on tests, the dishonest coworker who receives multiple promotions, the morally tainted pastor whose church grows exponentially, or the adulterous spouse who winds up with an attractive new partner and apparently happy new marriage.

How do we reconcile sinful behavior with outward success? The psalmist observed wicked people in power, comparing them to a "green tree" towering in its "native" soil. Should it be any wonder that sinful people, operating sinfully, in a sin-fallen world, find earthly prosperity? Yet, the psalmist observes, that same prosperous, wicked person eventually meets an end. The impressive tree dies and falls, with no sign that it ever even stood. In God's timing, the prosperity of the evil will turn to judgment, while the blameless person will inherit God's peace. That's why God says, "Wait on the LORD, and keep His way." When we trust God to act and keep obeying Him, He will judge wickedness and exalt faithfulness.

....

Lord, provide me patience to wait on You, even when I see evil people prospering. Open my heart to see You at work in all my circumstances, and lead me to obey You fully. In Jesus' name, amen.

Everyday Joy and Peace

Assuming the Best

We have been comforted in your comfort. And we rejoiced exceedingly more for the joy of Titus, because his spirit has been refreshed by you all. For if in anything I have boasted to him about you, I am not ashamed. But as we spoke all things to you in truth, even so our boasting to Titus was found true.

2 CORINTHIANS 7:13–14

Tyler texted his buddy a question. He got no answer for an hour, and then for several weeks. Tyler's assumptions ran wild. At first he was sympathetic: *He must be busy, but he'll get in touch soon.* After a few days, he told himself, *He should have replied. Something's wrong.* When two weeks passed, he thought, *This guy doesn't value me at all.* Finally, Tyler's better judgment prevailed. He called and learned his buddy's phone had been on the fritz. He hadn't gotten the message to begin with. Tyler could have avoided weeks of angst by simply assuming the best.

The apostle Paul assumed the best about the Christians at Corinth. Knowing they had serious problems, Paul wrote them a tough letter and sent his companion Titus to address the situation. Paul told Titus the Corinthians would respond positively. In our text, Paul rejoiced that they had proved him right. Paul's example provides a case study for assuming the best in others. He shows us that when we assume the best, we will speak positively about others. We will also take the risk to help, even when helping involves correction. Finally, assuming the best will cause us to find joy when others succeed.

....

Lord, may I see others as You see them, with compassion and grace. Give me wisdom and kindness to help them when they are on the wrong path. In Jesus' name, amen.

Dr. Stephen Rummage, Quail Springs Baptist Church, Oklahoma City, OK

Shining in Darkness

Remind them to be subject to rulers and authorities, to obey, to be ready for every good work, to speak evil of no one, to be peaceable, gentle, showing all humility to all men. For we ourselves were also once foolish, disobedient, deceived, serving various lusts and pleasures, living in malice and envy, hateful and hating one another. But when the kindness and the love of God our Savior toward man appeared, not by works of righteousness which we have done, but according to His mercy He saved us, through the washing of regeneration and renewing of the Holy Spirit.

TITUS 3:1–5

R ecently my wife and I helped lead a conference for ministry couples in New England. Many were serving in places where the culture strongly opposes Christ and spiritual darkness is overwhelming. Our host arranged a spectacular fireworks display, beginning after dusk at the close of the retreat. As the sky grew darker, the illuminations became ever more brilliant. It reminded me that the darker culture becomes, the more occasion believers have to shine for Jesus.

Paul instructed Titus to "remind" believers to be faithful citizens. That meant conscientiously placing themselves under the authority of their government, obeying laws, helping their community, and resisting temptations to be contentious. They had been given new life and cleansed by Jesus Christ, saved out of the same darkness that surrounded them. Now, they could show others God's kindness and peace. Our world today, dark as it may be, is no darker than theirs. God wants us to find opportunities to demonstrate Christ's transforming love as well.

Lord, thank You that no darkness can overcome the light of Your love. Use me today to honor You, bring peace to those around me, and draw people to Your salvation. In Jesus' name, amen.

Everyday Joy and Peace

Joy Because of Jesus

All these men of war, who could keep ranks, came to Hebron with a loyal heart, to make David king over all Israel; and all the rest of Israel were of one mind to make David king. And they were there with David three days, eating and drinking, for their brethren had prepared for them. Moreover those who were near to them, from as far away as Issachar and Zebulun and Naphtali, were bringing food on donkeys and camels, on mules and oxen—provisions of flour and cakes of figs and cakes of raisins, wine and oil and oxen and sheep abundantly, for there was joy in Israel.

1 CHRONICLES 12:38-40

David was God's anointed king, called by God to bring unity to the kingdom that was on the verge of civil war. We read that all Israel had great joy at the prospect of David's kingship. But the bride of Christ has a much greater joy now because of David's greater Son, the King Messiah, the Lord Jesus Christ. The prophet Zechariah tells us, "Rejoice greatly, O daughter of Zion! Shout, O daughter of Jerusalem! Behold, your King is coming to you; He is just and having salvation, lowly and riding on a donkey, a colt, the foal of a donkey" (Zechariah 9:9). As much joy as King David brought to Israel, there is a greater joy to be had through Jesus Christ. For He brings unity through His Spirit as He offers salvation to all those who will trust Him and follow Him with their lives. This salvation is from our sin; from eternal death; and from our greatest spiritual Enemy—the devil. There is joy because of Jesus Christ.

....

Lord, thank You that we have joy because of Jesus Christ. Amen.

Dr. Aaron D. Burgner, Lakes Church, Lakeland, FL

God's Abiding Peace

Above all these things put on love, which is the bond of perfection. And let the peace of God rule in your hearts, to which also you were called in one body; and be thankful. Let the word of Christ dwell in you richly in all wisdom, teaching and admonishing one another in psalms and hymns and spiritual songs, singing with grace in your hearts to the Lord.

COLOSSIANS 3:14-16

L ove is the manifest outflow of God's abiding peace in my heart. Without the peace of God, I know little of love, especially the perfect love of the Savior. Through His living Word, as I stay tethered to it every day, I learn more of His grace, mercy, and love for lost humanity and His love for me. This love that Christ gives me makes itself known in so many ways in my life. It causes me to be the person I would not be, left to my sin. But thanks be to God, He has called me out of darkness into His marvelous light; He has caused this dead man to be alive. His love therefore should be a pillar of my life, causing me to sing and pronounce His glorious salvation to others.

This abiding peace and love is yours too, as a believer in Christ. Let His Word dwell in you as you read the Scriptures, pray, and praise Him in thankfulness for what He has done for you.

God, I thank You that love is the manifest outflow of Your abiding peace in my heart. Through the perfect love of the Savior, You came to me to deliver me from my sin, to give me peace. God, thank You that as I stay tethered to your living Word every day, it transforms me into a new person, rich in Your wisdom and grace. May I rejoice and praise you daily. Amen.

Our Helper in the Midst of Sorrow

"Hear, O LORD, and have mercy on me; LORD, be my helper!" You have turned for me my mourning into dancing; You have put off my sackcloth and clothed me with gladness, to the end that my glory may sing praise to You and not be silent. O LORD my God, I will give thanks to You forever.

PSALM 30:10-12

God's deliverance of David was an act of mercy. David had sinned greatly against God, which caused him to not be allowed to build the temple himself. His son Solomon would have that joy. Still, David did not ignore God's hand of faithfulness on his life and continued to trust Him with his life. When God delivered David again in this song, there is no missing the gladness it brought to David's life. But there is One who has come and offered us a greater mercy. This greater Son of David, the Lord Jesus Christ, has offered us salvation. He has come to be our Helper in the midst of our sorrow. He has truly gone down to the pit and pulled us out and given us new life. How can we be silent? How can we not sing His praises? How can we not give thanks to Him forever and proclaim to all those who will listen the great deliverance He has brought to our lives?

God, You are my Helper in the midst of my sorrow. God, I pray that You would give me a spirit that's willing to cry out to You, even if it's a spirit with little faith—that I would cry out to You, experience Your salvation, and begin to worship You once again. In Jesus' name I pray, amen.

Dr. Aaron D. Burgner, Lakes Church, Lakeland, FL

Repent, Trust Him, and Rejoice

Do not rejoice, O Israel, with joy like other peoples, for you have played the harlot against your God. You have made love for hire on every threshing floor. The threshing floor and the winepress shall not feed them, and the new wine shall fail in her.

HOSEA 9:1-2

Hosea was commanded by God to marry a prostitute. His relationship with her symbolizes the relationship that God had with His people. They were an unfaithful people. It was at the threshing floor and the wine press that pagan worship took place through sexual sin. How could an unfaithful people rejoice in the Lord? It's important to understand that God is always faithful even though we are unfaithful. All persons have been unfaithful in some way in our lives. But God is faithful to us. We must come to Christ in repentance, thanking Him for His faithfulness to forgive us of all unrighteousness. We must strive to live each day surrendered to Him. As we strive for faithfulness to the Lord Jesus Christ, He will bring His blessing to our lives. His blessing comes in the form of a life that is overflowing with the joy of His Spirit. We will rejoice and be glad because of the faithfulness of our Savior. Remembering that "all have sinned and fall short of the glory of God" (Romans 3:23), remembering that "by grace you have been saved through faith, and that not of yourselves; it is the gift of God, not of works, lest anyone should boast" (Ephesians 2:8–9), repent, trust Him, and rejoice.

....

Lord, I pray that You would help me be light in the darkness. Thank You for Your faithfulness to forgive me of all unrighteousness, as I repent, trust You, and rejoice. Amen.

Everyday Joy and Peace

Walk in Integrity

Know that the LORD has set apart for Himself him who is godly; the LORD will hear when I call to Him. Be angry, and do not sin. Meditate within your heart on your bed, and be still. Offer the sacrifices of righteousness, and put your trust in the LORD.

PSALM 4:3-5

Although he wasn't perfect, David sought holiness in his life. As Israel's leader, David found himself in many moments of distress. But it seemed that David always knew where to turn amid turmoil. David understood that his walk with the Lord and his character would be the thing that would allow him to sleep at night (Psalm 4:8). You and I will face many troubles in this life. But one thing that cannot be taken from us is our character. Our character is an outflow of walking with God in holiness. Striving for holiness daily should be our aim. To walk in integrity before Him who is the joy of our salvation. To meditate on His Word and let it live inside of us. To look more like Christ every day and look less like ourselves. I want to walk with the Lord so intimately and closely that I know He hears me when I call to Him. This is the peace that God gives us through His Spirit. As David exclaims at the end of the fourth Psalm, "I will both lie down in peace, and sleep; for You alone, O LORD, make me dwell in safety" (v. 8).

....

God, I love you, and I praise you. Lord, I thank You for Your grace. You've given me all I need. Help me meditate on Your Word and let it live inside of me. Help me walk in integrity before You, as You are the joy of my salvation. Amen.

Dr. Aaron D. Burgner, Lakes Church, Lakeland, FL

Created For Worship

Oh come, let us sing to the LORD! Let us shout joyfully to the Rock of our
salvation. Let us come before His presence with thanksgiving; let us shout joyfully
to Him with psalms. For the LORD is the great God, and the great King above all
gods.

PSALM 95:1–3

We were created for worship. All throughout the Old Testament, God makes Himself known as the true and living God. We recall the plagues of Egypt. We recall the fire from heaven on Mount Carmel. We think of God's great and mighty deeds that He has explained to us throughout the Old Testament and see that He alone is worthy of our praise. But we do not live in the Old Testament, and we have greater reason and understanding to worship God. For He has sent us His Son. He has brought down from heaven not fire, but the bread of life. Jesus came to dwell among His people. Jesus comes and offers us salvation through the cross. He has become the rock of our salvation. How can we not come into His presence with thanksgiving? Our hearts overflow with shouts of joy. He is the King of our souls, and the King of kings and Lord of lords will one day rule from His throne as we come to Him and worship. Let us worship Him today; let us find moments of silence to give Him the praise due to Him.

....

God, I come to you right now, begging for Your mercy and grace, thankful that I was created for worship. Give me a heart that longs to come into Your presence with thanksgiving, overflowing with shouts of joy. Help me find moments of silence today to give You the praise due to You. Amen.

Everyday Joy and Peace

Staying Close with the Lord

All the kings of the earth shall praise You, O Lord, when they hear the words of Your mouth. Yes, they shall sing of the ways of the Lord, for great is the glory of the Lord. Though the Lord is on high, yet He regards the lowly; but the proud He knows from afar.

PSALM 138:4-6

Have you ever felt invisible? Have you thought that no one noticed you? I played on the offensive line in college football. We would joke that the only time we were recognized was when we did something wrong. As we walk upon the earth, we may feel invisible to those around us, but our scripture promises that when we seek to walk humbly before the Lord, He is very close to us. Of the proud and arrogant, who are most often seen in this world, it says they are dealt with from far off. If you want to experience peace and joy in our world, don't make it your goal for everyone to recognize you, but make it your goal to glorify Christ. Walk humbly before him and experience His presence in your life.

....

Lord, so often I am tempted to glorify myself to those around me. Help Me resist this temptation and to walk humbly before You. Help me glorify You and make You known to those around me. Thank You for the promise of Your close presence in my life when I walk humbly before You.

Dr. Marty Jacumin, Trajectory Ministries, Rutherford College, NC

How Fear and Peace Live Together

"Then you shall know that I have sent this commandment to you, that My covenant with Levi may continue," says the LORD of hosts. "My covenant was with him, one of life and peace, and I gave them to him that he might fear Me; so he feared Me and was reverent before My name. The law of truth was in his mouth, and injustice was not found on his lips. He walked with Me in peace and equity, and turned many away from iniquity."

MALACHI 2:4-6

Malachi 2:4–6 seems to present a dichotomy of terms. It says Levi had peace because he feared God. You may wonder, How can fear and peace go together? Many people would say that fear keeps them from having peace, but for Levi it went hand in hand. We must understand what a healthy fear of the Lord looks like. This fear is an awe and reverence of who God is. He is all-powerful, all knowing, and the Creator of everything. I once heard this fear described as a fear God might take his hand off us more than taking his hand to crush us. Because Levi had this fear, it caused him to walk in a reverent way before God. He kept God's truth in his mouth, and no injustice was found in him. This reverence for God so consumed him that it caused his life to be lived in a manner that pleased God. Because he pleased God, he had a peace in his life. He walked into each day knowing that God was pleased with him, and that brought him this sense of peace. The same thing will work for us. If we have this healthy fear of God, it will affect how we live our lives and can give us the same peace Levi had. Are you searching for peace? See God for who He is and live with the reverence that He requires.

....

Father, help me have a healthy fear of You. Help me be in awe and reverence because of who You are. I desire peace, and I know that comes from You.

True Joy in a Reality-TV World

Many sorrows shall be to the wicked; but he who trusts in the LORD, mercy shall surround him. Be glad in the LORD and rejoice, you righteous; and shout for joy, all you upright in heart!

PSALM 32:10-11

Much of reality television loves to glamorize the wicked things of this world. It paints a picture that someone can live according to his or her own rules and be extremely prosperous. The wicked seem to have it all, and those seeking to walk with God are portrayed as foolish. Although Proverbs 24:1 warns us not to be envious of evildoers, we can often desire the things they have. What the media doesn't betray is the devastation, destruction, and depression that often follows the individuals they are glamorizing. Sometimes we will read stories much later of the shambles that have become of their lives.

The Lord promised Levi in yesterday's reading from Malachi that he would experience true life and peace if he would have a reverent awe before the Lord. If he would live with integrity, the Lord would bless him. And as today's reading says, we must also trust and rejoice in the Lord. True joy doesn't come from the wicked things of this world. Let's make our goal not to have the glamorized life of those who are far from God. Let's experience His peace by rejoicing in Him and walking in a way that glorifies Him.

....

Lord help me not envy evildoers, no matter how glamorous they may appear. Help me walk reverently before You and experience Your peace.

Dr. Marty Jacumin, Trajectory Ministries, Rutherford College, NC

Where Is Your Focus?

Finally, brethren, whatever things are true, whatever things are noble,
whatever things are just, whatever things are pure, whatever things are lovely,
whatever things are of good report, if there is any virtue and if there is anything
praiseworthy—meditate on these things. The things which you learned and
received and heard and saw in me, these do, and the God of peace will be with you.

PHILIPPIANS 4:8-9

Have you ever tried to teach a child how to hit a ball? It really doesn't matter if it's a baseball or a softball; the instruction is the same. When teaching the skill, a word you often hear is *focus*. We tell the child to make sure he or she is focusing on the ball. Don't focus on the picture, the outfield fence, or any of the opposing players. Don't focus on first base, but simply focus on the ball. We will go as far as saying to watch the ball hit the bat. We know it will be hard to be successful if we don't focus on the goal (hitting the ball). Paul gives a similar instruction to believers about where their focus needs to be. The world will tell us to focus on ourselves and what we desire. The Bible contrasts this by saying we should focus on things that are true, noble, just, lovely, virtuous, and praise-worthy. These are things that point us to Christ. If we will focus on these things, Paul says the God of peace will be with us. The question we must ask ourselves is, Where is our focus?

....

Lord, help my focus to be solely on You. Help me long for the things
that give You the most glory.

The Way of Escape

Submit to God. Resist the devil and he will flee from you. Draw near to God and He will draw near to you. Cleanse your hands, you sinners; and purify your hearts, you double-minded. Lament and mourn and weep! Let your laughter be turned to mourning and your joy to gloom. Humble yourselves in the sight of the Lord, and He will lift you up.

JAMES 4:7-10

Flip Wilson was a tremendously funny comedian, popular in the 1970s and 1980s. One of the funniest parts of his routine would be when he was confronted with something he had done wrong. He had a famous line that eventually made it onto T-shirts, coffee mugs, and posters. When he was caught, he would simply reply, "The devil made me do it."

When we are confronted with sin in our own lives, we may desire to say it's the devil's fault. He made us do it. This may be funny in a comedian's act, but it's not biblically accurate. The Bible speaks of a way of escape. In our text for today, James says we can resist the devil and when we do, he will flee from us. God's grace should humble us and create a desire to purge sin from our lives and to walk with the Lord each day. That's where our true peace and joy will come from.

Lord, thank You for the grace you pour out on my life. Let this cause me to desire You more than anything I could have. Help me resist the devil as he seeks to tempt me. Help me humble myself and to walk in a manner worthy of Your grace. Thank You for a way of escape when I am tempted.

Dr. Marty Jacumin, Trajectory Ministries, Rutherford College, NC

The Ultimate Peace

Behold, this is the joy of His way, and out of the earth others will grow. Behold, God will not cast away the blameless, nor will He uphold the evildoers. He will yet fill your mouth with laughing, and your lips with rejoicing. Those who hate you will be clothed with shame, and the dwelling place of the wicked will come to nothing.

JOB 8:19-22

A s we conclude this week of devotions about true peace, we read verses that may seem troubling and lead us to a lack of peace. Job's acquaintance Bildad reminds him God will not cast away the blameless nor uphold evildoers. He is actually bringing a charge against Job. What's troublesome about these verses as we examine our own lives is we know we aren't blameless. We know the desires of our heart can be evil, so how does this bring us peace? For believers in Jesus, here's where we must trust the atoning work of Christ in the crucifixion and resurrection. We should work every day to remove sin from our lives, but we know we still commit sin. When we trust Christ as our Savior, our sins past and present are covered by the blood of Jesus. When God sees us, He sees the righteousness of His Son, and in Him, we are blameless. Take time to thank God for His sacrifice or ask God to forgive you and cleanse you by placing your faith in Him.

Lord, thank You for Your atoning sacrifice on the cross. Thank You for Your grace and forgiveness that You would die for us even in our sin. I am thankful that when You look upon believers, You don't see our sin, but You see the righteousness of Christ. Help me walk worthy of Your sacrifice.

The Joy of Fellowship

That which was from the beginning, which we have heard, which we have seen with our eyes, which we have looked upon, and our hands have handled, concerning the Word of life—the life was manifested, and we have seen, and bear witness, and declare to you that eternal life which was with the Father and was manifested to us—that which we have seen and heard we declare to you, that you also may have fellowship with us; and truly our fellowship is with the Father and with His Son Jesus Christ. And these things we write to you that your joy may be full.

1 JOHN 1:1-4

The apostle John was inspired by the Holy Spirit to write five books of the New Testament. He was a part of the inner circle of Jesus' disciples along with Peter and James. He also referred to himself as "the disciple whom Jesus loved" (John 21:7, 20). Without a doubt, John had an intimate relationship with Jesus. In the opening verses of today's epistle, he wrote to testify of Jesus Christ and of the purpose for which He came to earth. Jesus came for the express purpose of redeeming us from our sins, that we might enjoy the blessed privilege of having a relationship with Him. When we have fellowship with our heavenly Father, we can also experience the blessing of having fellowship with other believers. True joy is only possible when we are rightly connected with our Lord and His people. John encouraged fellowship with God and with others, "that your joy may be full." So as you gather together with others, you'll experience the fullness of joy through the relationship you share.

....

Lord, help me to remember the blessing of being Your child and a part of Your family.

Brent Thompson, Heflin Baptist Church, Heflin, AL

Godly Testimony

Blessed is the man who walks not in the counsel of the ungodly, nor stands in the path of sinners, nor sits in the seat of the scornful; but his delight is in the law of the LORD, and in His law he meditates day and night.

PSALM 1:1-2

The psalms bring much comfort and instruction for followers of Jesus Christ. Our text today describes for us the way a godly man conducts his daily life. It is very interesting to note that the longest book in our Bible opens with an emphasis on the testimony of a godly servant.

The psalmist makes us aware of the need to avoid dangerous situations by describing three areas of temptation. We must avoid those who seek to falsely advise us. We must avoid people or places that might tempt us toward sin. We must avoid seeking positions that would cause us to compromise our dependency on Christ. And we must trust the godly counsel of the Word of God to avoid any allurements that might draw us away from the Lord.

The psalmist also instructs us in the way to stay focused and faithful. We must find our standing and security in God's Word. Godly men and women will do much more than read the Word. They will meditate on the Word and allow its truth to sink deep within their souls to the point that they are completely saturated and overflowing. With so many voices competing for our attention, we must avoid ungodliness and find true joy in serving a risen Savior.

Lord, help me to focus my eyes, ears, heart, mind, and soul on seeking Your perfect will for this day. I deeply desire to honor You with my life. Amen.

Everyday Joy and Peace

Share Your Story

Nebuchadnezzar the king, to all peoples, nations, and languages that dwell in all the earth: Peace be multiplied to you. I thought it good to declare the signs and wonders that the Most High God has worked for me. How great are His signs, and how mighty His wonders! His kingdom is an everlasting kingdom, and His dominion is from generation to generation.

DANIEL 4:1-3

Nebuchadnezzar was one of the most wicked and notorious kings of all time. He was very prideful and arrogant as he sought to promote himself while ignoring the power of God. Our text today takes place some thirty years after the events of the fiery furnace, when Shadrach, Meshach, and Abed-Nego refused to bow before the golden image Nebuchadnezzar had erected. Those events began to move the heart of Nebuchadnezzar to the point where he wanted the nations of the known world to hear how God had worked in his life. He had a story to tell, and he wanted it told.

How about us? Do we have a story to tell? Do we really want it to be told? Sure we do—and we must be the ones to share it! We can tell the story of the love of a Savior who came from the realms of glory to take upon Himself the rags of humanity. He humbly submitted to the will of His Father and gave Himself as a sacrifice for the sins of the world. He came, He died, was buried, rose from the dead, ascended to the Father, and is soon to return for His own. His story is too glorious not to be told! Let us tell it with joy, that "peace be multiplied" among our hearers.

Lord, help me to faithfully share Your story today. Amen.

Brent Thompson, Heflin Baptist Church, Heflin, AL

Protect Your Joy

O vine of Sibmah! I will weep for you with the weeping of Jazer. Your plants have gone over the sea, they reach to the sea of Jazer. The plunderer has fallen on your summer fruit and your vintage. Joy and gladness are taken from the plentiful field and from the land of Moab; I have caused wine to fail from the winepresses; no one will tread with joyous shouting—not joyous shouting!

JEREMIAH 48:32-33

Jeremiah had the difficult task in today's passage of delivering God's message of judgment upon those who continued to reject His call for repentance. Even though the people of Moab had rejected the Lord, Jeremiah still wept for them. They had demonstrated some of the same characteristics that can cause us to lose our joy. Whenever we become overconfident in our own abilities, overjoyed by our abundant resources, or overtaken by our foolish pride, we are in danger of losing our joy. Our abilities are limited and our resources are finite. Our material blessings are from the Lord and will eventually wither and fade.

As a young pastor, I struggled with the tendency to lose my joy in the work of ministry. The pressure and stress were often overwhelming, and I really struggled when the attacks came from the people I served. The Lord helped me to realize that I could not control others, and the only way they could steal my joy was if I gave them access to it. He taught me that my relationship with Him would be more than enough to insulate me from the attacks of the enemy. Don't let anyone or anything steal your joy today. Place it firmly in the Lord.

Lord, help me remember that focusing on Your eternal promises is the pathway to living with joy. Amen.

Joy in God's Protection

Let all those rejoice who put their trust in You; let them ever shout for joy,
because You defend them; let those also who love Your name be joyful in You.
For You, O LORD, will bless the righteous; with favor You will surround him as
with a shield.

PSALM 5:11–12

I remember being told years ago that a promise is only as good as the person making the promise. How quickly we learn in this life that not everyone can be trusted to remain true to the promises they make. But when it comes to our Lord, we can live with bold confidence and blessed assurance that He has never made a promise that He did not keep. Our Lord is our holy example of unwavering integrity. He has been faithful and will always be faithful to His children. Paul declared in 2 Timothy 2:13, "If we are faithless, He remains faithful; he cannot deny Himself."

Today's psalm declares that those who place their total trust in God can visibly express their joy due to the abundance of His blesssings and the security He provides. With as much uncertainty and insecurity as are present in our world today, it is a tremendous blessing for followers of Jesus Christ to live with the promise of knowing that our heavenly Father surrounds us to shield us from the attacks of Satan. I pray today that you will commit your heart and life completely to the lordship of Jesus Christ so that you may live with an abundance of joy.

....

Lord, thank You for remaining faithful regardless of my inadequacies. Thank You for loving me and giving me the blessing of true joy. Thank You for giving me hope and peace. Amen.

Brent Thompson, Heflin Baptist Church, Heflin, AL

The Wonder of Worship

Those who live according to the flesh set their minds on the things of the flesh,
but those who live according to the Spirit, the things of the Spirit. For to be
carnally minded is death, but to be spiritually minded is life and peace.

ROMANS 8:5-6

E ach weekend we have the privilege of preparing our hearts to join with
the body of Christ and worship together on the Lord's Day. Many families
today live with such a hectic weekly schedule that attending a worship service
can become more of a mechanical exercise than a spiritual experience. Our text
today comes from one of the great chapters in our Bible. Romans 8 is filled with
teaching on the freedom we enjoy in Christ, admonitions on how to approach
suffering, and the promises of God's eternal love and care.

One of the greatest reasons we can worship God this weekend is because
He has set us free from the condemnation that was upon us (Romans 8:1). Every
person on earth stands in need of a relationship with Christ. This special relationship is only possible through the repentance of our sin. Before we repent, we live
under the heavy condemnation of the guilt and shame that sin brings. But when
we repent, we are completely set free to experience the joy that Jesus Christ made
possible through His finished work on Calvary's cross.

As you approach the Lord in corporate worship this weekend, take time to
allow the Holy Spirit to search your heart and reveal any hindrances that might
prevent you from experiencing His powerful presence. Be "spiritually minded,"
for it is "life and peace." Receive His Word gladly, and respond as He leads you.

....

Lord, help me to daily follow Your heart with all of mine. Amen.

Everyday Joy and Peace

The Struggle of Envy

So David went out wherever Saul sent him, and behaved wisely. . . . Now it had happened as they were coming home, when David was returning from the slaughter of the Philistine, that the women had come out of all the cities of Israel, singing and dancing, to meet King Saul, with tambourines, with joy, and with musical instruments. So the women sang as they danced, and said: "Saul has slain his thousands, and David his ten thousands." Then Saul was very angry, and the saying displeased him; and he said, "They have ascribed to David ten thousands, and to me they have ascribed only thousands. Now what more can he have but the kingdom?"

1 SAMUEL 18:5-8

Comparing yourself to others can lead to envy—an emotion of unhappiness caused by desiring what someone else has. The dangers of envy include relational division, resentment, and discontentment. And if unaddressed, envy can even lead to anger and hostility, eventually poisoning our hearts and leading us on a path that is far from God's peace. Proverbs 14:30 warns, "A sound heart is life to the body, but envy is rottenness to the bones."

Saul struggled with envy and become jealous of David, who had been a faithful servant. The people gave David more credit for accomplishments in battle than Saul, and Saul became angry and prideful, fulfilling the truth of Proverbs 16:18 (CSB): "Pride comes before destruction, and an arrogant spirit before a fall."

Envy is a serious sin and must not be overlooked. Let us examine ourselves, and if any symptoms are found, may we confess it to God and repent. Then we can experience the joy and peace that God intends for us.

Dear Lord, search my heart for any hidden envy, and give me the courage and wisdom to deal with it appropriately!

Jamie Altman, Bethlehem Community Church, Laurel, MS

Joy and Sadness

Many of the priests and Levites and heads of the fathers' houses, old men who had seen the first temple, wept with a loud voice when the foundation of this temple was laid before their eyes. Yet many shouted aloud for joy, so that the people could not discern the noise of the shout of joy from the noise of the weeping of the people, for the people shouted with a loud shout, and the sound was heard afar off.

EZRA 3:12-13

As we see in today's verses, once God's people returned from exile to their land and began to rebuild the temple, there were cries of joy and sadness. Some were thankful they would soon have a temple of worship again, but others couldn't get over the fact that whatever they built would never compare to what they had in Solomon's temple. It's possible that some were filled with mourning for what they had lost, as well as thankfulness for what was to come.

Perhaps we've all had those experiences in which we were grateful for our present blessings, but also filled with grief because we longed for what we had in the past. Scripture doesn't allude to the idea that these emotions are wrong or that God was displeased with His people. Joy and sadness can both be healthy if kept in proper perspective.

There are going to be those times in our lives when we miss the days of old, but we must not allow that to overshadow what God wants to do in our lives today and tomorrow. Change is not always easy, but as we look back and thank God for our past, we must look forward and trust Him with our future.

....

Lord, I pray that You keep me joyful, even in the midst of my grief and sadness.

Everyday Joy and Peace

The Heart of Prayer

"Hear my prayer, O LORD, and give ear to my cry; do not be silent at my tears; for I am a stranger with You, a sojourner, as all my fathers were. Remove Your gaze from me, that I may regain strength, before I go away and am no more."

PSALM 39:12–13

In today's passage we find David asking the Lord not to be silent, as David had been earlier when he should have spoken (Psalm 39:2, 9). He prayed that God would hear his cry and not treat him like a stranger, but rather show him favor in his remaining days.

At times, you may find yourself praying prayers like this. Sometimes life calls for short prayers filled with desperation and grief. Other times may call for long prayers filled with emotion and requests. Some prayers may be joyful and thankful, and others may be sad and worrisome.

The impact of a prayer is not based on the amount of words used, the tone of our voice, or the grammar of our phrases. What matters most is that our communication with God comes from the heart. God encourages us to do just that in Psalm 62:8 (NIV): "Pour out your hearts to him, for God is our refuge."

David had become a stranger to God, but at least he realized it and prayed for restoration. Has God heard from you lately? Do you need to reconnect with Him and experience His joy and peace again in your life? Take time with heartfelt prayer to reach out to God today. He can bring you peace.

....

Dear Lord, today I pray . . . [pray from your heart].

Jamie Altman, Bethlehem Community Church, Laurel, MS

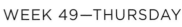

The Peace of Submission

"Now acquaint yourself with Him, and be at peace; thereby good will come to you. Receive, please, instruction from His mouth, and lay up His words in your heart."

JOB 22:21-22

Today's passage is a quote from Job's friend Eliphaz, pleading with Job to repent. These would have been tough words for Job to hear at such a time of loss. He had lost his fame, his fortune, and members of his family. His good health was taken from him, his faith was being tested, and perhaps he was wanting comfort and not commands during this tragic time in this life.

But God is more interested in our needs than our wants, and perhaps what Job needed more than anything at this point in his life was a lesson in submission during even the worst of times. Remember, it's the Holy Spirit's job to produce peace within us, but we have to submit everything to Him—the good and the bad. Peace in bad times? Peace in times of loss? Peace in times confusion? Peace in times of sadness? Yes, for it's then you can proclaim what Paul meant in Philippians 4:7: "And the peace of God, which surpasses all understanding, will guard your hearts and minds through Christ Jesus." I would encourage you to have some friends in your life that will tell you the truth in love even when you don't want to hear it.

Heavenly Father, I pray that You help me to submit to Your instructions at all times. Help me to never allow my desire to prosper to disrupt Your ultimate plan for my life.

Let's Be Salt

"Everyone will be seasoned with fire, and every sacrifice will be seasoned with salt. Salt is good, but if the salt loses its flavor, how will you season it? Have salt in yourselves, and have peace with one another."

MARK 9:49-50

The word *salt* in today's passage suggests that we are to live our lives sacrificially and peacefully. Just as sacrifices in the Old Testament were offered with salt (Leviticus 2:13), so Christians today must live their lives with sacrifice. As Paul said in Romans 12:1, we are to "present [our] bodies a living sacrifice, holy, acceptable to God, which is [our] reasonable service."

Salt was also used in biblical times as a type of medicine, a seasoning, and a preservative. In the same way, we as followers of Christ are to be like salt in promoting peace among fellow believers. This illustrates the preserving power of God. Scripture says that we "are the salt of the earth" (Matthew 5:13) and commands us to "[have our] conduct honorable" (1 Peter 2:12). Promoting peace with others enhances our godly influence, which in turn brings peace and joy to others.

....

Dear Lord, I pray that You will increase my godly influence. I want to be a promoter of Your peace rather than a disrupter of it. And I pray that You protect me from losing my godly influence and give me the strength to sacrifice my own desires for what You want for me.

Jamie Altman, Bethlehem Community Church, Laurel, MS

The Delight of God's Good News

"I delight to do Your will, O my God, and Your law is within my heart." I have proclaimed the good news of righteousness in the great assembly; indeed, I do not restrain my lips, O LORD, You Yourself know.

PSALM 40:8-9

Today's passage comes from a psalm written by David. As we can see from his words, David could not remain silent about God's good news, and we should not either. David was unapologetic and passionate about telling others about God and what his Lord had done for him. This was a breath of fresh air to have the king of Israel give glory to God in the midst of all the worshipers in the sanctuary. We should pray for more leaders like that today.

Have you ever found yourself holding back your praise or proclamation of what God has done for you? Do you allow your environment to dictate what you say about God and how much credit you give Him? If so, I want to encourage you to follow David's example and remember the words of Paul to the Romans: "For I am not ashamed of the gospel, because it is the power of God that brings salvation to everyone who believes" (Romans 1:16 NIV). Sharing the gospel story and how God has worked in your life can bring great joy both to you and to those who hear your story!

....

Dear Lord, thank You for being so good to me. I pray that You give me a joy and passion to share Your Word and my testimony.

Everyday Joy and Peace

Covenant Fulfillment: Place of Peace

"Behold, a son shall be born to you, who shall be a man of rest; and I will give him rest from all his enemies all around. His name shall be Solomon, for I will give peace and quietness to Israel in his days. He shall build a house for My name, and he shall be My son, and I will be his Father; and I will establish the throne of his kingdom over Israel forever."

1 CHRONICLES 22:9-10

A place of peace is the fulfillment of God's covenant promise for those who submit to His divine rule. In today's verses, God promised David, because of his devotion to His divine direction, that he was to have victory over his enemies and that God would bring him to a place of peace. He would not have to continue to fight for victory. David would now live in a place of victory, built by God through his own son Solomon.

God continued His fulfillment of that promise to David when He gave us His Son, as described in Isaiah: "Unto us a Child is born, unto us a Son is given" (9:6). This Prince of Peace, Jesus, will eventually bring a final peace and rest on earth, the final dwelling place for God and His people. This peace will not be a man-manufactured peace. It will be a God-created peace built by a Man of rest, a Savior who is the ultimate Victor over all enemies. But we can experience His peace and rest today too, as we listen to His divine direction and submit to His will.

....

Lord, thank You for Your established peace and rest from my labors and the continued assault from my enemies. Help me to trust the born Prince of Peace who has been given, that I might rest in Your victory. Amen.

Dr. Marcus Glass Sr., New Seasons Church at Radium Springs, Albany, GA

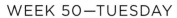

A Continuous Protocol: "Pro to Call"

As for me, I will call upon God, and the LORD shall save me. Evening and morning and at noon I will pray, and cry aloud, and He shall hear my voice. He has redeemed my soul in peace from the battle that was against me, for there were many against me.

PSALM 55:16–18

What is the protocol for surviving friendly fire? As we see from today's verses, David always had a "pro to call" in times of trouble: God Himself. No enemies can have triumph against a constant God-consulting Christian. Consistency is the common denominator for victory in the conversation between the caller (us) and receiver (God). David's consistent cry to God suggests that we can consult God constantly for every calamity.

But what do we do when the foe is a so-called friend? David's battle in today's psalm is personal. Nevertheless, he shows us that despite the circumstances the protocol (pro to call) for circumstances is still the same. David's advice is constant conversation with the Almighty. No matter who the foe, the pro to call is God. No matter what the time, the pro to call is God. No matter what the circumstance, the pro to call is God. The remedy for a continous attack of the enemy is always a continuous call to the pro, God. And the result is His redeeming peace.

....

Lord, I am calling You every day, in every circumstance. Help me hear Your direction for protection against enemies foreign and near. Guide my behavior and redeem my soul in peace from the battle against me. Amen.

The Strength to Understand

Again, the one having the likeness of a man touched me and strengthened me. And he said, "O man greatly beloved, fear not! Peace be to you; be strong, yes, be strong!" So when he spoke to me I was strengthened, and said, "Let my lord speak, for you have strengthened me."

DANIEL 10:18-19

God's process of our journey to a place of peace may be difficult to withstand. When we consider the encounters that we must have in this life in order to rest, it may prove difficult to remain strong. Our opposition in the world may debilitate our willingness to accept and undertake God's plan for our journey to peace.

In today's verses, the pressure to perform in Daniel's situation had drained him, due to his unusual visions. In the midst of Daniel's dilemma, God sent an angelic visitor to encourage Daniel. This encounter shows us that God has a remedy for our inability to stand in uncertain times.

As with Daniel, often it is our inability to understand and accept what God is showing us that has us weak to the point of failure. We too are admonished to receive a touch from God in times when it is difficult to understand our circumstances. This touch comes from reading and meditating on God's Word, and it opens up His flow of divine strength and peace, which is needed to stand when we don't understand. If you are struggling today with weakness and confusion, turn to God's Word and look for His strength and peace.

....

Lord hold me up with Thy touch of lovingkindness and tender mercies, so I may endure the journey that will bring me into a place of strength and peace in my struggle. Hold me with Thy right hand that I might stand when I don't understand. In Jesus' name, amen.

Dr. Marcus Glass Sr., New Seasons Church at Radium Springs, Albany, GA

No Other Compasses

The heavens are Yours, the earth also is Yours; the world and all its fullness, You have founded them. The north and the south, You have created them; Tabor and Hermon rejoice in Your name. You have a mighty arm; strong is Your hand, and high is Your right hand. Righteousness and justice are the foundation of Your throne; mercy and truth go before Your face.

PSALM 89:11–14

There is none like the Lord. Because of this statement, all men must stand in awe of His ownership and creation. No matter where we find ourselves wandering in the heaven or earth, His wonders cannot be compassed. Just as every point on the compass from the north, south, east, and west are made to point to His praise, we as His creation should make a point to give Him the praise that is due Him for His majesty and almighty power. Praise Him for His mighty arm that reaches to the lowest times in our lives. Praise Him for the strength of His hand that carries us through our dark times and our troubles. Praise Him and rejoice in His faithful hand of righteousness and justice, which establishes our ways and brings mercy and truth to light in our lives. No other compasses His wonders, and He deserves all our praise.

Lord, thank You for Your glorious creation that brings a constant reminder of our need to praise and rejoice in You. Thank You for continuously carrying me away from moments of derision from others into the marvelous light of Your presence. You are worthy like no other. Amen.

Everyday Joy and Peace

Unemployed Faith

What does it profit, my brethren, if someone says he has faith but does not have
works? Can faith save him? If a brother or sister is naked and destitute of daily
food, and one of you says to them, "Depart in peace, be warmed and filled,"
but you do not give them the things which are needed for the body, what does it
profit? Thus also faith by itself, if it does not have works, is dead.

JAMES 2:14–17

D oes your faith work? Or is it unemployed? To be unemployed, according
to *Merriam-Webster*, means "not engaged in a gainful occupation."[20] It is
to be available, but out of work. The faith James illustrates in today's text is one
that seems available, but it does not work or produce gainful profits. The claim of
acquiring the saving works of faith should be expressed in the profit those works
yield. Therefore, an unemployed faith, though readily expressed, will always make
no cents, or sense, because it does not yield profit. It has no substance of things
hoped for or evidence seen (see Hebrews 11:1). It will boast of its availability without the opportunity to work. It is, by its very nature, not gainfully employed.

On the other hand, true faith has the ability to begin a work that produces
something profitable in the end for God's will and kingdom. Is your faith
employed, or is it unemployed? If the latter, I encourage you to spend some time
in God's Word, and ask Him to guide you to gainfully employ your faith. It will
bring much peace and joy in your life.

Lord, thank You for a saving faith that changes me from the inside
out. Give me the strength to work while it is day. Lead me to the
people and places where others may profit from my saving faith.
Amen.

Dr. Marcus Glass Sr., New Seasons Church at Radium Springs, Albany, GA

Think About It

This Book of the Law shall not depart from your mouth, but you shall meditate in it day and night, that you may observe to do according to all that is written in it. For then you will make your way prosperous, and then you will have good success.

JOSHUA 1:8

What has the most attention in your mind? What do you meditate on the most? Is it your problems, your present predicament, or future placement? In today's verses, Joshua was mandated to meditate on what true prosperity and success look like. God's instruction was to meditate, think on, and replay His manual for success—His Word—to ensure progress in this Christian life. Is that where your focus is in your life?

Think about the Book of the Law, God's Word. Think about how it has never been broken; only men have broken themselves over it. Think about how many times God has delivered His people out of the hands of enemies. Think about how prosperous God has made those who followed His commands. Think about the difference a personal relationship with the almighty God can make in your own life. Think about how many times God has brought great success out of chaos. In every waking moment of your life, you can have peace and good success if you just develop a habit of thinking about it! It's all there in His Word! Think about it.

....

Lord, thank You for giving me a manual for life that counters all my fears of moving forward in good success. Lead me in Your will and Your ways through the Book of the Law. Give me Your presence, that I may have a personal relationship with You every day and night. Amen.

Joy in the Hope to Come

Oh, let the nations be glad and sing for joy! For You shall judge the people righteously, and govern the nations on earth. Let the peoples praise You, O God; let all the peoples praise You. Then the earth shall yield her increase; God, our own God, shall bless us. God shall bless us, and all the ends of the earth shall fear Him.

PSALM 67:4–7

What a consistently faithful God we serve. There's great hope in knowing that no matter how unpredictable and challenging life may become, God is faithful and mindful of the needs of His people.

There's a word used in the above verses that could easily be overlooked. Notice how many times the word *shall* is used. Five times in four verses the psalmist uses the word. The writer chose to find joy in the promise of the things God was *going* to do rather than fall into frustration at what God had *yet* to do around him.

There is great debate in our day about justice, fairness, and equity. Some believe it is attainable through social reform. Some who are cynical may think the ideals are so far removed from us that the world will never truly know them. But the Christ-follower knows that the promise of perfect righteousness and justice is promised in the Lord both now and throughout eternity. And with this, there's joy for the present and hope for tomorrow. We cannot afford to lose faith for what God alone can ultimately provide. Our joy depends on it.

....

Father, help me find joy in what You've promised to do while I faithfully trust in the righteousness to come, throughout the ages, through Your Son, Jesus Christ. I ask this in Jesus' name, amen.

Steven Blanton, Ebenezer Baptist Church, Hendersonville, NC

Diligent Toward Peace

Beloved, looking forward to these things, be diligent to be found by Him in peace,
without spot and blameless; and consider that the longsuffering of our Lord is
salvation—as also our beloved brother Paul, according to the wisdom given to
him, has written to you.

2 PETER 3:14-15

F ew spiritual disciplines in the Christian life come without labor, devotion, and an ongoing commitment toward developing them. Finding and knowing the peace of God is no exception. Isn't it amazing to observe what some will do, and the lengths they will go to, to find something or someone who will provide peace and security in their lives? It is an innate desire of the soul.

As believers we must learn the discipline of peace in the Lord while we observe the world churn, cycle, and spin around us. In today's verses, we're challenged to be diligent in the work of peace. Peace in the Lord doesn't always come easily. We've got to work at it and ask for it in the strength of the Lord.

One of the motivators driving a believer's diligence is in knowing that Jesus is coming again. Jesus asked His disciples in Luke 18:8, "When the Son of Man comes, will He really find faith on the earth?" So how about you? When Jesus comes, how will He find you? Hectic, frantic, without faith in the moment? Or diligently working toward the spiritual disciplines of peace and blamelessness at the promise of His coming?

Father, we need Your help. In a world giving us everything but peace, help us to be diligent to settle our hearts with the promise that You will never leave or forsake us. I ask this in Jesus' name, amen.

The Perfect Couple

Surely His salvation is near to those who fear Him, that glory may dwell in our land. Mercy and truth have met together; righteousness and peace have kissed. Truth shall spring out of the earth, and righteousness shall look down from heaven.

PSALM 85:9–11

Before the days of on-demand mobile newsfeeds, many received a hard copy of their local newspaper delivered to their door. It was the daily habit of many to wake each morning, slip on their shoes, walk out to get the paper, to then return to the kitchen table and, after a quick observation of the front-page story, flip to the "Local" section to learn of engagements and anniversaries in the area.

In today's verses, the Lord would like to announce and honor the love between two couples who have been together a very long time. They are not actual people; they are ideals and characteristics of the very nature and attributes of God. But it would be God's desire for you to build lifelong relationships with these two couples. Learn their names. Invite them over often. Know their nature and develop their ways. It is true you have no greater friend than Jesus, but today, He'd love to connect you with two couples worth befriending. Meet "Mercy and Truth" and "Righteousness and Peace." These couples complement one another perfectly. They'd love to get to know you, and better yet, for you to know them.

Father, help me learn and display the attributes of mercy, truth, righteousness, and peace throughout my life, for my good and Your glory. I ask this in Jesus' name, amen.

Steven Blanton, Ebenezer Baptist Church, Hendersonville, NC

From Judgment to Joy

Then the word of the LORD of hosts came to me, saying, "Thus says the LORD of hosts: 'The fast of the fourth month, the fast of the fifth, the fast of the seventh, and the fast of the tenth, shall be joy and gladness and cheerful feasts for the house of Judah. Therefore love truth and peace.'"

ZECHARIAH 8:18-19

There aren't many places in scripture where God issues a word of judgment without following the sentence with a word of hope. Throughout time, God's people have experienced His judgment in their disobedience while also receiving a promise of His forgiveness and restoration. Zechariah 8 is no exception to the rule.

God had told His people through the prophets that He would send His judgment because of their waywardness and rebellion against Him. However, He would follow His word of judgment with a word of hope, should the people be willing to repent and follow Him once again. In today's text, God promised the people of Judah that one day their labor to know Him in fasting and repentance would turn to days of great celebration and joy.

Thank God for the finished work of His Son on the cross. Jesus endured all the judgment we deserved because of sin, for any who would repent and believe in His death and resurrection. God's wrath and the requirement for our restoration are satisfied through the person of Jesus Christ.

....

Father, thank You for Your Son, who has brought us from judgment to joy. Help me hold to the eternal promise that one day we will trade fasting and waiting for the pure joy of Jesus' glory and redemption in a place called heaven. I ask this in Jesus' name, amen.

Overwhelmed by Glory

Shout joyfully to the LORD, all the earth; break forth in song, rejoice, and sing praises. Sing to the LORD with the harp, with the harp and the sound of a psalm, with trumpets and the sound of a horn; shout joyfully before the LORD, the King.

PSALM 98:4–6

Has there ever been a time you were so overwhelmed with happiness you just wanted to shout? Maybe you had just received a bit of amazing news. Or perhaps you were in a time of worship and you just felt compelled to raise your voice in praise to the Lord. If you've ever felt this way, you and the writer of today's verses have something in common.

Many of the psalms are the product of a heart overwhelmed at the goodness and faithfulness of God. Recognition of the work and power of God stirs the heart so deeply the soul is moved to express what it feels. Worship offered to God can be unique from person to person. Some feel led to sit in quiet reverence before the Lord. Some silently meditate and think on the truths of God in gratitude for who He is. But the writer of today's psalm had reached a level of worship that could only be expressed as a shout of joy and adoration to God.

What causes an emotion to run so deep that the heart is compelled, almost involuntarily, to sing and shout aloud to God? The glory of God. When the heart has experienced the glory of God, one can't help but declare the experience joyfully.

....

Father, help us take inventory of how faithful You have been to us. So overwhelm our hearts with Your faithfulness that we sing and shout to the glory of Your name. You deserve nothing less. I ask this in Jesus' name, amen.

Steven Blanton, Ebenezer Baptist Church, Hendersonville, NC

No More Sorrow

A woman, when she is in labor, has sorrow because her hour has come; but as soon as she has given birth to the child, she no longer remembers the anguish, for joy that a human being has been born into the world. Therefore you now have sorrow; but I will see you again and your heart will rejoice, and your joy no one will take from you.

JOHN 16:21-22

Difficulties, tragedies, and burdens sometimes blind our hearts from seeing the goodness of the Lord. This was all too true for the disciples the night before the Lord's crucifixion. Jesus had plainly told His disciples that the time of His departure was at hand, and because of this, their hearts were overwhelmed with sadness. But Jesus wanted His followers to know that hope was not lost.

Consider the phrase in today's passage: a mother "no longer remembers the anguish, for joy that a human being has been born." The joy of the Lord is powerful in the believer's heart. It is so strong it overpowers the deepest hurts and sorrows so that the heart forgets what disturbed it because of the glory it has encountered. Jesus pointed His disciples to the fact that just as their hearts were heavy, the joy of the Lord would supersede any sorrow they would experience.

And so it is with us. Once we see Jesus face-to-face, every hurt and difficulty in this life will fade in the light of His glory. We find joy in knowing one day the burdens and pains of this life will give way to the glory of being in the eternal presence of Jesus.

Father, help my joy to be full and greater than any difficulty I may face. I ask this in Jesus' name, amen.

Everyday Joy and Peace

To Know and Be Known

Beloved, now we are children of God; and it has not yet been revealed what we shall be, but we know that when He is revealed, we shall be like Him, for we shall see Him as He is.

1 JOHN 3:2

We will know one another in heaven. In fact, the Bible says we will be known as we are known (1 Corinthians 13:12).

When Peter, James, and John stood with Jesus on the Mount of Transfiguration, Moses and Elijah appeared before them in their glorified forms, and both of them were recognizable (Matthew 17).

No one, then, will have to introduce me to Paul or Peter or anyone else who loves the Lord—and these heroes of the faith will know you and me. It is one thing for us to know who the president of the United States is, but it is something quite different for him to know us, to call us by name. In heaven we will know and be known. We will be home.

In heaven there will be no need for any introductions. We will be "like Him," and He knows us all and loves us all equally.

....

Lord, what joy to know I will see family and friends again . . . but even more to know that one day I will look upon Your face! In Jesus' name, amen.

O. S. Hawkins, PhD, Bestselling Code Series Author, Dallas, TX

God's Boundaries for Us

"I am the LORD your God, who brought you out of the land of Egypt, out of the house of bondage. You shall have no other gods before Me."

EXODUS 20:2-3

The Torah—the Jewish Scripture—is comprised of Genesis, Exodus, Leviticus, Numbers, and Deuteronomy. Those five books contain more than six hundred laws, but the Big Ten are found in Exodus 20.

These ten ancient laws are, in twenty-first-century America, experiencing an intense assault. Listings of and even references to them are being systematically removed from public view. Yet in our nation's capital, the Ten Commandments are carved in granite on government buildings and in mahogany in public libraries. The commandments are also on the wall above where the Supreme Court justices sit and hold court. These public displays testify to our founding fathers' faith and to the principles that made this the greatest nation on earth.

The Ten Commandments have served as the building blocks of almost every civil society for more than three thousand years. Our American experiment in democracy is just one example.

Football, basketball, and baseball are played within boundary lines. And so it is with life. God has set some boundaries for you (the Ten Commandments), and if you play within them, you will win at this game called life. That is the only way to true joy and peace.

....

Lord, Your laws are a testimony of Your great love and concern for me. In Jesus' name, amen.

God Is with Us

Yea, though I walk through the valley of the shadow of death, I will fear no evil;
for You are with me; Your rod and Your staff, they comfort me.

PSALM 23:4

A lot of voices tell us how to live, and self-help books flood the marketplace. But only one Book tells us how to die. And no verse in that Book of books is more relevant to the subject than the verse above.

Tradition tells us that David penned these words about the "valley of the shadow of death" while sitting in the Judean wilderness between Jerusalem and Jericho. The spot—known today as Wadi Kelt—is a long valley about four and a half miles long, and its canyons run as much as fifteen hundred feet in depth. The sun casts a shadow over the canyon and on the sheep trails across the way, which snake their way up, down, and through the rugged terrain.

Aware of how deep the valleys around him were, David knew he would walk with his Lord through the deepest "valley of the shadow of death."

When you see a shadow, let it always remind you that you will never walk through the valley of death. Jesus did that for you. You will walk only through the valley of the "shadow" of death. And you have His peace in your heart as assurance.

....

Lord, a shadow might frighten me, but it can never hurt me, and You are with me. Thank You for Your peace in my heart. In Jesus' name, amen.

O. S. Hawkins, PhD, Bestselling Code Series Author, Dallas, TX

Finding Bethlehem

"You, Bethlehem Ephrathah, though you are little among the thousands of Judah, yet out of you shall come forth to Me the One to be Ruler in Israel, whose goings forth are from of old, from everlasting."

MICAH 5:2

Long centuries before His birth, the prophets foretold that Christ would be born in Bethlehem. But how? Joseph and Mary resided seventy miles north, in Nazareth. God put the whole world in motion to fulfill His Word. A decree went out from Caesar Augustus that everyone was to go to the place of their family lineage to pay taxes. So Joseph, because he was in the line of David, left Nazareth with his very pregnant wife on a long journey.

Many of the things in our lives that on the surface appear inconvenient may just be the hand of God's providence getting us to our own Bethlehem.

Bethlehem reminds us that what God promises, He performs—no matter what. Bethlehem is a place of providence, and so are you.

God is at work, behind the scenes in your life, right now. He has not abdicated His throne. He is at work in your life when you are not even aware.

Lord, what You have promised You will perform. Make me a Bethlehem today. In Jesus' name, amen.

Everyday Joy and Peace

Blessed Assurance

I know that my Redeemer lives.

JOB 19:25

Notice that Job did not say, "I think" or "I hope." Job was rock-solid certain that his Redeemer would live again.

And this confident proclamation comes from a man who had lost his wealth, his friends, most of his family, and his health. Yet his answer to his original question—"If a man dies, shall he live again?" (Job 14:14)—is an unwavering "Absolutely!"

Yes, there is life after death. God wants us to know that truth; He wants us to live with certainty that life continues after our earthly existence. The apostle John put it like this: "These things I have written to you who believe in the name of the Son of God, that you may know that you have eternal life" (1 John 5:13).

The Bible you often hold in your hands was written to you so that you would have absolute assurance not only that there is life after your time on earth, but that you will spend it with Jesus.

God doesn't want you to hope, but to *know* that you have eternal life. The reality is you are not really ready to live until you are ready to die and have that assurance and peace in your heart.

....

Lord, thank You that I can know I have eternal life because Your Word says so! In Jesus' name, amen.

O. S. Hawkins, PhD, Bestselling Code Series Author, Dallas, TX

Goodbye to Anger

It displeased Jonah exceedingly, and he became angry.

JONAH 4:1

I t was God's decision to extend kindness and mercy to the people of Nineveh. And Jonah's heart overflowed with anger. Earlier Jonah had refused to preach a message of repentance to Nineveh. Jonah ended up in the belly of a big fish for three days. Then Jonah did obey and preach.

One would think that after all Jonah had been through, his heart would be softer and overflowing with praise when he learned that God had sent revival to the people of Nineveh. Instead, we see a sharp contrast between God's heart of grace and Jonah's heart of anger.

God's mercy "displeased Jonah exceedingly, and he became angry" (Jonah 4:1). The Greek word for *angry* means "to burn." Jonah was fuming; smoke was pouring out his ears. This is the first by-product of harboring resentment and anger: it takes away our own peace of heart and mind. Someone filled with God's Spirit has a heart of love, joy, and peace.

Anger is like a cancer. It doesn't affect the other person, it simply eats away at you. Don't allow anger to find a root in your heart. As soon as it appears, wave it goodbye.

Lord, fill me with Your love, joy, and peace so that there is no room for anything else. In Jesus' name, amen.

Contributors

Scripture Index

MARK

LUKE

JOHN

Notes

1. Edward Mote, "My Hope Is Built on Nothing Less," 1834, public domain.
2. I encourage you to visit the whole writing in Article XVII. https://bfm.sbc.net/bfm2000/.
3. Helen Howarth Lemmel, "Turn Your Eyes upon Jesus," 1922. Public domain.
4. Adapted from author's blog: https://libertylive.church/2022/01/06/blog-whatdoesthebiblesayaboutgodspromises/. Used by permission.
5. Karen Nitkin, "Alzheimer's Disease: Frustration and Hope," Johns Hopkins Medicine, November 19, 2018, https://www.hopkinsmedicine.org/news/articles/alzheimers-disease-frustration-and-hope.
6. "Facts and Figures," Alzheimer's Association, accessed February 25, 2022, https://www.alz.org/alzheimers-dementia/facts-figures.
7. Matthew Henry, *A Commentary upon the Holy Bible: Isaiah to Malachi* (London: Religious Tract Society, 1834), 142.
8. Frederick Bruner, *The Gospel of John: A Commentary,* The Pillar New Testament Commentary (Grand Rapids: Eerdmans, 2012), commentary on John 14:15–17.
9. "Silent and Solo: How Americans Pray," Barna, August 15, 2017, https://www.barna.com/research/silent-solo-americans-pray/.
10. Robert Robinson, "Come Thou Fount of Every Blessing," 1758, public domain.
11. Adrian Rogers, *The Adrian Rogers Legacy Bible* (Nashville: Thomas Nelson, 2009), 1344.
12. Max Lucado, *Jesus: The God Who Knows Your Name* (Nashville: Thomas Nelson, 2020), 119.
13. Ron Wolfe, "200 Million of These Self-Help Books Have Been Sold in 20 Years," *Arkansas Democrat Gazette*, May 1, 2011, https://www.arkansasonline.com/news/2011/may/01/200-million-these-self-help-books-have-be-20110501/.
14. Colin Schultz, "The Oldest Olive Oil Ever Found is 8,000 Years Old," *Smithsonian*, accessed March 2, 2022, https://www.smithsonianmag.com/smart-news/oldest-olive-oil-ever-found-its-8000-years-old-180953678/.

15. From Kuyper's inaugural address at the dedication of the Free University. Found in *Abraham Kuyper: A Centennial Reader*, ed. James D. Bratt (Grand Rapids: Eerdmans, 1998), 488.

16. Excerpted from Dr. Stephen G. Cutchins, *Prove It: Defend the Christian Faith* (Independently published, 2015), 31–32.

17. Adapted from author's blog: https://stephencutchins.com/2021/03/19/do-not-quit/. Used by permission.

18. Adapted from author's blog: https://stephencutchins.com/2019/12/17/grace-without-holiness/. Used by permission.

19. Adapted from author's blog: https://stephencutchins.com/2020/01/03/trust-god-with-your-fear/. Used by permission.

20. https://www.merriam-webster.com/dictionary/unemployed